Teaching Culture

Strategies for Intercultural Communication

H. Ned Seelye

National Textbook Company
NTC a division of *NTC Publishing Group* • Lincolnwood, Illinois USA

1994 Printing

Published by National Textbook Company, a division of NTC Publishing Group.
© 1993 by NTC Publishing Group, 4255 West Touhy Avenue,
Lincolnwood (Chicago), Illinois 60646-1975 U.S.A.

4 5 6 7 8 9 0 VP 9 8 7 6 5 4 3 2

Dedication

Sometimes it takes a lot of patience to deal with a foreigner, and I want to recognize the virtue of countless, mostly anonymous, people in a hundred countries who have befriended me while I was in that role. Some of them in countries where I have had the good fortune to spend years rather than days have become close friends and sharing time with them is one of my greatest pleasures.

Contents

Foreword to This Edition

"What we do not know can harm us."

When Stephen K. Bailey shared this insight with the American Council on Education in 1975, the world was much different than today. The Soviet Union menaced our national security. The Cold War struggle for the loyalties of countries around the world dominated foreign policy. As we strove to better understand our military enemies, we came to recognize the importance of expanding foreign-language and cultural education.

Today we live in a different world. The demise of the Soviet Union has left the United States the sole military leader of the world, but this distinction is not as important as in 1975. Today, the global community is the arena in which we make our friends and enemies, and the global economy is much of the solution to a secure future for our country.

Knowledge of the world's languages and cultures is more vital than ever. In order to compete in the global community, we must be able to communicate effectively and to appreciate, understand, and be able to work in the framework of other cultures. *Teaching Culture: Strategies for Intercultural Communication* provides educators— particularly teachers of foreign languages, social studies, literature, and art—with tools for developing intercultural skills as well as concrete, creative ideas for helping students understand and appreciate other cultures.

As the twentieth century comes to an end, the United States is in a unique position: We are the greatest economic power in the world. We are fortunate to have a population composed of people of various racial, ethnic, and social backgrounds. Seelye knows that our diversity can be one of our greatest strengths. He recognizes that in order to prepare our children for the challenges ahead, we must teach them to understand and appreciate other languages and cultures. Our competitors already realize the importance of this. In Japan, every public school student starts studying English in the seventh grade. And all students in the nations of the European Community are expected to learn two languages, in addition to their native tongue.

Seelye goes beyond focusing only on the facts that students should learn. He focuses also on the importance of instilling in students an intellectual and emotional appreciation of cultures other than their own.

Seelye underscores the need for quality multicultural instruction and provides useful recommendations for achieving this. *Teaching Culture: Strategies for Intercultural Communication* provides sound ideas that can be helpful for teachers of all subjects who want to enhance their students' understanding of other cultures. Seelye is wise to begin with suggestions for students at the elementary level.

The book includes discussion on understanding bicultural identity, writing performance objectives, and ways to achieve them. "Suggested Activities" at the end of each chapter show teachers how best to apply these concepts in the classroom. The book includes an extensive bibliography.

Seelye's qualifications for writing this book are clear. As a professor, lecturer, and writer, he has a strong background in multicultural education. Seelye also draws on the experiences and expertise of other educators, including participants in workshops he has led on teaching culture.

The first edition of *Teaching Culture* was published in 1974. Since then, it has contributed to the increased recognition by educators that we must enhance our ability to communicate with people from other nations. Seelye's belief in the importance of multicultural education was right two decades ago, and he is right today.

Paul Simon
U.S. Senator
Illinois

Excerpts from the Foreword to the Second Edition

Back in 1971 Ned Seelye masterminded for the American Council on the Teaching of Foreign Languages what must have been the first preconference workshop on the teaching of culture. About ten of us who were interested in the area of cross-cultural understanding were asked to serve as resource people at the workshop. I arrived on the scene a bundle of nerves—in awe of Seelye, in awe of Chicago, in awe of the sharp-beaked chambermaid who replenished my towel supply. Most of all, I doubted my own ability to respond intelligently in my role as workshop group leader. That night Seelye called a preworkshop briefing for all resource people involved. I watched them come in to the meeting room—the great and the near-great in the teaching of culture. They exuded an aura of expertise. Their heads seemed to bulge with stores of wisdom. They fairly radiated confidence in matters cultural. I looked at that glittering cavalcade and my heart sank. Then Ned Seelye took me aside and indicated the group with a discreet nod of his head. "Genelle," he whispered, "about half of those folks know what it's really about when it comes to teaching culture. The other half I invited here to make sure they found out." Ned Seelye has been helping us find out how to teach culture ever since.

The first edition of this book has fulfilled every expectation Emma Birkmaier held out for it in her original Foreword to the volume. It has opened the eyes of undergraduates to a critical area of their training in foreign language methodology; it has inspired research topics in the graduate seminar; it has salvaged the battered enthusiasm of dedicated in-service teachers. [The second] edition promises even more. Seelye has not only updated the original materials designed for foreign language teachers, he has added new chapters which made the book immediately useful to those who work in any capacity with people of other cultures.

This book supplies not only the rationale for the development of intercultural skills, but concrete suggestions for attaining them. It offers, too, an extraordinarily rich bibliography. Throughout the text, pertinent references are seeded as closely as clover along an Iowa highway.

I have been using the first edition of this volume as a text in courses on "Teaching for Cross-Cultural Understanding" for almost ten years. As one student recently wrote in critiquing the materials used in the course, "Mr. Seelye's book helps us know more than the facts of culture; it helps us *see* what to do and *feel* how to do it." This student happened to be from Taiwan. But knowing, seeing, and feeling are the critical components of learning and teaching across all cultures. Seelye's consistent empathy for the teacher and the learner shines through in the valuable new edition.

Genelle Morain
Professor of Language Education
The University of Georgia

Excerpts from the Foreword to the First Edition

Ned Seelye, the author of this volume, is a distinguished spokesman for the learning and teaching of foreign languages and cultures. He has been honored by learned societies and conferences in foreign language education for his yeoman work in the field. Outstanding anthropologists have taken cognizance of his work. He speaks to us as one who has helped students and teachers use foreign languages for the development of *humane* individuals and the achievement of *humanistic* goals.

In preparing this volume he has drawn upon his rich experience as a classroom teacher, as a keen observer and participant in many cultures, especially the Latin American, and as a director of many workshops devoted to the teaching of culture.

Some of the materials written by the participants in these workshops are used to illustrate and bring home to us the cultural hypotheses the author advances in this volume. Because these illustrative reports are written by groups of teachers who have had actual experience in working with students at various age and ability levels, the reader will find many encouraging examples of ways and means for making his or her program a truly cultural experience for his or her students.

The book is written primarily for the teacher. It will help teachers grow in their ability to comprehend what culture is all about, to help the student help himself by perfecting his ability to work out the processes and use the tools needed to penetrate a culture, and to assist the student in uncovering reasons for a culture and why its members behave as they do.

I consider this volume to be a top-level how-to-do-it book that is readable, practical, informative, and enjoyable. It has treated a most vexing area of teaching: student attitudes. I am sure it will be underlined and dog-eared by professional teachers of cultural persuasion who want to produce students whose future actions will demonstrate how well they have learned, not only by their competency in subject matter, but also by their behavior when facing the dynamic cultural changes we will be experiencing in a future one-world society.

Not since the Stanford Language Arts Investigation in the late 1930s and early 1940s with its resultant two volumes, *Modern Languages for Modern Schools* and *Foreign Languages and Cultures in American Education*, has a powerful, insightful, practical study been made of the role that foreign languages and cultures can play in the development of human relationships. The present volume is such a study.

Emma Marie Birkmaier
Professor of Foreign Language
Research and Education
University of Minnesota

Preface

Adrift on a Sea of Data

Culture shapes our thoughts and actions, and often does so with a heavy hand. How do we as teachers and trainers enhance communication with people conditioned by other systems of thought and behavior? One of the vexing problems I have wrestled with is what to do with the huge amounts of cultural data that besiege us in this Age of Information. We need, I reasoned, a *parsimonious* model to focus on relevant things.

One cannot (at least I cannot) isolate a manageable stack of facts that will turn into the magic elixir that would, if properly applied, increase our ability to communicate across cultures. Even knowledge of the language is not enough. Instead of key facts, therefore, I looked for key skills: There are a lot fewer skills than facts. Skills that are begun under the tutelage of a mentor (you, the reader) can be honed against the whetstone of one's own ensuing experience. That's what I wanted. A few critical skills we can help folks begin to develop, skills that they can refine later, skills that will improve the quality of their intercultural communication.

This book identifies a half-dozen skills that nurture and support intercultural communication. Implicit where it is not explicit, underpinning these skills is one basic act—personal interaction with someone from another culture. These six skills give us a simple way to deal with the mass of detail that confronts all students of intercultural communication.

The skills are:

- Cultivating curiosity about another culture (or another segment or subculture of one's own culture) and empathy toward its members

- Recognizing that role expectations and other social variables such as age, sex, social class, religion, ethnicity, and place of residence affect the way people speak and behave

- Realizing that effective communication requires discovering the culturally conditioned images that are evoked in the minds of people when they think, act, and react to the world around them

- Recognizing that situational variables and convention shape behavior in important ways

- Understanding that people generally act the way they do because they are using options their society allows for satisfying basic physical and psychological needs, and that cultural patterns are interrelated and tend to support need satisfaction mutually

- Developing the ability to evaluate the strength of a generalization about the target culture (from the evidence substantiating the statements), and to locate and organize information about the target culture from the library, the mass media, people, and personal observation

Many of these appear, at first glance, to be concepts rather than skills. You could lecture on them for 45 minutes, then give your students a multiple-choice test calibrating their understanding. This would be like testing a student on swimming techniques by asking him or her to write an essay on how you swim the butterfly. You wouldn't need pools of water. Just paper and pencil. This book champions getting your feet wet in the waters of another culture. Seeking out people from another cultural background and talking (or signing, if you are deaf) to them. It advocates doing activities associated with the above six concepts often enough to develop facility in integrating them into our interaction with people from other cultures. Effort spent in developing these skills will be rewarded by face-to-face interactions that are more effective and fun.

Reorganization of the Goals

Instructors who have used previous editions of this book may wonder what happened to the *seven* goals of instruction highlighted earlier, since this edition describes *six* goals. I collapsed, rather arbitrarily, into one goal (goal 6 in the current edition) what had previously been divided into two: evaluating statements about a culture, and researching another culture. The order in which the goals are presented and their exact wording in the current edition also differ somewhat from the prior editions.

Classroom Activities

A word about the book's many sample learning units, units that can be used to help students appreciate some of the ways that understanding the cultural context of communication is vital to decoding the message. These illustrative units, unless clearly identified otherwise, were prepared by participants during courses and workshops I directed. In a few cases, the immediate supervision was done by a teaching assistant. In all cases I have tried to give appropriate credits.

Acknowledgments

Since this book first hit the publisher's catalog twenty years ago it has undergone many printings but this is only the second time the original has undergone major revision. During this score of years, reviewers and readers from all over the world have been extremely kind and generous in their feedback. Their encouragement has given me energy to do the present revision.

Previous editions of this book have acknowledged my debt to individuals who aided me and I will not repeat their names here. I do want to thank Howard L. Nostrand, Margaret Pusch, William DeLorenzo, and V. Lynn Tyler for bringing many excellent works to my attention for inclusion in the current edition. My niece, Olga Elena Díaz Oliva, transcribed the previous edition onto a computer disk to greatly facilitate my editing the present book. Shannon Robson and R. J. Smith helped with the library research. From National Textbook Co., Tim Rogus (along with his predecessor, Michael Ross), Geoffrey T. Garvey, and Michael O'Neill have contributed superb editing talents. Karen E. Christoffersen (NTC's art director) has enhanced the visual literacy of the book. I must also thank the three eminent VIPs who wrote such glowing forewords to various editions of this book—Dr. Emma Marie Birkmaier, Dr. Genelle Morain, and Senator Paul Simon. Theirs is the only part of the book my mother reads.

1 Cultural Context, the Key to Comprehension

When communication is between people with different world views, special skills are required if the messages received are to resemble the messages sent. The most important overriding skill is understanding the context within which the communication takes place. This context is to a large extent culturally determined. This chapter illustrates this concept. The relation of language to thought is explored.

Context in Communication

The key to understanding what people say is context. If someone says "Let's go to McDonald's for a milkshake," the meaning seems clear. But is it? It is only clear if you make certain assumptions about the context of the statement. You may assume, for example, that the speaker refers to McDonald's Restaurant and not to John McDonald, an accommodating friend. One assumes that there is a McDonald's readily available. Were the statement made in the middle of the Sahara by an intrepid tourist, the meaning would be intentionally ironic. Without knowing the context of a statement, we can only guess at its meaning.

What provides this meaningful context?

Sometimes it is just getting oriented enough to know what topics the person is addressing. When I was a teenager, I met a charming

Brazilian. She did not speak English, but we communicated in a kind of Spanish, mine engagingly Mexican with traces of American English, hers a breathtaking mixture of Argentine, Paraguayan (including sprinklings of Tupí-Guaraní), and ample doses of São Paulo Portuguese. At one point early in our relationship, our jobs interposed a continent between us. She cheerfully announced that I could write to her in Spanish and that she would write to me in Portuguese. Protestations about my ignorance of Portuguese were brushed aside. She gave me a comprehension aid—a list of twenty common Portuguese words translated into Spanish (e.g., não=no, muito=muy, eu=yo). Other than this brief list, I had no other source for divining the meaning of the language of Camões (Portugal's Shakespeare). Her first missive arrived. I read it and understood about 20 percent. (Spanish was helping.) I then reread it and understood about half. The third reading, immediately after the first two, yielded about 80 percent understanding. (The other 20 percent I either ignored or, if the context seemed intriguing, asked her about in our next round of correspondence.)

The Portuguese letter lark illustrates one of the most important concepts in communication: redundancy. As message redundancy increases, so too does message comprehension (as long as you can avoid boring the person into a trance). In this case, just by developing a sense of context—getting (and refining) the general idea of what the letter dealt with—dramatically increased my understanding of it.

Understanding the words is not the same as understanding the message, however.

I asked a Brazilian friend of my correspondent how things were going.

"*Tudo azul*," he replied. "All blue."

Oh, that's too bad, I said. I told him that when Americans feel depressed they go shopping.

"*Não, não*, I feel *tudo azul*—great!"

Whether blue lifts you up or puts you down must depend on where you are. Even how you talk about color depends on circumstances.

Years later, passing time while riding the Washington, D.C., metro with my eldest son, I began waxing poetic about the different metro lines, all color-coded. I told him that the red line isn't so much red as it is red with a pinch of ochre to give it depth and a touch of violet to give it energy. I went on in that vein through all the metro's colors. When I wore myself out, David, a graduate of Rensselaer Polytechnic Institute, turned to me and said, "It's clear you weren't a science major."

"Why?" I asked. "How would a scientist talk about it?"

"Well first," he said, "we wouldn't call it red."

"What color is it?"

"It'd be some wavelength measured in nanometers. Probably somewhere between 600-700."

"What are nanometers?" I asked, rapidly falling in over my head.

"They are one-billionth of a meter, or about 1/25,000,000 of an inch. Different wavelengths between 400-700 are perceived by humans as colors." He went on like this for a while.

"Uh huh," I mumbled. There were serious subcultural differences in color perception, I noted. Brazilians weren't the only people to look at color differently.

Meaningful context often is provided by the culture. Some years ago several teachers of Spanish visited me in Guatemala, where I was teaching. The maid asked them if they would like something to drink and they requested *agua* (water). About fifteen minutes later the maid returned with Coca-Colas. In Guatemala, although *agua* means "water," it commonly refers to soft drinks. To get H_2O, *agua pura* should have been requested. But once the language barrier has been hurdled and a glass of water has been obtained, what does one do with it? Can it be drunk? In some parts of the world, camel blood is the beverage of choice. (It is drunk for the food value rather than to quench thirst.)

An interesting example of misunderstanding prompted by ignorance of the cultural connotations of a word was afforded in an advanced undergraduate class in Latin American literature. In preparation for this course (in a U.S. college), a number of paperbacks were ordered from Mexico for the college bookstore to sell. After the titles were announced in class, the students dutifully trekked to the bookstore, made the required purchases, and retired to their dormitories. Within an hour, three-fourths of the class had attempted to return the paperbacks to the bookstore because the books were "defective"—the pages had not been cut! Although these Spanish majors had been using the word *libro* for at least seven years, they were not able to distinguish, in the Hispanic world, a defective book from a "normal" one.

The most immediately overwhelming context that faces one in a foreign country is the foreign language. This fact forces serious students of the culture—or even unserious souls who need to live in the culture—to set about acquiring another language. A great teacher helps, or even a mediocre teacher if you are learning the language where it is spoken. There are books that can help language learners get motivated and develop useful language-learning strategies (e.g., Rubin and Thompson, 1982; T. Marshall, 1990; H. Brown, 1991).

The Cultural Nature of Language

Dewey's (1897) famous essay "My Pedagogic Creed" appeared in an educational journal about a century ago. Dewey observed that "language is almost always treated in the books of pedagogy simply as the expression of thought. It is true that language is a logical instrument, but it is fundamentally and primarily a social instrument." If language is "primarily a social instrument," how can it be divorced from the society that uses it? Writing more than seventy years after Dewey, Chao (1968) emphasizes in his study of language that "action and speech are thoroughly mixed." Chao further observes that language is not even usually in the form of connected discourse such as sentences or paragraphs.

When for one reason or another members of one language community are forced to function either within or alongside another language, both their language and way of life inevitably change. There is probably considerable positive correlation between linguistic change and social change.

Ilbek (1967) offers an interesting discussion of the effect of English on the home language of French-speaking minorities residing in the United States. Ilbek gives examples of shifts of meaning caused by the presence of cognates in the language, direct borrowing of lexical items to designate new things, and borrowing of patterns through translation. Instead of using these data to arrive at insights into the nature of linguistic change or biculturation, however, the author disappointingly concludes that "as teachers of French we are pledged to fight this kind of interference and to keep our language pure."

Many teachers make this same mistake. While intrigued with the cultural implications of linguistic data, they get hung up on the form and fail to reach a cultural comprehension of the data beyond an assessment of its snob appeal. Despite five decades of modern linguistics, a lot of normative puritanism remains. Chao (1968) correctly characterizes language when he says that "there is no complete uniformity in any speech community; there is always mixture of dialects in the same locality; there is class difference; there is difference in the speech of different personalities even within the same dialect or the same class; above all, there is difference in style in the same individual." Chao adds that besides talking with people and hearing them talk with you, one should overhear them talk among themselves to learn to understand the nonstandard dialects. (Linguists call switching between two varieties of the same language "diglossia.")

Moreover, since much of the world's population speaks more than one language, studies of bilingual situations in which a choice is made of which language to employ help us understand the cultural functions of language. Rubin's (1968) classic study of bilingual people in Paraguay describes the social context and consequences of switches between Spanish and Guaraní, an indigenous language widely spoken among Paraguayans in many social classes. Spanish typically is used for formal occasions, in schools, in government, and in the transaction of most business. Guaraní, on the other hand, is spoken with friends, with servants, when telling a joke, in intimate situations, and in most casual situations. (See also Farb, 1973, for a paraphrase of parts of Rubin's study.)

In an excellent anthology on cross-cultural communication (Smith and Luce, 1979), each contributor gives many concrete examples of how language and culture interact. One such interaction occurs in public advertising and street signs. Publications dealing with advertising for the foreign language classroom are available for many languages. (For Spanish see Bawcutt, 1977, and for French see Paoletti and Steele, 1981.)

Every language has devices—a sound system and intonation patterns, function words (e.g., *of*)—that are indispensable elements of the language but that lack meaning in and of themselves. Words in isolation convey *potential* meanings. Verbs tend to convey so many meanings that in isolation they rarely communicate much. The word *get*, for example, has several hundred potential meanings; only in context is a particular meaning communicated: "He got two years for hitting his semantics teacher." Even common nouns in isolation are slippery. The word *house* may communicate "abode," but what kind of abode are we talking about? Stone? Mud? Cave? Mansion on the hill? Only within a larger context do individual words mean anything precise enough for reasonably accurate communication.

Is Speaking the Language the Same as Thinking like a Native?

One naïve assumption occasionally made by teachers is that a mastery of the linguistic patterns of a foreign culture leads in itself to "thinking like a native." As Lewald (1968) properly points out, this belief is unwarranted. Unless the student is learning the language in the target culture, the cultural referents necessary to understanding a native speaker must be learned in addition. Jay (1968) argues the point in pertinently broad terms:

> It should be made crystal clear, however, that
> bilingualism itself does not insure ipso facto a respect for
> other cultural patterns. The traditional hostility between
> France and Germany has been until recently a bitter reality,
> even though the language of each was commonly taught and
> understood by the other. . . . Bilingualism is not in itself
> the answer to cultural understanding among people. An
> indispensable asset, it must be fortified by the strongest
> possible sensitivity education. With knowledge of the
> language must exist a similar knowledge of the social,
> religious, and economic attitudes of a people. [pp. 85-86]

Some years ago Benjamin Lee Whorf (cf. J. Carroll, 1956), citing the earlier work of Sapir (1921), theorized that the world view of a speech community is reflected in the linguistic patterns they use. The implication was that the "reality" that is categorized in the underlying patterns of a language is an indication of how speakers of that language view the world; and, inversely, how they view the world depends on the language system they have. The proliferation of Eskimo words for snow (over 400 different words), according to what was to become known as the Sapir-Whorf hypothesis, reflects the importance snow has in Eskimo culture. Similar instances are the Trobriand Islanders' multiplicity of terms for yams, the basis of their economy, and the truckloads of terms to designate automobiles current in contemporary United States culture.

Perceptions of colors, kinship relations, space and time—all differ from language to language and from culture to culture. The trick is to demonstrate an association between language and culture. (It may be recalled that Whorf advocated contrasting languages such as Navaho and English, or French and Chinese, and not languages within the Indo-European family.) Unfortunately, off-the-cuff pronouncements on the relation between language and culture are the rule in social studies and in language classes. The fact that the linguistic structure of some languages enables the speaker to become the object of the action ('The glass broke on me'), to take an example, does not in itself demonstrate that the speaker views nature as an active agent and the human being as a passive one even while he or she is using a reflexive form (Seelye, 1966). To draw a behavioral inference legitimately from an analysis of language structure, a language pattern must be associated empirically with a behavioral pattern. This rarely is done.

That the Sapir-Whorf hypothesis has been accepted as truth by so many communication teachers may be an interesting example of the tendency toward wish fulfillment. The theory is exciting; there is some corroborative evidence and, perhaps inevitably, a body of contradicting evidence also; the idea has been around long enough for most teachers to have forgotten its highly speculative nature; and if the theory were true it would imbue language and communication courses with newfound importance.

Unfortunately, few writings by linguistic specialists are, at this stage in the science's struggle for respectability, comprehensible to most classroom teachers, and few classroom teachers have shown enough familiarity with the linguistic literature to be "linguistically respectable." Consequently, our acceptance of the Sapir-Whorf hypothesis must await either more empirical evidence or improved communication with linguists. Some books that treat this area include Hoijer (1954), Carroll (1956), Gumperz and Hymes (1964), Romney and D'Andrade (1964), Hammel (1965), Greenberg (1966), Lander (1966), Witucki (1966), Mathiot (1967), Manners and Kaplan (1968), Niyekawa-Howard (1968), Pike (1971), Penn (1972), Rossi-Landi (1973), Gutiérrez López (1975), Kelling (1975), Jones (1976), Pinxten (1976), Mathiot (1979), Scollon and Scollon (1979), Rollins (1980), Friedrich (1986), Grace (1987), and Schultz (1990).

Farb (1973) summarizes the importance of these theories in this way: "The true value of Whorf's theories is not the one he worked so painstakingly to demonstrate—that language tyrannizes speakers by forcing them to think in certain ways. Rather, his work emphasized something of even greater importance: the close alliance between language and the total culture of the speech community" (pp. 186-187).

Context Is a Powerful Organizer of Experience

In my own home, my wife, Clara, and I converse in Spanish, she talks to our three kids in Spanish, I talk to them in English, and they usually talk in English among themselves when they are in the United States. When my oldest two boys were preschool tykes, I asked them how many languages they spoke. After a minute or two of silence, one said "Two." That's very good, I said. Which two? Another silence. Then the other child said "Mami and Papi."

Some people have an advantage in seeing more of the context than others. Let me give an example. In a course I taught on race relations, I had the students prepare psychodramas illustrating the behavioral patterns of an out-group. Students would pair off, by race. Whites portrayed African-Americans in some social interaction, and African-Americans portrayed interaction with whites. Typically, the psychodrama presented by whites would feature students passing each other giving high fives and saying things like "What's shaking, man?" The African-Americans, on the other hand, would dramatize subtle put-down power moves of white bureaucrats as they deal with minority peoples.

If the context of your life is played out under the heel of another group that is favored with a disproportionate share of your country's power, prestige, and wealth, you will tend to develop into better observers of the human scene. The dominant culture (in the United States this is often white, male [heterosexual], middle-class [suburban], Protestant [Episcopalian]) sees a few primary colors but misses many of the connecting hues.

This difference in how much of the social background one discerns extends beyond subordinate-dominant class divisions. Some cultures as a whole teach that an abundance of the social background is germane to any contemplated action while other cultures see less of it as relevant. Sojourners who are socialized in a high-context culture (e.g., Hispanic, Arabic, Japanese) and then travel to a low-context one (the United States or Germany) often erroneously perceive slights and insults where none were intended. Conversely, the low-context person often misses the barbs in interactions in a high-context culture. It's like someone from a nontonal language such as English trying to hear the difference between two utterances that appear identical save a tonal difference. (Whether *ma* means mother or horse in some Chinese dialects, to take one example, is a function of tone.)

In many cultures (if not most) women are trained to be more context-sensitive than men.

While a convenient place to begin learning about another culture is in a language or social studies class, both the language and its cultural context ideally are learned together. They are linked. Just as culture cannot be ignored in foreign language classes, the role of language in human thought cannot be ignored in social studies classes—at least not if the classes aspire to develop intercultural communication skills.

And don't kid yourself. You are not going to become an expert in another culture without learning to talk to the people in their own vernacular.

Paul Simon (1980)—the U.S. senator, not the musician—pithily begins his book *The Tongue-Tied American* with the admonition that we should erect the following sign at each port of entry into the United States:

—Welcome to the United States—

We Cannot Speak Your Language

It seems obvious enough that to penetrate another culture, one must understand what its people are saying and make oneself understood. I don't know how this can be done without a knowledge of the target language or dialect. (A dialect is a variety of a language; everyone who has speech speaks at least one dialect of at least one language. The belief that dialects are structurally different from languages—perhaps linguistically primitive forms of speech—is hogwash.)

This is not to say that our need to know culture for effective communication automatically guarantees that we will pick up the culture as we learn a second (or third) language. This is one of the principal differences between learning a language within its indigenous setting and learning it in an alien cultural context. Learning a language in isolation of its cultural roots prevents one from becoming socialized into its *contextual* use. Knowledge of linguistic structure alone does not carry with it any special insight into the political, social, religious, or economic system. Or even insight into when you should talk and when you should keep your mouth, er, shut.

Understanding the way of life of at least one group of people socialized in another culture is important to survival in a world of conflicting value systems, where the boundaries that formerly isolated and protected people from alien ideas have been eroded by advances in the technology of communication or have been struck down by the angry clamor of the downtrodden in their search for a better life. Transistor radios and FAX machines are revolutionary tools.

How is one to liberate one's ideas from the stagnant eddies of ethnocentrism, from what Francis Bacon called the "fallacy of the tribe," if not through a study of other cultures? It is this "foreign" context—linguistic and cultural—that provides the key to understanding other peoples.

Suggested Activities

1. List ten ways in which language and culture are linked.
2. Give an example of a misunderstanding that occurred because you and the person you were talking to were thinking of different contexts. (In other words, you were each talking about different things.)

3. Give two examples of a misunderstanding you experienced until more of the context was revealed. (People who are hard of hearing can give thousands of examples.)

References Cited

Bawcutt, G. J. 1977. *Spanish Sign Language: Reading Comprehension Activities.* London: Harrap.

Brown, H. Douglas. 1991. *Breaking the Language Barrier.* Yarmouth, ME: Intercultural Press.

Carroll, John B., ed. 1956. *Language, Thought, and Reality: Selected Writings of Benjamin Lee Whorf.* Cambridge, MA: MIT Press.

Chao, Yuen Ren. 1968. *Language and Symbolic Systems.* New York: Cambridge Univ. Press.

Dewey, John. 1897. "My Pedagogic Creed." *The School Journal* 54: 77-80. Reprinted in Kahil I. Gezi and James E. Myers, eds. *Teaching in American Culture.* New York: Holt, 1968, pp. 408-11.

Farb, Peter. 1973. *Word Play: What Happens When People Talk.* New York: Knopf.

Friedrich, Paul. 1986. *The Language Parallax: Linguistic Relativism and Poetic Indeterminacy.* Austin: Univ. of Texas Press.

Grace, George William. 1987. *The Linguistic Construction of Reality.* New York: Croom Hellm.

Greenberg, Joseph H., ed. 1966. *Universals of Language.* 2nd ed. Cambridge, MA: MIT Press.

Gumperz, John J., and Dell Hymes, eds. 1964. *The Ethnography of Communication.* Special publication of *American Anthropologist* 66, 6 (Dec.), Part 2.

Gutiérrez López, Gilberto A. 1975. *Estructura de lenguaje y conocimiento sobre la epistemología semiótica.* Madrid: Editorial Fragua.

Hammel, E. A., ed. 1965. *Formal Semantic Analysis.* Special publication of *American Anthropologist* 67, 5 (Oct.), Part 2.

Hoijer, Harry, ed. 1954. *Language in Culture: Conference on the Interrelations of Language and Other Aspects of Culture.* Chicago: Univ. of Chicago Press.

Ilbek, Jacques. 1967. "A Case of Semantic Interference." *The French Review* 41: 368-76.

Jay, Charles. 1968. "Study of Culture: Relevance of Foreign Languages in World Affairs Education," pp. 84-92 in Pat Castle and Charles Jay, eds., *Toward Excellence in Foreign Language Education*. Springfield, IL: Office of Public Instruction.

Jones, John. 1976. *Classification Systems, Vernacular and Education in Papua New Guinea*. Port Moresby, PNG: Educational Research Unit, University of Papua New Guinea.

Kelling, George W. 1975. *Language: Mirror, Tool, and Weapon*. Chicago: Nelson-Hall.

Lander, Herbert. 1966. *Language and Culture*. New York: Oxford Univ. Press.

Lewald, H. Ernest. 1968. "A Tentative Outline in the Knowledge, Understanding, and Teaching of Cultures Pertaining to the Target Language." *Modern Language Journal* 52 (May): 301-9.

Mandelbaum, David G., ed. 1962. *Edward Sapir: Culture, Language and Personality, Selected Essays*. Berkeley: Univ. of California Press.

Manners, Robert A., and David Kaplan, eds. 1968. *Theory in Anthropology: A Sourcebook*. Chicago: Aldine.

Marshall, Terry. 1990. *The Whole World Guide to Language Learning*. Yarmouth, ME: Intercultural Press.

Mathiot, Madeleine. 1967. "An Approach to the Study of Language-and-Culture Relations." *Dissertation Abstracts* 27, 3765B, Catholic University of America, Washington, DC.

Mathiot, Madeleine, ed. 1979. *Ethnolinguistics: Boas, Sapir and Whorf Revisited*. The Hague: Mouton.

Niyekawa-Howard, Agnes. 1968. *A Psycholinguistic Study of the Whorfian Hypothesis Based on the Japanese Passive*. Educational Research and Development Center, University of Hawaii, Honolulu.

Paoletti, Michel, and Ross Steele. 1981. *Civilisation française quotidienne*. New York: Hatier.

Penn, Julia M. 1972. *Linguistic Relativity versus Innate Ideas: The Origins of the Sapir-Whorf Hypothesis in German Thought*. The Hague: Mouton.

Pike, Kenneth L. 1971. *Language in Relation to a United Theory of the Structure of Human Behavior*, 2nd rev. ed. The Hague: Mouton.

Pinxten, Rik, ed. 1976. *Universalism versus Relativism in Language and Thought: Proceedings of a Colloquium on the Sapir-Whorf Hypothesis*. The Hague: Mouton.

Rollins, Peter C. 1980. *Benjamin Lee Whorf: Lost Generation Theories of Mind, Language, and Religion*. Ann Arbor, MI: Published for Popular Culture Association by University Microfilms International.

Romney, A. Kimball, and Roy Goodwin D'Andrade, eds. 1964. *Transcultural Studies in Cognition*. Special publication of *American Anthropologist* 66, 3 (June), Part 2.

Rossi-Landi, Ferruccio. 1973. *Ideologies of Linguistic Relativity*. The Hague: Mouton.

Rubin, Joan. 1968. *National Bilingualism in Paraguay*. The Hague: Mouton.

Rubin, Joan, and Irene Thompson. 1982. *How to Be a More Successful Language Learner*. Boston: Heinle and Heinle.

Sapir, Edward. 1921. *Language: An Introduction to the Study of Speech*. New York: Harcourt, Brace.

Schultz, Emily A. 1990. *Dialogue at the Margins: Whorf, Bakhtin, and Linguistic Relativity*. Madison, WI: Univ. of Wisconsin Press.

Scollon, Ronald, and Suzanne B. K. Scollon. 1979. *Linguistic Convergence: An Ethnography of Speaking at Fort Chipewyan, Alberta*. New York: Academic Press.

Seelye, H. Ned. 1966. "The Spanish Passive: A Study in the Relation between Linguistic Form and Worldview." *Hispania* 49, 2 (May): 290-92.

Simon, Paul. 1980. *The Tongue-Tied American: Confronting the Foreign Language Crisis*. New York: Continuum.

Smith, Elise C., and Louise Fiber Luce, eds. 1979. *Toward Internationalism: Readings in Cross-Cultural Communication*. 2d ed. New York: Harper & Row.

Witucki, Jeannette Renner. 1966. "Personal References and Personal Security: An Experiment in Language and Culture Research," University of California, Los Angeles. *Dissertation Abstracts* 27, 1707B.

2 What Is Culture?

This chapter looks at what "culture" is, examining anthropological and literary approaches to defining—and teaching—culture. Culture is seen to include everything people learn to do.

The Teapot Tempest

This book uses the word *culture* a lot. Just what does it mean?

Practically all the discussions on culture by teachers during the 1950s and 1960s gyrated around the question of how culture should be defined. Two distinct insights became, in the minds of many, antagonistic to each other. On the one hand were humanists concerned with the liberating effect of humanity's commendable accomplishments. Alfred North Whitehead (1929) stated this position succinctly: "Culture is activity of thought and sensitiveness to beauty and human feeling. Mere scraps of information have nothing to do with it. The merely well-informed man is the most useless boor on God's green earth." On the other hand are social scientists concerned with the details of all human learning—the good, the bad, and the ugly. (See H. Nostrand, 1989, for more on this divergence of approaches.) These argumentative, often hotly polemic, discussions served to keep the question of culture before the reluctant audience of a profession preoccupied with grammar, literature, geography, and history.

One such characteristically unsuccessful attempt to coordinate the teaching of language and culture occurred at the 1960 Northeast Conference on the Teaching of Foreign Languages (Bishop, 1960). Livid professors, acting as though their basic value system were under attack from imperfectly socialized upstarts, defended with righteous indignation the appropriateness of a literary approach (versus a social science approach) to cultural matters. A dozen years later a second Northeast Conference on culture (Dodge, 1972) was characterized by greater acceptance of the legitimacy of culture in language classes, but there was little sign of progress in integrating it into the classroom. The most recent Northeast Conference report to focus on language and culture (Singerman, 1988) does deal directly with the integration of language and culture and does suggest that the language profession may have reached a critical point in integrating culture into the classroom.

The first really contemporary effort to define culture was exerted by anthropologists. Culture, they reasoned, was what their science was all about. It was, therefore, imperative to define it precisely. How else, theoretical-minded anthropologists were prone to ask, could valid research be accomplished in the area? It seemed logically evident, at the time, that to talk about culture one has to know what culture is. But each anthropologist had his or her own definition. Prompted by a desire to isolate the common denominator in the many diverse definitions of the term, two well known anthropologists, Kroeber and Kluckhohn (1954), examined approximately 300 definitions in a study entitled *Culture: A Critical Review of Concepts and Definitions*.

Alas, a precise common denominator was not found. Culture emerges from these analyses as a very broad concept embracing all aspects of human life. The anthropologist Leslie White (1968) concludes an article on this problem by quoting Alfred North Whitehead: "It is a well-founded historical generalization that the last thing to be discovered in any science is what the science is really about."

Many teachers have been slow to accept culture as a broadly defined concept. For much of the profession culture has been defined almost exclusively in terms of the fine arts, geography, and history. This narrow definition of culture, unfortunately, does not fully prepare a student to understand the wide range of behavior exhibited by our species.

The late Nelson Brooks, who has been so influential in causing teachers to recognize the importance of culture and its link with language, identified five different types of culture: biological growth, personal refinement, literature and the fine arts, patterns for living, and the sum total of a way of life. Brooks (1968) stressed the importance of never losing sight of the individual when we talk about culture as it is relevant to language classes. The same point is relevant to any program concerned with enhancing intercultural communication.

The type of culture Brooks identified as most appropriate for intercultural classes is "patterns for living," a concept defined as "the individual's role in the unending kaleidoscope of life situations of every kind and the rules and models for attitude and conduct in them." These patterns enable the individual to relate to "the social order to which he is attached." Culture should be broadly sampled. As Brooks said, culture in the classroom "must not only answer the question: 'Where is the bookstore?' It must also answer the question: 'Where is the bathroom?' "

Murdock's famous *Outline of World Cultures* (1983) lists 900–odd distinct categories of behavior. It is the ultimate laundry list of things cultural. Avoid being a wimp! Reach for as broad an understanding of the target culture as your interests and energies will allow.

Can Culture Be Taught through Literature?

Some professors dedicated to an analysis of literary style claim that literature affords the best tool to teach about the life of the people. Here we need to be cautious, Howard Nostrand (1966) advises, "in generalizing from literature. Many Russians [of the day] have formed their idea of the American businessman and of Wall Street partly from American novels such as Babbitt which reflect a hostile attitude on the part of one subculture in the United States, the writers, toward another subculture, the businessman." Although Russo-American relations have changed drastically since the late 1980s, the point is still valid: Literature often deals with past societal settings, rather than with contemporary structures. (As any school-teacher knows, the length of time "contemporary" culture extends into the past is measured in minutes by many of their charges.)

Lewald (1968), in an article that expertly reviews the problems associated with teaching about culture in language classes, observes that using fiction to illustrate a target culture "has been defended on the grounds that all art is based on a conscious or unconscious contact with social reality and cultural patterns, present in the mind of the creative writer. Here the problem arises of determining which types of literature or art forms are most suitable to elicit cultural patterns or indicators. A case might be made for those forms that strongly reflect an outer reality." Lewald elaborates by suggesting that the contribution of psychological, surrealistic, or experimental writing would be questionable. If the interest is in contemporary culture rather than in a preindustrial period, the number of qualifying documents shrinks greatly.

One should be careful, in emphasizing the universal aspects of culture, not to minimize the variety of values and behaviors manifested within the target culture. Literary works become important as they develop themes of universal interest, but to understand a culture's uniqueness, study also must be directed to the role local idiosyncratic cultural patterns play in achieving universal needs.

Even in situations where the legitimate objective of a course is the study of fine literature, a knowledge of culture is not an irrelevant digression. One writer whose sympathies were clearly literary in nature came to the conclusion through teaching a course in English as a second language that, in the study of literature, the whole area of cultural comprehension is more likely than language to cause difficulty (Povey, 1967).

Another writer not only reached the same conclusion but for that very reason sees harm in attempting to rely too heavily on cultural generalizations abstracted from literature. In describing the experience of some teachers involved in teaching adult Arab employees of an American company, Yousef (1968) recounts that

> it was clear to the teachers that literary values were not universal. These students of English as a foreign language would never be able to reach an understanding of the people and the culture of the United States by studying

American literature. Instead, the study of American literature
actually seemed to increase misunderstanding and confusion.
It was apparent that the students would need pertinent
cultural orientation before they could attempt any meaningful
literature course.

The quarrel is not with the value of literature or art as a means
to illustrate how people in another culture live, but rather with
the limited range of insights fiction offers as the major source of
information. Since many language teachers feel uncomfortable
dealing with concepts and data of the social sciences, they tend
to rely too heavily on literature to teach culture. Culture cannot
be dealt with as a series of disconnected footnotes to literature.
However, "the study of culture and that of literature, which must
be clearly separated, are neither irreconcilable nor antagonistic"
(Beaujour and Ehrmann, 1967).

Literature can best be seen in the present context as illustrating
the cultural patterns of a society once the patterns have been
identified by the methods of the social sciences: social science as
source, literature as example. Nevertheless, literary approaches to
understanding the human condition can be powerfully insightful.
A sociologist of some fame remarked to me once that one good
novel is worth ten sociological monographs. Marquardt (1967)
suggests the value of certain carefully selected literary works as an
aid to teaching cross-cultural communication and this is discussed
in chapter 5. Lewis and Jungman (1986) use short pieces of literature to prepare one for culture shock. Just as we need to be
open to the many ways literature and art can help us understand
other cultures, so must we remain open to the insights of the social
sciences.

Folklore: An Ideal Compromise?

Genelle Morain (1968) and J. Dale Miller (1973) convincingly argue
that folklore offers a logical bridge to service language teachers
trained in literary analysis who are interested in getting closer to
an anthropological understanding of culture but who are not equipped

by disposition or background to deal with the empirical orientations of the social scientist.

Morain takes as her definition of folklore the comfortably loose description by Archer Taylor (1965):

> Folklore is the material that is handed on by tradition, either by word of mouth or by custom and practice. It may be folk songs, folk tales, proverbs, or other materials preserved in words. It may be traditional tools and physical objects like fences or knots, hot cross buns, or Easter eggs; traditional ornamentation like the walls of Troy; or traditional symbols like the swastika. It may be traditional procedures like throwing salt over one's shoulder or knocking on wood. It may be traditional beliefs like the notion that elder is good for ailments of the eye. All of these are folklore.

Morain argues that when it comes to mirroring the attitudes of large groups, folklore is superior to literary writing. The very durability of folktales, proverbs, slurs, and jests is an indication of the validity they have for a given people. A study of carefully selected folk materials could illuminate some of the important cultural themes that underlie a country's thought and action. While Morain's examples are taken from the French, Campa (1968) demonstrates how an analysis of folklore can illuminate the main themes of Hispanic culture. One-line proverbs, brief verses, narrative ballads, and riddles all afford lively illustrations of themes such as the "picaresqueness of the Spaniard," or his sense of "self-assurance."

An article in *Soviet Education* by Khanbikov (1967) calls the folklore that is relevant for instructional purposes "folk pedagogy." He goes on to say that this folk pedagogy is of a democratic nature; it is the result of the creative contribution of many generations of working people to spiritual culture, its inalienable component. Many thousands of folk philosophers, folk psychologists, and folk educators have worked on its creation. It is the expression of the ideals of the toiling majority, and it puts forward, in correspondence with the needs of the people, the most humane and democratic ideals in the education of the rising generation.

It is a great disappointment for many students, who have developed fluency in the language after four to twelve years of sequential study in primary and secondary schools, and have passed the advanced placement test, to go on to advanced classes only to discover in college that if they are to continue taking courses in their second language, they have to study literature or "advanced grammar." Even the somewhat isolated Civilization and Culture course usually bases itself "solidly" on literature. If a student wants to satisfy any of the many interests he was led to expect from his high school teachers, he must often leave or avoid altogether the college foreign language department, for frequently it is easier to locate professors who are both fluent in the foreign language *and* interested in its culture in other college departments. Perhaps folklore is a door through which more culturally pertinent materials can be introduced into the rather arid genre-oriented college foreign language offerings.

Communication and Understanding

Besieged by an endless procession of cultural studies from anthropology, art, history, sociology, economics, political science, social psychology, music, and literature, teachers must ask themselves what knowledge is relevant and what skills should be developed in students. Nostrand (1966b) proposed that teachers concentrate on two goals in teaching about a foreign way of life: cross-cultural communication and understanding.

Cross-Cultural Communication

The basic aim of an intercultural communication class is to have the students learn to communicate with people who do not share their own hue of cultural conditioning. If people from the target culture do not speak your language, you've got to learn another language. This is not as difficult as many believe it to be. The Mexican movie comic Cantinflas once said that *gringos* are so intelligent—he visited New York City and discovered that even the children spoke English! One could add that even idiots in the United States speak English.

Obviously, since fairly common emotions and thoughts cannot be understood apart from their cultural connotations, these connotations also must be learned. Examples of difficulties in cross-cultural communication that arise from ignorance of the target culture are recounted by many authors.

Debyser (1968) offers examples from the French to illustrate how the cultural connotations of common terms and phrases can be taught on the elementary level. To know the words denoting the various members of a family (mother, child, uncle) is not enough. To be able to use the words with impunity one must also know the specific social context within each can be employed. The word *maman*, for instance, may be used by a person when he talks to his mother, but would rarely be used by him when talking about her to others.

Much misunderstanding in the communication professions concerning the degree of effort that should be spent to get the students to act like natives is the result of confusing the ability to communicate accurately with the attitudes dictated by the mores of the target culture. There should be no controversy about the aim of accurate communication, and this includes understanding the culturally based mores of the target people but does not necessarily include professing or internalizing them.

Cross-Cultural Understanding

Nostrand's second basic purpose in teaching the foreign culture—understanding—can imply a restructuring of our attitudes and world view. Nostrand includes under the rubric of understanding, for example, such intangibles as "the psychological capacity to be magnanimous toward strange ways" (1966b). In the final analysis, no matter how technically dexterous a student's training in the foreign language, if the student avoids contact with native speakers of that language and lacks respect for their world view, of what value is the training? Where can it be put to use? What educational breadth has it inspired?

Unfortunately, some communication teachers themselves do not feel comfortable in the presence of people of other cultures. This may be because the teachers have not yet learned to follow speech at conversational speed, have not yet learned what to talk about and what to avoid, have not yet accustomed themselves to the amount of space separating them from the native or to the rules governing eye-to-eye contact, have not yet learned to share the target sense of humor or its taste in songs, have not yet learned about the cultural referents in the topics of discussion. And they may have succumbed to a regrettable ethnocentric tendency to underestimate the intelligence of members of the other culture.

Reaching a Consensus

The most widely accepted usage now regards culture as a broad concept that embraces all aspects of human life, from folktales to carved whales. What is culture? It is everything humans have learned. Even in a few published articles concerned with teaching the older concept of culture as the limited but praiseworthy production of creative artists, the importance of a knowledge of patterns of everyday life as a prerequisite to appreciating the fine arts is recognized to an increasing degree.

In short, it is becoming increasingly apparent that the study of language cannot be divorced from the study of culture, and vice-versa.

Intercultural communication teachers have not necessarily been able to define culture where others have not; we have finally been content to shrug our shoulders and admit that it doesn't really matter how it is defined as long as the definition is broad. The important thing to note is that intercultural communication involves many characteristics not often present in our classes.

Culture is seen to involve patterns of everyday life that enable individuals to relate to their place under the sun. When we peek in on people "relating," we see them mixing action and speech. They do ingenious things to foreign words to incorporate them into their own idiom. They talk in nonstandard dialects within the same speech area; they talk one way to strangers and another way among themselves. The words they use evoke cultural images of novel shapes and sizes. The speech of a person indicates one's sex, age, social class, and place of residence and often conveys information concerning one's religion, occupation, and other interests.

The controversy over the definition of culture has led to a dead end. The parameters of a culture-based instruction are limited only by the experiences and imagination of the teacher-guide. The subsequent chapters begin to describe in detail how skill in communication is enhanced enormously by intimacy with the cultural context of thought and behavior.

In chapter 9 I try to bridge the humanist and social science traditions by looking at culture as knowledge and behavior patterns provided by differing traditions to enable their culture bearers to satisfy basic physical and psychological needs.

The intercultural communication teacher can make it easier to understand someone from another culture by building bridges from one cognitive system to another. Stay tuned; this book will suggest practical ways to do this.

Suggested Activities_____

1. What are five extralinguistic cultural connotations of *child* in one of your languages (other than your first)?

2. Through an example, illustrate how an element of folklore may mirror the attitudes or cultural themes of some segment of a nation's thought and action.

3. Identify in writing twenty-five ideas for cultural activities. Each idea should relate to a different category of Murdock's (1983) *Outline of World Cultures*.

4. Give three examples of how you would speak in one way in a formal situation and another way in a less formal situation.

References Cited_____

Beaujour, M., and J. Ehrmann. 1967. *La France contemporaine*. Paris: Armand Colin.

Bishop, G. Reginald, ed. 1960. *Culture in Language Learning*. Report of the Northeast Conference on the Teaching of Foreign Languages. New York: MLA Materials Center.

Brooks, Nelson D. 1968. *Language and Language Learning: Theory and Practice*. New York: Harcourt, Brace.

Campa, Arthur L. 1968. *Teaching Hispanic Culture through Folklore.* ERIC Focus Report No. 2. New York: MLA/ACTFL Materials Center.

Debyser, Francis. 1968. "The Relation of Language to Culture and the Teaching of Culture to Beginning Language Students." *Language Quarterly* 6: i-ii.

Dodge, James W., ed. 1972. *The Case for Foreign Language Study.* New York: MLA Materials Center.

Khanbikov, Ia. 1967. "Folk Pedagogy," *Soviet Education* 9, 1: 32-41.

Kroeber, Alfred L., and Clyde Kluckhohn, eds. 1954. *Culture: A Critical Review of Concepts and Definitions.* New York: Random House.

Lewald, H. Ernest. 1968. "A Tentative Outline in the Knowledge, Understanding, and Teaching of Cultures Pertaining to the Target Language." *Modern Language Journal* 52 (May): 301-9.

Lewis, Tom, and Robert Jungman. 1986. *On Being Foreign: Culture Shock in Short Fiction, an International Anthology.* Yarmouth, ME: Intercultural Press.

Marquardt, William F. 1967. "Literature and Cross-Culture Communication in English for International Students." *The Florida FL Reporter* 5, 2: 9-10.

Miller, J. Dale. 1973. "Proverbs Supply Gems of Culture." *Accent on ACTFL* 3, 4: 9.

Morain, Genelle G. 1968. "French Folklore: A Fresh Approach to the Teaching of Culture." *The French Review* 41 (April): 675-81.

Murdock, George P., et al. 1983. *Outline of World Cultures.* 5th ed. New Haven, CT: Human Relations Area Files.

Nostrand, Howard L. 1966a. "Audiovisual Materials for Teaching the Social and Cultural Context of a Modern Foreign Language: Their Bearing upon Preservice Education." *The Department of Foreign Languages (DFL) Bulletin,* National Education Association, 5, 3 (May): 4-6.

Nostrand, Howard L. 1966b. "Describing and Teaching the Sociocultural Context of a Foreign Language and Literature," pp. 1-25 in Albert Valdman, ed., *Trends in Language Teaching.* New York: McGraw-Hill.

Nostrand, Howard L. 1989. "Language Learning and the Perils of Pluralism." *The Canadian Modern Language Review* 45,4 (May): 703-14.

Povey, John F. 1967. "Literature in TESL Programs: The Language and the Culture." *TESOL Quarterly* 1,2: 40-46.

Schmittroth, Linda, ed. 1991. *Statistical Record of Women Worldwide.* Detroit: Gale Research.

Singerman, 1988. NE Conf report

Taylor, Archer. 1965. "Folklore and the Student of Literature," in Alan Dundes, ed., *The Study of Folklore.* New York: Prentice-Hall.

White, Leslie A. 1968. "On the Concept of Culture," pp. 15-20 in Robert A. Manners and David Kaplan, eds., *Theory in Anthropology*. Chicago: Aldine.

Whitehead, Alfred North. 1929. *The Aims of Education, and Other Essays.* New York: Macmillan.

Yousef, Fathi S. 1968. "Cross Cultural Testing: An Aspect of the Resistance Reaction." *Language Learning* 18, 3-4 (Dec.): 227-34.

3 The Cultural Mazeway: Six Organizing Goals

What skills do we need to increase our ability to communicate across cultures? This chapter provides a framework to facilitate the selection of cultural data that will increase student skill in intercultural communication.

What Are the Most Important Cultural Facts?

The last chapter argued that cultural behavior is learned behavior. And culture is anything the species has learned. What, many ask, are the most important facts that repose in earth's diverse cultures and how does one identify them?

One approach advocated from time to time is that for any given culture a core of information exists that one must share in order to participate meaningfully (i.e., not marginally) in that culture. Two examples will illustrate some of the difficulties in this approach.

An Englishman who devised and widely administered among academicians a test to measure cultural knowledge concludes his study by indicting the academic elite for their "modest accomplishments" (Richmond, 1963). Richmond states that ". . . only one person in a hundred will have a clean bill of health." He defines culture as "a broad intellectual awareness founded on informed opinion." Even within one relatively narrow segment of the population (i.e., the academic elite) there is little agreement on which facts constitute a common culture. The "one hundred books that any educated [Western] person must have read" falls into this tradition.

A more recent example is provided by a U.S. educator, who, in the face of "the decline of literate knowledge," argues that changes in the educational system are required to increase the level of "cultural literacy" among all segments of the society (Hirsch, 1988). Hirsch sees increasing the citizenry's shared core of knowledge as a way to a more viable society: "We will be able to achieve a just and prosperous society only when our schools ensure that everyone commands enough shared background knowledge to be able to communicate effectively with everyone else."

To this end, Hirsch's bestselling *Cultural Literacy* inventories 4,600 items that every educated American should be able to identify. These are listed in an alphabetized appendix titled "What Literate Americans Know." These items range from people and places (Hank Aaron, Achilles, Maya Angelou, Adirondack Mountains, Argentina) to sundry concepts (act of God, adagio, animism) to songs ("Amazing Grace") to science and medicine (antigen, anthropomorphism, arthritis) to adages ("All work and no play make Jack a dull boy") and so on. Some other items under the letter A are Jane Addams, Addis Ababa, AEC (Atomic Energy Commission), Aeschylus, amniotic sac, "As flies to wanton boys are we to the gods," and Atlantic Charter.

Putting aside the larger issue of "How much shared knowledge is necessary for a society's viability?" these lists do provide useful insights into the education of one sector of a population: Those with the most institutional instruction. Communication with these people *is* facilitated by sharing this part of their socialization with them. Formal education does not constitute the whole of their socialization, of course. And unfortunately, the sector that can remember esoteric bits and pieces of their formal education more often than not is poorly (but admirably) representative of a nation as a whole. Historical biases conspire to deny many sectors equal access to formal education. Rural people, working-class people, women, indigenous peoples, and linguistic minorities often suffer in this regard. (As do those individuals who fall below average in intelligence—and, by definition, as many fall below the average as fall above it.)

At any rate, 'tis a long list of t'ings to learn. Hirsch argues that merely recognizing the meaning of the terms will aid communication among the populace. In-depth knowledge of an item is not required, according to Hirsch; "just a few bit of associated information" will suffice. Other educators are more concerned with the linkages among isolated facts. The significance of knowing any given laundry list of facts, the synergism their integration might inspire, does not seem to be a prominent concern of list makers.

Facts are tricky little things, though. There are so many sources to help us understand any given culture that it is necessary to develop a method for cutting the number down. We cannot assign ten thousand titles to our students. (At least not if we want to avoid mass exodus.) Modern teachers who see their role as that of preparing students to survive future shock, the trauma that results from having to face too much change in too short a time (see Toffler, 1970), seek to avoid having students develop an undue respect for obsolescent "facts." (Excellent materials for teaching about future change has been prepared by Hass et al., 1987.)

The misspent search for an authoritative tome of the "fifty most important facts" of the target culture brings to mind a parlor game popular in some circles, Trivia. Trivia requires the successful participant to be the first to respond correctly to a question whose answer is not worth knowing. Some teachers play the game of "Filling Freddie Farkle Full of Fickle Facts." This is commonly accomplished through superficial units on art, food, the marketplace, the War of Independence, and above all, on the principal navigable rivers and their seamy ports. These teachers ask questions such as "What is the principal river of Germany and what is its principal port?" or "In what country of Latin America is tin the principal product?" Trivia gives the illusion of learning something. Any educational objective that promotes the learning of facts for their own sake is enhancing the probability of a severe case of future shock. It takes more than the illusion of learning to justify schooling.

Before pertinent sources are identified, the student must learn to ask intelligent questions. The real issue is: What's worth knowing? Only after this is answered can we go about the task of assembling sources to respond to the questions.

One of the best sources of information is somebody who lives or who has lived in the target culture.

How Do We Focus on Something as All-Inclusive as Culture?

Cultural instruction must be purposeful if it is to lead anywhere. It should be apparent—at least to the instructor—what the reason is for doing any given cultural activity. While good programs to engender intercultural communication maintain enough flexibility to house the occasional whimsy of aimless activities, aimlessness must not characterize more than a minuscule proportion of the time spent on building a context for understanding what's going on in the target culture. There should be a sound reason behind each and every cultural activity.

It has been said that the beginning of wisdom is to separate things into two categories. I propose a simple way of dividing the gigantic world of cultural phenomena. I will divide the world into six different "piles" of activities. Each pile represents a goal of cultural instruction. And each goal focuses on a skill that can increase intercultural communication and understanding.

To be purposeful, instructional activities should relate in a reasonable way to a defensible goal such as the six proposed in this book. While one goal (showing curiosity about the target culture) does offer some justification for the learning of facts for their own sake, none of the other five goals is concerned with this in the slightest.

The First Task: Identifying Goals

In writing cultural goals one generally begins with some large, innocuous-sounding statement replete with "understandings" and "appreciations"—a supergoal! Here is my supergoal:

All students will develop the cultural understandings, attitudes, and performance skills needed to function appropriately within a segment of another society and to communicate with people socialized in that culture.

Supergoals must be delineated to be useful. The Nostrands (1970) identify culturally relevant skills that can be developed in the classroom, and this is the logical place to begin identifying the basic cultural purposes, or goals, upon which teachers can base their instruction.

The six goals listed below are a modification of the Nostrands' "kinds of understanding to be tested" and they have, over the years, evolved considerably from the Nostrands' original set. These goals are sufficiently detailed to enable a teacher to focus on a justifiable reason for using most any illustration or artifact of the target culture.

The goals are not measurable in their present form. To keep the focus where it belongs, they are nonetheless stated in terms of student achievement rather than in terms of teacher process. I am proposing that they be employed as the basic frame for courses in intercultural communication. They can also serve as a model of how to organize courses in intercultural learning, which may have different goals. The six organizing goals presented on page 31 can be reworded or otherwise modified or expanded to tailor them to the needs of any particular instructional program.

In other words, we can help the student develop *interest* in *who* in the target culture did *what, where* and *when*, and *why*. (That summarizes the first five goals.)

Further, we can help the student develop some sophistication in evaluating statements about the culture and in finding out more about it. (And this summarizes the sixth goal.)

These six goals involve skills that are associated with intercultural communication and understanding and are skills that can be developed in our classes and workshops. Each goal is the subject of its own chapter(s) starting with the next chapter. Helping students achieve some degree of skill in each of these goals of cultural instruction becomes an integral part of any program aimed at enhancing intercultural communication.

Goal-Relating "Trivial" Topics

"How do I work my favorite unit on food into the framework of these six goals?" panic-stricken teachers ask. Indeed, how do any of the activities generally carried out in the name of culture fit into the goals described above? The answer lies in the way teachers relate their favorite units to a cultural goal. Table 3.1 shows how several common, often purposeless, activities can be made goal-related.

Six Instructional Goals

Goal 1—*Interest*: The student shows curiosity about another culture (or another segment or subculture of one's own culture) and empathy toward its members.

Goal 2—*Who*: The student recognizes that role expectations and other social variables such as age, sex, social class, religion, ethnicity, and place of residence affect the way people speak and behave.

Goal 3—*What*: The student realizes that effective communication requires discovering the culturally conditioned images that are evoked in the minds of people when they think, act, and react to the world around them.

Goal 4—*Where and When*: The student recognizes that situational variables and convention shape behavior in important ways.

Goal 5—*Why*: The student understands that people generally act the way they do because they are using options their society allows for satisfying basic physical and psychological needs, and that cultural patterns are interrelated and tend mutually to support need satisfaction.

Goal 6—*Exploration*: The student can evaluate a generalization about the target culture in terms of the amount of evidence substantiating it, and has the skills needed to locate and organize information about the target culture from the library, the mass media, people, and personal observation.

Table 3.1

Goal Relating "Trivial" Topics

Topic

	Food	Cities, Rivers, Harbors
Goal 1	How much interest does the student show in trying out new target foods? Does he or she develop a taste for something new?	What effort had the student exerted to make contact with someone from X? Has the student visited or does he or she plan to visit X?
Goal 2	How does what target people eat depend on the country, or part of the country, in which they live? Do teenagers eat anything the rest of the population doesn't? How would a typical middle-class dinner differ from a working-class dinner?	What locales are agricultural? Industrial? Especially wealthy? Impoverished? How is the mode of intercity travel in X city affected by age and social class?
Goal 3	What do different foods look like in the target culture? Do any of the foods figure in common jokes? What kind of meals does one associate with exceptionally opulent eating? With impoverished eating? With family meals? With snacks?	Do target people consider the people of X city to possess any special attributes? What images does a native think of when Y city is mentioned?
Goal 4	What etiquette is usually observed at different meals? What are the common phrases one uses at mealtime or at the market?	To what extent does the way one greets someone in X city differ from the "textbook standard"? Do the rituals accompanying marriage and death differ from area A to area B?
Goal 5	What behavior patterns are associated indirectly with the production or consumption of food in the target culture (e.g., truck transportation, manufacture of utensils)?	What would one have to get done that would require a trip to Xique-Xique? How would one go about getting from X city to Y city?
Goal 6	Is any given statement (provided by the teacher) about food in the target culture sympathetic or ethnocentric? On how much evidence does it seem to be based? Are variables such as circumstances and social class taken into consideration?	What seems to be the most significant statement made from a text about X city/harbor/river? Can the statement be substantiated objectively?
	How aptly can a student locate information concerning food in the target culture? To what extent are both print and human resources utilized? How does the student relate his or her report to significant issues?	Same questions as those opposite in the left-hand column, substituting the city/river/harbor for food.

The trick in doing this lies in which questions you ask. It is easy to relate the same artifact or photograph or magazine advertisement, for instance, to two or more different goals just by varying the questions you pose. For example, let's say you have a picture clipped from a foreign language magazine.

Goal 1 (*interest*): You would ask what the photo makes the student curious about, or ask about the student's willingness to become personally involved in some way with some activity or encounter in the photo.

Goal 2 (*who*): Ask "*Who* does it or uses it?" Probe the relevance of social variables such as age, sex, social class, religion, or race or ethnicity to what is pictured in the photo.

Goal 3 (*what*): Probe for any special connotations or reactions the target people might have toward some aspect of the photo.

Goal 4 (*where and when*): Query the circumstances of doing or using what they see in the photo. Is "it" associated with crises or mundane situations? With common or infrequent happenings? Is it associated with any particular segment of the population? Do people expect a conventional response to the situation? If so, what is the anticipated response?

Goal 5 (*why*): Ask how the observed behavior may fit into the need-gratification system of the target culture.

Goal 6 (*exploration*): Ask how you would find out more about the aspect of the culture portrayed in the photo. What cultural generalizations can be hypothesized from the photo? How much evidence supports the generalization?

The next two chapters describe goal 1—developing curiosity about another culture and empathy toward its members—in more detail.

Suggested Activities

1. Choose a trivial topic and relate it to each of the six goals as suggested by Table 3.1.

2. Choose a random photograph from a magazine and relate it to each of the six goals.

3. Choose a gesture or other behavioral pattern (e.g., a t'ai chi "dance" movement, or, body language that shows deference to another person) and relate it to each of the six goals.

References Cited

Hass, John D., Jacqueline Johnson, Robert LaRue, Barbara Miller, and Ron Schukar. 1987. *Teaching about the Future: Tools, Topics and Issues for the Future.* Center for Teaching International Relations (CTIR), University of Denver.

Hirsch, E. D., Jr. 1988. *Cultural Literacy: What Every American Needs to Know.* New York: Vintage.

Nostrand, Frances, and Howard L. Nostrand. 1970. "Testing Understanding of the Foreign Culture," pp. 161-70 in H. Ned Seelye, ed., *Perspectives for Teachers of Latin American Culture.* Springfield, IL: Superintendent of Public Instruction.

Richmond, K. 1963. *Culture and General Education.* London: Methuen.

Toffler, Alvin. 1970. *Future Shock.* New York: Random House.

4 I Am Curious, Blue

This chapter examines three approaches to motivating students to explore the target culture: Showing curiosity about the basic human geographical character of the country; making personal contact with people from the culture; and language, including skill in appropriately asking questions.

Cultural Goal 1—Interest: The student shows curiosity about another culture (or another segment or subculture of one's own culture) and empathy toward its members.

The Atlantis Syndrome: Just Where Is the Target Culture?

Judging from surveys, the location of other countries is a closely held secret, inscrutable to the ordinary American citizen. In college classes on intercultural communication I often give students blank outline maps of the world for them to fill out at the beginning and at the end of the course. The pretest results are startling. One college student identified Mexico as bordering the United States to the north, and Italy as reposing on the United States' southern border. Most can identify only a handful of countries. Africa, they reason, is one of the countries. In a recent Gallup poll, one in four Americans could not locate the Pacific Ocean on a world map. One in five could not locate the United States!

Odd that this novel sense of the world's political boundaries should be so irritating to the inhabitants of these "lost continents"!

Global perspectives cannot develop in ignorance of how the globe is partitioned into nation-states. In fact, this abysmal ignorance of geography is so offputting that the first step in demonstrating interest and goodwill toward other peoples becomes one of studying the atlas.

There are many ways to do this. There are map games. One weekend training program that orients college students who are planning to go abroad begins the sessions by posting several world maps on the wall, then pinning the name of a country to each participant's back. The participants are allowed to ask each other yes-no questions, in attempts to identify the country assigned to them. "Is it an island?" "Is is in Africa?" "Is it a big country?" And so forth. Needless to say, answering other participants' questions often is as hard as figuring out your "own" country. I survived my own initiation into this training program by identifying the political entity a colleague had pinned on my back: Timor.

Computer atlas programs, and there are many of them, can be a lot of fun to play. They bear names such as PC Globe, World Atlas, Geo Jigsaw, and the engagingly entitled BushBuck Charms, Viking Ships and Dodo Eggs. The Carmen Sandiego series (e.g., Where in the World Is Carmen Sandiego?), which began as a computer game and then went on to become a TV series, is both interesting and instructional. Carmen is an arch-criminal who roams the globe wreaking havoc with her henchmen. Your assignment, if you choose to accept it, is to use the provided cultural clues to find the doer of dastardly deeds.

When one enlarges the focus on a particular country, ethnic issues often pop into view. One geography book (Demko et al., 1992) shows Africa as it would look were it divided into tribal affiliations. My youngest son Michael spent the turbulent summer of 1991 in the [former] Soviet Republic of Georgia teaching English as a second language. His attempts to clarify meaning by resorting to Russian were always rejected by the nationalistic Georgians. They insisted he use either Georgian or English.

Coaxing students into an international perspective is made much easier by a series of publications sold by the Center for Teaching International Relations (CTIR), University of Denver (Denver, CO 80208). *The New State of the World Atlas* (Kidron and Segal, 1991), in conjunction with *Activities Using "The New State of the World Atlas"* (Hursh and Prevedel, 1991) offers secondary and tertiary students a graphic ways to become acquainted (through maps) with many interesting issues (e.g., geopolitical and cultural groupings, stereotypes). In fact, there are too many issues to deal with them all. By having students select a small number of issues, perhaps one from each major geographical area, students will get an interesting introduction to geography (without turning the communications course into a geography course). Both publications are available through CTIR Publications.

Of the many exciting titles in the CTIR Publications catalog, some of my favorites include *Demystifying the Chinese Language* (by a Stanford University team, 1983), *Teaching about Cultural Awareness* (Smith and Otero, 1989), and *Japan Meets the West: A Case Study of Perceptions* (by a joint Stanford and University of Washington team, 1987). These publications come complete with lesson plans and classroom handouts. I have used some CTIR lessons with undergraduate students that were designed for elementary school children and have found the lessons appropriate after making a few simple and intuitive modifications.

Three other highly commendable books that offer geographical aid for the internationalist are Kidron and Smith (1991), Marshall (1991), and Demko, Agel, and Boe (1992). Teacher units focusing on geography and our interrelationships have been prepared by Hursh, Schukar, and Simmons (1991). CTIR also publishes computer software (Apple and MS/DOS) that heightens student understanding of geography and international issues; send for their catalog.

Making Personal Contact

Who Cares about Foreigners?

On each evening news broadcast, satellites beam the day's weather into our living rooms. In Detroit, a couple of minutes' ride from

Canada, the camera zooms in to exclude the weather outside the U.S. political boundaries. The same thing happens in El Paso, where weather in Mexico appears irrelevant to the TV audience, many of whom are from Mexico or have relatives in Mexico. In the Washington, D.C., area, there are 200,000 Central Americans, none of whom get to see on the evening weather reports whether it is storming in their home countries. For a sizable segment of the United States, interest in events affecting their loved ones does not end at the U.S. border. Why isn't the news more inclusive?

According to a *Time* Magazine cover story in 1990, in thirty or forty years the majority of the United States will be what are now regarded as "minorities." Asians and Hispanics will form the largest segments. "Minorities" are already the majority in many if not most U.S. cities. Inevitably, one would expect, the United States will develop a more international perspective. On the other hand, this did not occur after the large immigrations over the past century. Instead, the country became provincial and rather intolerant of the foreign-born. My mother's Welsh grandparents, reflecting the pressures of the times, proclaimed that "We are in America now: We will speak American." And with that nationalistic sentiment, their descendants lost a language whose written literature goes back to the eighth century. My Welsh linguistic heritage is limited to a dozen words and one brief verse that can't be recited in polite company.

Writing in *Time* Magazine (Oct. 9, 1989, p. 106), William A. Henry III reports that one of the first axioms of U.S. reporters is that a fender bender on Main Street is bigger news than a train wreck in Pakistan. Henry compares the U.S. media coverage of two airplane crashes, one of which resulted in two deaths, the other in the death of all 171 passengers due to a terrorist bomb. The accident that killed two got more than twice the coverage of the other. The well-publicized accident happened near New York City, the other in Chad.

Henry goes on to cite a study (Herbert Gans, 1980) called *Deciding What's News,* in which the author noted that network journalists of the 1960s tried to prick their bosses' consciences by assembling a "Racial Equivalence Scale, showing the minimum number of people who had to die in airline crashes in different countries before the crash became newsworthy. . . . One hundred Czechs were equal to 43 Frenchmen, and the Paraguayans were at the bottom." Hurricane Hugo, Harris notes, which killed 51 people, got about as much coverage across the United States as the 1985 Mexico City earthquake that claimed 20,000 lives.

It is uncertain whether the fault lies with news editors or news consumers.

Sometimes just having a strange-sounding name is enough to incur disdain. A study of American attitudes toward 58 ethnic groups included the fictitious entry "Wisians." Although 61 percent of the respondents said they didn't know enough to rank them, the other 39 percent went ahead and gave them a low rating (reported in *Time* Magazine, Jan. 20, 1992, p. 25).

The long form in current usage that aliens seeking entry into the United States are required to complete at their point of entry states, with mindboggling parochialism: "Please use only English [in completing the form]." The U.S. Immigration and Naturalization Service often provides the applicant for citizenship with a traumatic introduction to U.S. government. In an article entitled "America's Unwelcome Mat," Sheng-mei Ma (1992), a Ph.D. college professor, describes the humiliating trials of obtaining permanent residence (a "green card"). As a result of his experiences, he states that "All immigrants are created equal; one is just as worthless as the other." He adds, "Abandon all dignity ye who enter here [the INS offices]."

How to help our students take more interest in people from other countries? People of our own country who belong to an ethnic community—those who hail from Spanish-, French-, German-, Hindi-, Thai-, Vietnamese-, Korean-speaking homes, or those who come from working-class African-American or white Appalachian backgrounds—provide a place to begin.

Activities that place the student in the position of having to interact with someone from another culture can be very powerful. There is even some reason to think that the single most influential activity a student can engage in to affect his fluency in a target country's idiom is to spend some time in it (Carroll, 1967; Gardner and Taylor, 1968; Gezi, 1965; Seelye, 1969; Seelye and Brewer, 1970).

Facilitating student contact with the target culture is easier to accomplish than it may appear to be.

Who Are the New Immigrants?

People who have recently arrived from abroad are wonderful sources of information. Immigrants sometimes get a bad rap, especially in times of economic hardship. It may help to break down several offputting stereotypes to mention a few findings by an economist, Julian Simon (1989), in his book about immigrants to the U.S., *The Economic Consequences of Immigration.*

- More immigrants than natives have less than 5 years of elementary school (3 percent of natives, 13 percent of immigrants).

- In spite of this, on the average, immigrants are better educated than natives (8 percent of natives with 5 or more years college compared to 13 percent of total immigrants and 20 percent of Asian immigrants). (There is a bi-modal distribution: more immigrants than U.S. citizens have less than 5 years of education, and more immigrants than natives have more university education.)

- Contemporary immigration is not high by historical U.S. standards. Immigrants between 1901 and 1910 arrived in numbers equal to about 10 percent of the population; between 1970 and 1980, only 2 percent. In 1910, 15 percent of the population was foreign born; in 1980 only 6 percent.

- Immigrants on the whole use tax monies—the public coffers—much less than the nonimmigrant population. Comparing immigrant and native families of similar education and age, there is almost no difference in usage levels of welfare, unemployment compensation, Aid to Families with Dependent Children, and food stamps. The costs of schooling are somewhat higher for immigrants after the first few years in the United States because their families are younger than the average native families. When Social Security, Medicare, and similar programs are considered, immigrant families on average receive much less in total welfare payments and public services than do average native families.

- Undocumented immigrants pay five to ten times as much in taxes as the cost of the welfare services they use.
- In the long run, the beneficial impact upon industrial efficiency of additional immigrant workers and consumers is likely to dwarf all other effects.

Assignments

Virginia Zanger (1984) has written a superb manual to guide second-year (or beyond) students of Spanish into interaction with Hispanic peoples. Each chapter focuses on a topic such as greetings, gestures, politeness, family structure, or roles of males and females. The chapter begins with an insightful reading on the topic, followed by questions that probe how the student feels about different issues raised by the reading.

The heart of the chapter contains relevant questions for the student to ask of Spanish-speaking people in his or her community. (Most communities in the United States count Spanish-speaking people among its residents. In Chicago, for example, one out of every five inhabitants lives in a Spanish-speaking home.) The results of these interviews can be processed in class. Zanger provides questions to help the student analyze individual and group differences in the responses and which patterns are associated with one social variable (e.g., age, sex) more than another.

Zanger has a second book in print (Zanger, 1985) that is aimed at ESL students. These students interview English-speaking people on various cultural topics. One also could use this book for English-speaking students of intercultural communication who want a structured approach to interviewing people from any other cultural group.

Exchange between ESL and FL Classes

For years I have thought that most U.S. students of a foreign language seriously underestimate the utility of what they have learned. In even a year or two of FL study students learn a lot. They just don't think so. This is for several reasons, one of which is that the instruction has occurred within a "hot house," too far removed from the give and take of real communication with a native speaker of the language. The students leave our FL classes psychologically blighted. They know a lot but they fall into a self-fulfilling prophecy of paralysis because they don't think they can do it. What they need is more face-to-face contact with folks from the target culture while they are studying the language (Flori, 1982).

In this context, one fall day I was approached by a nervous coordinator of language courses (Spanish and English as a second language) from a community-based agency. Although the ESL courses were robust, the enrollment for the Spanish courses was listless. I asked where the courses were offered. In two different buildings, Spanish in one and English in the other. The first thing to do, I suggested, was to have Spanish and ESL students share the same facilities. The second thing, I ventured, was to totally revamp the Spanish curriculum. I outlined a new approach. She took both suggestions and the story has a happy ending.

This is the approach I suggested: Put yourself in the student's position. Beginning the first day of class—whether beginning, intermediate, or advanced—the teacher announces that in one half hour you will be going to a classroom down the hall where Hispanic students just recently arrived in the United States are studying ESL. We'll stay there for 10 minutes, where you will be paired with someone who doesn't speak English. Your job for the next 30 minutes is to prepare for that interview. Let's break into small groups and start preparing. Students who didn't know any Spanish at all would prepare things such as "My name is _____. What is your name?" "Do you have brothers? How many?" "What time is it?" More advanced students might prepare questions around a topic. Then, since turnabout is fair play, the teacher announces a change in language and the ESL students talk to the Spanish students in English.

The class then returns to their own room and the teacher debriefs them. How do they feel? Were there things they tried to say but that couldn't be understood? The teacher deals with those elements of communication that the students have developed a need to know. Every class period had the same routine. About once a month on nice days, the teacher takes the students for a stroll in an ethnically mixed neighborhood and students approach people who look as though they speak Spanish and ask them for directions or the time or anything that occurred to them.

When this approach was first implemented, the agency did not tell the students what was in store. It was felt that if students knew that during every class they would have to converse with a real, live Spanish-speaking person, enrollment would be jeopardized. And there *was* student anxiety. One student reported that before each "interview" his stomach would turn in knots; it wasn't until the end of the course that he became inured to it, and even then he was nervous. It soon became apparent to the agency, however, that this face-to-face interaction was a selling point. When prospective students were told about it, enrollment tripled!

I don't know if these students learned any more Spanish than students in a traditional course. Maybe they learned a lot less. But they sure learned how to use what they did know, something I don't see traditionally taught students doing much of.

There are other ways to engineer contact.

Studying Abroad

It is surprisingly easy to arrange to study as a special student in a university in Europe, Latin America, or Asia. (I am uncertain about the situation in Africa.) For liberal arts majors it is especially easy. But even for majors in subjects such as science, medicine, or engineering a semester abroad can be arranged if the student begins planning early enough.

One may forget any given year of study in your native country, but you will never in your life forget the experiences gained by studying abroad. A female friend of mine who years earlier had spent a semester of secondary school in Austria became close to one of the daughters of the host family. Today, her son is visiting the daughter's family, continuing a friendship into the third generation. (Next summer a teenage son of the Austrian family will stay with my friend's family.)

Some resources for preparing to study abroad are Beckman et al. (1986), Cassidy (1988), Griesar (1992), Howard (1989), Institute of International Education (1992), Judkins (1989), and UNESCO (1992).

Working Abroad

One recent book on working abroad (Seelye and Day, 1992) contains a chapter on volunteer jobs available in the United States with service agencies that work with immigrants. It suggests serving as a paid or volunteer worker in these U.S.-based agencies to learn the target language. Other books of interest to people seeking employment abroad are Win (1986), *Teaching Abroad* (1988), Schuman (1988), and Krannich and Krannich (1990).

To encourage your students to meet people from other cultures, some record can be kept of the nature and extent of this interaction, and academic credit may be given for this behavior. However, the instructor may want to base the credit on the quantity of interaction rather than on an attempt to judge its quality. (Not because quality may be absent, but because attempting to measure it in newly formed relationships may be premature. Besides, it is technically laborious to measure the quality of these relationships.)

One easy approach to interacting with people is to ask them questions.

Asking the Right Questions

"What is the answer?" Gertrude Stein asked. And in the absence of a response she continued, "In that case, what is the question?"

Any question is the right question as long as it doesn't irritate the person so much that he or she ends the conversation, or worse. In fact, one of the first things to learn about the target culture is whether it is appropriate to ask questions at all in any particular situation, and if so, to whom. For example, students in many cultures will not pose a question during class but will ask teachers questions after class. In some cultures (e.g., Japan, Native American) one is expected to learn primarily from observing the behavior of others.

A major learning strategy consists first in motivating students to formulate productive questions and then in teaching them skills that will enable them to find answers to their questions. Yet it is common practice to give students answers before they have formulated the questions. Little wonder that a frequently heard classroom adage is "It goes in one ear and out the other!" One of the most significant answers given in the twentieth century, Einstein's famous $E=mc^2$, is utterly meaningless to those of us who have not formulated the necessary questions in advance of hearing the "answer."

The Exotic as Springboard

What immediately hits the student of a second culture is that things are done differently there. These exotic differences are two-edged swords. They provoke interest but they reinforce the ethnocentricity of the learner. ("Those Frenchmen are really crazy—the men kiss each other!" "Latin Americans are really lazy—they're always taking siestas." "Italians are so emotional—always waving their hands around.") Culturally contrastive patterns can best be exploited for their motivating interest by using them as points of entry into the target culture. Once inside, the student should be helped to discover that even seemingly bizarre behavior usually makes perfect sense once it is seen within the context of the rest of the culture. Once its relationship to other patterns and to universal needs is seen, it makes sense. (This point is discussed in more detail in chapter 9.)

The two principles that people everywhere satisfy the same basic needs (although the relative importance of these basic needs and the patterns available to satisfy them differ from culture to culture) and that many different patterns interact in concert for basic needs to be satisfied, along with Brooks's reminder to focus on the individual, help us ask significant questions about relationships in the target culture.

But, alas, human curiosity is not limited to "significant" questions. Curiosity, however perverse, is such a strong and useful motivator that it is not to be trifled with.

How can the teacher capitalize on a student's offbeat interest in something such as whether most belly buttons in Italy are inverted or protrude? To assist the student's perception of significant relationships in this patently absurd instance, he or she can be asked to list things that might affect the appearance of navels and, conversely, things that navels might plausibly affect. The list might include things such as whether it is a matter of genetic determination and, if so, whether the gene pool for inverted navels in Italy differs in frequency from that of other culture areas; whether techniques used by doctors or midwives during birth affect the phenomenon; whether infant care in Italy, such as swaddling, has an effect; whether one form or another is considered more aesthetic; and if so, whether this affects fashion in any way.

While any one of these topics may be interesting, plotting the interrelation of several topics affords practice in making guesses within a cultural context that is broader than the "we do it this way but they do it that way" of much contrastive analysis. The object is to get the student into the target culture in a way that makes it easier for him or her to see how behavior systematically and logically fits together. The teacher is not, of course, expected to know, or even care, what the answers are to most questions posed by students. Today's teacher is more interested in the process of inquiry than in having students memorize disembodied facts.

Another example of turning trivia into something more promising involves a student with no known academic or intellectual accomplishments or interests except two: girls and stealing cars. He might be cajoled into making a scrapbook of clippings of girls from the target culture and photos of cars culled from a stack of Mexican magazines. If the teacher is female, the student will undoubtedly try to test her sophistication with some of the pinups he has collected, so she might want to forget about part of the initial assignment and emphasize the inanimate. Pictures of cars can be catalogued according to make, model, year, number of occupants, whether male or female is driving, type of highway, and so on. The student's summary of this information (e.g., number of cars collected, number of females driving) can be presented to the class to see what kind of "conclusions" (hypotheses) might be ventured concerning the economic structure, transportation facilities, and position of women in the country based on the data. The class can be asked to suggest other kinds of information that might check the "conclusions" (e.g., number of licensed women, number of cars imported annually from Europe). Some of the South American magazines would be more interesting to old car buffs. Some Peruvian taxis, for example, are virtual antiques.

The main pedagogical point in these exercises is to (1) get the student interested in the target culture; (2) direct this interest, step by step, into pertinent areas of concern; and (3) develop student skill in discovering things about peoples and places.

The teacher's role in a problem-oriented approach such as this is to assist the student in defining the problem that interests the student. The more precisely a problem is defined, the less trouble a student will have in researching it and the more fruitful will be the outcome. (It is not desirable to have the student stymied by an extensive background search. As would be the case with the car pictures, sometimes it is advisable to jump in and begin manipulating the "documents" and fill in background as the need arises.) The teacher, with the cooperation of the school librarian, can guide the student in his or her bibliographic work. Rather than be told to read a book on the general topic chosen, students can be taught to skim and to read carefully only limited sections that are germane to their specific area of interest. Otherwise, the student will fast become bogged down in the fantastic explosion of knowledge that threatens to engulf all scholars, especially those in science and the social sciences. If the student report is to be written, the teacher can offer invaluable assistance and encouragement in the first draft. If the report is presented orally, sympathetic questions can help a student evaluate his or her own work.

Brooks (1964, pp. 82-96) asks many promising questions about some sixty-four different topics such as: "In what ways are age, provenance, social status, academic achievement, degree of formality, interpersonal relations, aesthetic concern, personality, reflected in . . . speech?" "What common words or expressions in English have direct equivalents that are not tolerated in the new culture, and vice versa?" "What objects are often found decorating the bureau and walls of a young person's bedroom?" "What careers have strong appeal for the young?"

The particular aspect of the target culture that initially motivates a given student is of little importance as long as some of the questions inspired by the interest lead to a discovery that cultural patterns interact (that is, are mutually supportive) and that they are used by people to satisfy universal needs.

An especially strong source to aid teachers in posing fruitful questions about any culture area has been prepared by Volunteers in Asia (Darrow and Palmquist, 1977). The hundreds of articulated questions are grouped under topics such as Roles of Women and Men, Religion and Beliefs, Food, Music and Art, Education. Another source for relevant cultural questions is available in Saville-Troike (1978). She asks, for example, how insults are expressed, who may talk to whom, what significance dress has for group identity. Still another fruitful source to aid asking questions in face-to-face contact was authored by Tyler (1987).

We did not get to the moon by holding sacred the scientific facts of the 1950s. We never move away from the cozy dark corner of the cave, where self-serving myths soothe our troubles, unless we are open to new facts as well as old facts in fresh combinations. The folk wisdom of many cultures tells us that experience is the best teacher. To learn from experience is to change our way of doing and understanding.

Interviewing Informants

The following exchange was overheard between a Korean elementary school student and a Chicago ESL teacher:

TEACHER: "How old are you?"

STUDENT: "I was ten but now I'm eight."

How to make sense of this? (And, it turns out, it makes perfect sense.) The obvious answer is to seek additional information from someone who has lived extensively in Korea. Fortunately, the ESL teacher had a Korean colleague in the same school. The answer was simple: Koreans consider themselves to be one year old at birth and two years old as soon as the New Year arrives. A person born the day before the lunar calendar New Year's Day would be two years old his or her second day of life. The "but now I'm eight" refers to the age adjustment made by the U.S. cultural system to the child's age.

Intercultural communication teachers possess an insatiable need for all kinds of culture-specific information to better fathom the behavior of the people they study. There are several ways teachers can put students into contact with perhaps the best source of information—natives of the target culture.

Locating native informants within the local community can become a class project. Once a directory is compiled, the teacher can enhance student interaction with bearers of the target culture by inviting them into class for visits, by encouraging students to talk to them out of class, by arranging visits to target institutions such as churches or social centers, and by establishing a strategy for communication via the telephone or mail. As with any other type of instructional device, purposeful activities that students pursue for credit should be planned. Students are assigned to interview native informants.

By secondary school age, the natural curiosity of primary school children often has degenerated into a self-conscious reticence that makes interviews with strangers difficult. Embarrassing silences and martyred attempts at yes-or-no questions characterize many classroom "confrontations" with natives. With a little bit of planning, much of this awkwardness can be avoided.

Spending an hour every two or three weeks with a classroom visitor from the target culture does not rob time from an in-depth analysis of the imperfect subjunctive so much as it dramatizes what intercultural learning is all about—direct personal communication with another culture. Regularly planned interviews with natives can become an integral part of any course about the target culture. (William F. Marquardt used to conduct whole ESL courses this way, with a different informant each day. Students subsequently wrote letters to each informant, making comments on the substance of what the informant said during the class interview.)

Culture shock is a two-way street, as many visitors to U.S. classrooms can painfully attest. Planning for an interview begins with concern for putting the guest at ease and establishing quick rapport. This is not so difficult to achieve. Everyone responds to people who are genuinely interested in them, especially when the interest is not marred by a display of ignorance so dismal as to be insulting. It does not generally go over very big to ask a visitor from Costa Rica about life in South America, or to assume that a Brazilian speaks Spanish.

Preparation begins with the students locating the most detailed map available of the guest's country and studying it to get a feel for the land and place names. Next, a brief survey of the vital statistics of the country should be read by all students. This need not exceed two pages in length; encyclopedias or almanacs are adequate sources. The background gleaned from the map and survey equips the student interviewer with the minimum necessary knowledge to begin the next step: preparing the initial interview questions.

Each student can prepare three questions on relatively neutral areas of the target culture that cannot be answered by yes or no. Questions that reflect a little background research concerning climate, food, music, and sports can be asked in the initial stages of the interview to break the ice. In addition to writing out these questions beforehand, each student should practice his or her questions orally. (I am assuming the interview will be effected in the guest's language.)

Each student next prepares three more questions (both in writing and orally) concerning the things people like and dislike and the way people (but not necessarily the person interviewed) relate to each other. Would a typical person from Aix want a large or small family? Where do teenagers go for recreation? Do wives like to hold jobs outside of the home? What are some differences between city and country people? How are children disciplined? By whom? For which meals does the whole family get together? What responsibilities does each member of a family generally have? What are the most popular religions? How much social contact does a family generally have with the church leader?

Some questions probably should be avoided. Areas that have some social stigma associated with them, or whose answers might demean the guest's dignity, obviously fall into this category. Potentially offensive questions include: How many years of schooling do you have? What do you [or your parents] do? Do you have you own house/car/TV? What are your ethnic origins? To what social or economic class do you belong? Discovering the taboos of questioning can itself become the basis of an exciting interview. When in doubt about how to word a question, try asking the guest "What question should I ask to find out _____?"

Each student can then prepare three more questions (this brings the total to nine) that directly relate to whichever of the six cultural goals is currently being studied in class. This task should be carried out in cooperation with the rest of the class to avoid asking the same question twice.

Each interaction with a stranger is an adventure into uncharted territory, and one cannot predict the turn of events. The informant should be invited to ask questions of the interviewers, too.

Nevertheless, the teacher should try to have students structure the session. A detailed how-to text on interviewing techniques has been prepared by a sociologist with extensive experience in cross-cultural interviewing (Gorden, 1987), and an extensive review of the area of face-to-face cross-cultural interactions has been prepared by a social psychologist (Brislin et al., 1986).

A simple interview objective might require students to write in English a minimum of four facts that they learned from the interview. A little more involved objective would require students to write the answers in the target language to those of the nine oral questions they prepared in advance and subsequently asked in the interview.

The following example of a performance objective on interviews was written in a workshop I directed.

Performance Objective for Native-Informant Interview

(prepared by Marsha Rybski)

Performance objective

The student will demonstrate his awareness of cultural meanings associated with everyday target words (goal 3).

Terminal behavior

The student will demonstrate his ability to describe the word *le déjeuner* beyond the translated meaning of "lunch."

Conditions

The student will write on a piece of paper a report on *le déjeuner* describing the following points: what is eaten, how long the meal lasts, what time of the day it is eaten, where it is eaten, who fixes the meal, how the student knows it is an important daily event. The student will write his report in 30 minutes in class the day after the informant's visit. The report will be written in English or in French.

Criterion

The student must describe in his report at least five of the points mentioned above. The description may be as simple as answering the who, what, or where in the question.

Interviews are structured, not to drive out the spontaneous, but to have something to fall back on to keep the conversation rolling, and to facilitate the gathering of specific information.

Our most becoming stance as students of culture is one of inquiry. This chapter has suggested several techniques to assist a student in asking questions about the target culture. The point of the chapter can be realized only in classrooms in which the process of inquiry is rewarded at least as much as the capture of ephemeral facts. I would advise that people who want to learn should do the following:

1. *Be interested in everything.* If spear-throwing is the treasured local skill, learn to throw them.
2. *Keep up to date.* Read the local newspapers, listen to the radio, read street graffiti.
3. *Learn from others.* Ask about their interests, share triumphs and disappointments with them, ask their views on current affairs.

In 1985 an innovative journal, *World Cultures* (P.O. Box 12524, La Jolla, CA 92037-0650), began "publishing" directly on personal computer diskettes (IBM-PC and other formats) rather than on paper. This electronic quarterly provides databases and accompanying codes on "any aspect of human groups" worldwide. Murdock's *Ethnographic Atlas* (which contains no maps) is one of the databases included. Students can begin by asking of the data base, "How common is [some cultural practice that interests me]?" They then can progress to hypothesizing what variables are most associated with the cultural practices that interest them. These hypotheses can easily be checked with the aid of any simple correlations program that will run on the school's or on the students' personal computers.

LEARNING ACTIVITY FOR GOAL 1

This goal is one that encourages empathy with people in the target culture. To facilitate this goal teachers can do the following:

A. Provide the students with a bibliography of interesting titles on the target culture.

B. Invite at least one person socialized in another culture into the classroom each month.

C. Keep students informed on the availability of movies and magazines in the target language.

D. Prepare a listing of local residents who belong to the target culture and facilitate getting your students to talk with them.

Curiosity enables us to be open to the contributions other peoples and cultures can make to our own lives. The next chapter deals with the fatigue—and sometimes the shock—that intercultural experiences so often offer as well.

Suggested Activities

1. From a trivial topic write five testable cultural hypotheses. (If you chose women, a starter might be: Women between the ages of 18 and 36 never wear their hair down to their shoulders.)

2. Prepare your own mini-media unit based on your chosen topic. (If you chose men, you could use photos showing their reactions to death, to children, to sports, etc.)

3. Carry your topic through to an interview with a native from the target culture. Prepare ten questions that would elicit information on it.

4. Prepare a performance objective for your intended interview.

5. Compile a human resources directory of community residents who were raised in the target culture.

6. Some anthropologists estimate that as much as 90 percent of any given culture is the result of cultural borrowing and the acceptance of technological innovations invented by people from different cultures. Prepare a list of fifty such traits currently observable in a country of your choosing.

References Cited_____

American Citizens Abroad: A Handbook for Citizens Living Abroad. 1988. New York: Doubleday.

Beckman, David M., Timothy J. Mitchell, and Linda L. Powers. 1986. *The Overseas List: Opportunities for Living and Working in Developing Countries.* Rev. and exp. Minneapolis: Augsburg.

Brislin, Richard W., Kenneth Cushner, Craig Cherrie, and Mahealani Yong. 1986. *Intercultural Interactions: A Practical Guide.* Newbury Park, CA: Sage.

Brooks, Nelson D. 1968. *Language and Language Learning: Theory and Practice.* New York: Harcourt, Brace.

Carroll, John B. 1967. "Foreign Language Proficiency Levels Attained by Language Majors near Graduation from College." *Foreign Language Annals* 1: 131-50.

Cassidy, Maggie Brown. 1988. *Taking Students Abroad: A Complete Guide for Teachers.* Brattleboro, VT: Pro Lingua.

Darrow, Kenneth, and Bradley Palmquist, eds. 1977. *The Trans-Cultural Study Guide.* 2nd ed. Stanford, CA: Volunteers in Asia.

Demko, George J., Jerome Agel, and Eugene Boe. 1992. *Why in the World: Adventures in Geography.* New York: Anchor.

Flori, Monica. 1982. "The Hispanic Community as a Resource for a Practical Spanish Program." *Foreign Language Annals* 15, 3: 213-18.

Gans, Herbert J. 1980. *Deciding What's News: A Study of CBS Evening News, NBC Nightly News, Newsweek, and Time,* New York: Vintage Books.

Gardner, Robert C., and Donald M. Taylor. 1968. "Ethnic Stereotypes: Their Effects on Person Perception." *Canadian Journal of Psychology* 22, 4: 267-76.

Gezi, Kahil I. 1965. "Factors Associated with Student Adjustment in Cross-Cultural Contact." *California Journal of Educational Research* 16 (May): 129-36. Also in Kahil I. Gezi and James E. Myers, eds., *Teaching in American Culture.* New York: Holt, 1968, pp. 254-61.

Gorden, Raymond L. 1987. *Interviewing: Strategy, Techniques, and Tactics.* Homewood, IL: Dorsey.

Griesar, William. 1992. *The Underground Guide to Study Abroad in Britain and Ireland.* Yarmouth, ME: Intercultural Press.

Howard, Marguerite, ed. 1989. *Vacation Study Abroad, 1989.* New York: Institute of International Education Books.

Hursh, Heidi, and Michael Prevedel. 1991. *Activities Using 'The New State of the World Atlas.'* Center for Teaching International Relations (CTIR), University of Denver.

Hursh, Heidi, Ron Schukar, and Barry Simmons. 1991. *Geographic Perspectives: Content-Based Activities.* Center for Teaching International Relations (CTIR), University of Denver.

Institute of International Education. 1992. *Academic Year Abroad.* New York: The Institute. (Revised annually.)

Judkins, David. 1989. *Study Abroad: The Astute Student's Guide.* Charlotte, VT: Williamson.

Kidron, Michael, and Dan Smith. 1991. *The New State of War and Peace.* New York: Simon & Schuster.

Kidron, Michael, and Ronald Segal. 1991. *The New State of the World Atlas.* New York: Simon & Schuster.

Krannich, Ronald L., and Caryl R. Krannich. 1990. *International Jobs and Careers.* San Luis Obispo, CA: Impact.

Ma, Sheng-mei. 1992. "America's Unwelcome Mat," pp. C1, C4, *The Washington Post,* May 17.

Marshall, Bruce, ed. 1991. *The Real World: Understanding the Modern World through the New Geography.* New York: Houghton-Mifflin.

Murdock, George P. 1967. *Ethnographic Atlas.* Univ. of Pittsburgh Press.

Saville-Troike, Muriel. 1978. *A Guide to Culture in the Classroom.* Rosslyn, VA: National Clearinghouse for Bilingual Education.

Schuman, Howard. 1988. *Making It Abroad: The International Job Hunting Guide.* New York: Wiley.

Seelye, H. Ned. 1969. "An Objective Measure of Biculturation: Americans in Guatemala, A Case Study," *Modern Language Journal* 53,7 (Nov.): pp. 503-14.

Seelye, H. Ned, and Marilynn B. Brewer. 1970. "Ethnocentrism and Acculturation of North Americans in Guatemala." *Journal of Social Psychology* 80 (April): 147-55.

Seelye, H. Ned, and J. Laurence Day. 1992. *Careers for Foreign-Language Aficionados and Other Multilingual Types.* Lincolnwood, IL: National Textbook.

Simon, Julian L. 1989. *The Economic Consequences of Immigration.* Cambridge, MA: Blackwell.

Smith, Gary R., and George Otero. 1989. *Teaching about Cultural Awareness.* Denver: Center for Teaching International Relations (CTIR), University of Denver.

Stanford University team. 1982. *Demystifying the Chinese Language.* Denver: Center for Teaching International Relations (CTIR), University of Denver.

Stanford University and University of Washington team. 1983. *Japan Meets the West: A Case Study of Perceptions.* Denver: Center for Teaching International Relations (CTIR), University of Denver.

Teaching Abroad: Opportunities for U.S. Teachers and Faculty Worldwide. 1988. New York: Institute of International Education.

Tyler, V. Lynn. 1987. *Intercultural Interacting.* Provo, UT: David M. Kennedy Center for International Studies, Brigham Young University.

UNESCO. 1992. *Study Abroad.* New York: UNESCO Publications Center. Published annually.

Win, David. 1986. *International Careers.* Charlotte, VT: Williamson.

Zanger, Virginia Vogel. 1984. *Exploración intercultural: Una Guía para el estudiante.* Rowley, MA: Newbury House.

Zanger, Virginia Vogel. 1985. *Face to Face: The Cross-Cultural Workbook.* Rowley, MA: Newbury House.

5 Building a Survival Kit for Culture Shock

This chapter continues the discussion of goal 1 (showing interest in the target culture) begun in the previous chapter. Chapter 4 argued that one important way to show interest in another culture is to seek out people from this culture. The present chapter describes two techniques to sensitize students to the miscommunication that always accompanies interaction with bearers of another culture. The first technique involves out-of-class reading of "empathic" literature; the second involves a specially designed class skit called a "minidrama." Examples are included of minidramas for French, German, and English as a second language.

When Cultural Assumptions Clash

Conflict is present whenever two cultures come into contact. This often is because of a clash of values—a cultural difference in the perception of the appropriate way to satisfy basic physical and psychological needs. Sometimes this conflict, played across the stage of daily interaction with people from another culture, provokes strong physiological and psychological responses in the sojourner. This phenomenon was called "culture shock" by Kalervo Oberg (1960), an anthropologist, and the name has stuck.

The symptoms of culture shock include a preoccupation with personal cleanliness and disease and dirt (and an inordinate fear of drinking the water and eating the food), a sense of being cheated, irritability with little provocation, hypersensitivity to perceived criticisms, and depression. Many suggest that there is an ebb and flow to these symptoms; culture shock is greater at some junctures than at others. Curves of various forms representing rising and falling emotional intensity across time have been hypothesized. Some see a "U-curve," with a steady depression that plateaus after a year or two, then steadily gets better as one adjusts to life under different ground rules. Others see a "J-curve," with things turning sour soon after arrival but improving steadily once you are over the hump. Some add a wrinkle by talking about a "W-curve," which is really two U-curves, with the second U referring to problems the sojourner often experiences when reentering his or her home culture.

There are five or six generally recognized stages of culture shock. The preliminary stage (events that occur before departure), the spectator phase (the initial weeks or months of living in another culture), the increasing participation phase, the shock phase, and the adaptation phase. Some add a sixth phase, the reentry phase. An excellent literary source that helps these phases come alive was edited by Lewis and Jungman (1986). These editors present four or five short pieces by major authors (e.g., Camus, Conrad, Borges) organized under each of the six phases of culture shock.

One businessman, Igor Lelchitsky, discussing the dynamics of doing business in Russia, puts the initial phases of second-culture adjustment this way:

> The first time you go to Russia you think you can do
> anything in the world. The second time, you start having
> your doubts. The third time, you think, 'These Russians
> don't know what the hell they're doing.' The fourth time,
> you think you don't know what the hell you're doing.
> (Don Steinberg, 1990)

Only one person ever persuaded me that he was going to avoid successfully the trauma associated with adjustment to another culture. He had a command of the target language, a well-paid professional position in the target culture, a personable manner, an excess of good will, and the boundless energy of the young. He would seek out natives with whom to converse, and when he was by himself he would practice out loud new idioms and difficult verb inflections. A little before completing two years of residence abroad ("abroad" in this case was the United States), he was hospitalized due to a nervous breakdown caused by the stress of adjusting to U.S. life.

Mildred Sikkema and Agnes Niyekawa tell the story of "an American girl [who] cleaned the room while her Thai roommate was having breakfast in the dormitory dining hall. When the roommate returned, she became upset, cried, and left the room. Later it became clear that the American girl had placed the Thai girl's skirt on the pillow portion of the bed. In Thai culture, the head is sacred and putting a piece of clothing associated with a lesser part of the body on a place reserved for the head was one of the worst possible insults. Friends and advisers tried to explain to the Thai girl that the American girl's intentions were only good, but the involuntary reaction was so deep that she refused to room with the American girl again" (Sikkema and Niyekawa, 1987).

At a New Year's Eve celebration in an exclusive Guatemalan hotel, one American was overheard telling another, "You see all these people? They're all my wife's relatives. And every damn one of them has kissed me tonight. If another Guatemalan man hugs and kisses me I'll punch him right in the face!" The irritated American was disturbed by two things: the extended kinship patterns of the group and the *abrazo de año nuevo* as executed by the men (he did not complain of the female *abrazos*). Both customs—close family ties that extend to distant relatives and the *abrazo* given as a greeting or sign of affection devoid of sexual overtures—elicited hostility in the American who was bored by unintelligible language and depressed by nostalgia and alcohol. After a good day's rest and a hot shower, the *yanqui* probably achieved a peaceful coexistence with his wife's relatives.

But a hundred other strange customs await his every venture outside his circle of American friends—the bureaucratic *qué vuelva usted mañana* ("Come back tomorrow"), the angry stares when he enthusiastically whistles at his favorite team's athletic triumph (whistling in this context belittles the players), the solicitous *es suyo* (it's yours) after he compliments someone's clothes, followed by his *no, gracias*, which is in turn met by confusion (he should have simply acknowledged the politeness by saying *gracias*).

A prominent member of the foreign language teaching profession tells of the frustration of a year's sabbatical in Germany. In his initial two months abroad he did not accomplish much that he had planned, and he blamed the host people. His hostility gradually increased until, one afternoon several months later, he came within a fraction of hitting a housewife who was blocking the sidewalk with a baby carriage. This so unnerved him that, out of fear of causing bodily injury, he kept himself locked up in his hotel room for the duration of the sabbatical, some six months (Seelye and Seelye-James, 1995).

Most cases of culture shock are not this severe. More generally, guests in another culture suffer from psychological weariness rather than from outright shock. Getting through the daily routine is so much more tiring in another culture!

V. Lynn Tyler (1987), a specialist in intercultural communication, prefers the terms "self-discovery shock," "role shock," and "transition shock." Whatever you call it, says Tyler, it all concerns dealing with diversity. The term *shock* may be a bit hyperbolic. *Culture fatigue* has been suggested by many as a more accurate description of what usually occurs. At the end of a day of dealing with myriads of new cultural patterns, you are worn out. Jacqueline Howell Wasilewski, an intercultural communication specialist teaching at International Christian University in Tokyo, approaches culture fatigue from a fresh perspective (personal communication, 1992). "Too much is made of it," she says. "Of course you get tired. You are learning new things and all learning is fatiguing."

Sojourners suffer from the inevitable malaise of cross-culturally induced fatigue for a number of reasons. The fatigue is occasioned by energies spent in an exaggerated concern for hygiene, by having to work harder to do simple things such as use the telephone or catch a bus, by the constant irritation of dealing with people who "don't know how to get things done." All those who venture abroad for any lengthy stay contract it. Most recover within a few years, but recovery is gradual. It makes little difference whether it is an American terrified by the traffic patterns of Guatemala or a Guatemalan perspiring with claustrophobic anxiety in the subways of New York. Culture fatigue is not a respecter of persons.

Geoffrey Garvey describes his bout with culture fatigue in terms many will recognize.

> My worst time with it came when I was working on a French farm, with no phone, no opportunity for hygiene beyond brushing my teeth, no bus . . . (personal communication, 1992)

That the people of one culture experience difficulty observing the same "reality" as natives of another culture has been demonstrated on many different levels. Linguistically, for example, the inability of many Chinese to distinguish between rice and lice or the problems Americans have differentiating the Spanish *bata* and *pata* or *pero* and *perro*, or the difficulty of speakers of Spanish to distinguish the two English words silly and Seelye. In fact, this very observation that different languages hear different sounds (i.e., that they hear certain phonetically distinct sounds as the same) has led to the fruitful concept within descriptive linguistics of the phoneme.

An acquaintance went blind shortly after birth but fortunately regained his sight at the age of 16. One of his major adjustments, he related, was then to learn not to see the inconsequential objects that came into his line of vision. For instance, while looking at a person across the room, everything within eyesight would demand equal visual attention. Our culture teaches us what to see and what to ignore. A newly arrived foreigner does not know what to see, let alone what to say.

Each of us experiences difficulties as we attempt to function effectively in another culture. Richard Brislin et al. (1986) identify many areas that are associated with cross-cultural adjustmental strains. These include the difficulty of

- *Dealing with anxiety whose origins are typically vague.* Brooding about their feelings leads sojourners to incorrect conclusions concerning their bind. Often the anxiety is produced by a loss of control over goal attainment (i.e., need satisfaction). You can get what you want so much easier in your own hometown.

- *Learning new culturally appropriate behaviors at a time sojourners may feel free of the constraints and social sanctions of their native culture.* The difficulty lies in missing the behavior that is appropriate to goal attainment in the second culture and, instead, engaging in behaviors that are atypical to both cultures.

- *Putting memorable events into proper perspective. Emotionally charged personal experiences, especially if they are negative, can take on a significance that misrepresents the host culture.* This tendency is exacerbated when one has a strong expectation that the experience violates.

- *Exercising the level of social skills needed to belong to host networks at a time when the sojourner is cut off from his or her support networks back home.*

- *Having to make decisions based on less information than one is accustomed to.*

- *Adjusting to different beliefs about how the workplace should be organized.* How is authority exercised? How much planning should precede action? How are incentives, rewards, and control effected? How much conformity and initiative are expected? What constitutes an appropriate work setting? How does gender affect expectations?

- *Recognizing how time is broken down in the host culture.* Brislin states that "the working unit of time for the Euro-American is the five-minute block." Some cultures have other "units." In the Arab and Hispanic business worlds, for instance, a 15-minute block may reign.

- *Understanding the meaning in an ambiguous statement such as "Let's have lunch together sometime."* Is the speaker just being polite or should a date be set?

- *Learning to feel comfortable with the greater or lesser physical distance that is observed between people in the host culture.* In Latin America this is typically six inches closer than is customary in the United States.

- *Recognizing new cues to role and how one is expected to interface with that role.* Some of the roles are novel (Guardian of the Beauty Path), others appear to be familiar but are defined differently (steelworker). A related area is how hierarchies are established and how status is apportioned.

- *Adjusting to sex roles that go against one's principles.* American females frequently have particular difficulty with behavior they classify as "sexist" (e.g., aspects of Islamic or Hispanic cultures).

An overriding element that provokes much cross-cultural fatigue, according to Triandis (1983), is the way different cultures organize experience into different categories. Triandis gives the example of how Greeks define in-groups and out-groups. In-groups are formed of family and close friends. Greeks often extend the possibility of in-group membership to foreigners by asking the sort of question that one only asks, in Greece, of in-group members: How much did that cost? How much money do you make? If the foreigner is reluctant to answer questions that are "too personal," he or she may be forgoing unwittingly the proffered acceptance as a friend.

When the wealthy retired vending-machine magnate leans back in his straw chair by the hotel swimming pool and lifts his martini to the rising mountains and exclaims, "This is a beautiful country; I like the people; they know how to take it easy; I understand this country," he is kidding himself. His illusion of empathy lacks the foundation of knowledge and experience. A Finnish poet (Hollo, 1977), writing in English about "sojourner microcosms," puts it this way.

> visible & invisible persons
> distributed in space
> according to principles unknown
> to either group
> guessing, nevertheless,
> at each other's existence

(Quotation of a portion of the poem "Mediations" by Anselm Hollo from *Sojourner Microcosms: New & Selected Poems, 1959–1977* [© 1977] is reprinted here by permission of Blue Wind Press, P.O. Box 7175, Berkeley, CA 94707.)

Other useful sources for understanding culture shock or fatigue include Furnham and Bochner (1986) and Bache (1990). This latter book deals with difficulties between refugees and their American sponsors. One book that deals specifically with reentry shock is Austin (1986).

Stereotypes

Stereotypes pose an interesting paradox. Although often woefully out of date or outrageously derogatory, they often capture characteristics that are common in the target society. Why are they so insidious even when they generalize accurately? Because stereotypes lead us to ignore the considerable variety of personalities that make up any society.

Kohls's (1984) popular booklet, *Survival Kit for Overseas Living*, lists a series of common descriptors of Americans: outgoing, friendly, informal, loud, boastful, hard-working, wasteful, confident they have all the answers, lacking in class consciousness, disrespectful of authority, ignorant of other countries, wealthy, generous, always in a hurry. Kohls then makes the point that to the extent an American fits the stereotypes he or she will be likely to experience problems abroad, since even our "virtues" may be considered liabilities by another society. It is disconcerting for someone reared in a culture that values the individual to have someone abroad treat you as a "typical American." Conversely, our own stereotypes of other peoples can rob them of much of their richness as individuals.

Intimacy with a variety of people, and in-depth knowledge of the institutions that help form their personalities, is a powerful antidote to generalizations gone wild. Ask students questions concerning the *range* of behaviors observable in the target culture, not just questions emphasizing central tendencies since these latter generalizations can lead to stereotyping.

One approach (Finkelstein, Tobin, and Imamura, 1991) to "demystification" (or "defanging" the stereotype) of Japanese education assembled an enlightening anthology on Japanese culture in general, followed by articles grouped around the topics of family and society, education and cultural transmission, educational policy and the dilemmas of reform, and intergroup tensions in Japanese school and society. Giving this book a read will put to rest the facile generalizations on Japanese education that appear again and again in the Western press.

In the spring of 1992, the Southern Poverty Law Center (400 Washington Ave., Montgomery, Alabama 36104) began publishing *Teaching Tolerance*, a commendable magazine provided free of charge to teachers who request it. It is published twice a year.

The best study to date of the phenomenon of intercultural communication difficulties within a home setting was done by a sociologist, Raymond Gorden. Gorden (1974) studied miscommunication that occurred while U.S. college students and Peace Corps volunteers resided in the homes of middle-class hosts in Bogotá, Colombia. Gorden focused on two elements that affect communication: space and role.

The first type of problem (space) occurred because the Americans did not know the proper way to behave in the living room, the bedroom, the bathroom, the kitchen, etc. For example, the Americans were considered unkempt because they put their shoes in the wrong place in their bedrooms. Others were considered either too forward or too introverted depending on when they kept their bedroom door open or closed—and how open or closed they kept it.

The second type of problem Gorden focused on concerned inappropriate role relationships the Americans tried to maintain with the various members of the host household. For example, one American male, after "a terrific dinner party" in the host home, attempted to help the señora and the maid afterward by carrying a tray full of dishes into the kitchen. Gorden reports that the sight of a man in the kitchen trying to scrape the dishes was too disturbing to the Colombian's notions of social status and was more distracting than helpful.

One startling discovery Gorden made was that miscommunication between the Americans and their hosts was greater when the Americans were more fluent than average in Spanish. Americans who spoke hesitantly with a heavy accent were misunderstood less. The reason? The Colombians assumed that the fluent Americans who sounded as though they knew what they were talking about *did* know what they were talking about. Unfortunately, they rarely did, for they had not been socialized into Hispanic life. They had acquired fluency in Spanish in a U.S. cultural setting. Their cultural referents were U.S., not Hispanic.

Why didn't the Americans who murdered the language get into more communication difficulties? Because when they spoke their halting Spanish they didn't sound as if they knew much. Consequently, the Colombian hosts assumed ignorance of everything, including many basic Colombian cultural assumptions. The Colombians worked harder to understand these innocents abroad.

Gorden concludes that the key to learning how to function effectively in another culture is to learn the discrete behavioral patterns that are employed there. His masterful book answers the question of just how this learning is to occur. It occurs when the right questions are asked in the right way. A reading of Gorden's book goes a long way toward helping one develop this skill. Another source for living in Colombia is Hutchison et al. (1987).

Ethnocentrism

The culprit behind much cross-cultural fatigue is an ethnocentric outlook. According to Sumner's (1906) classic definition, ethnocentrism may best be described as a syndrome involving at least three basic factors: integration and loyalty among in-group members; hostile relations between in-group and out-group members; and positive self-regard among in-group members in contrast to derogatory stereotyping of out-group characteristics. One important component of this syndrome is an acceptance of in-group values and standards as universally applicable.

An exhaustive compendium of social science propositions dealing with ethnocentrism has been prepared by an anthropologist and a social psychologist (LeVine and Campbell, 1972). An excellent junior high school social studies book that presents materials especially selected to reduce ethnocentrism and to provide insight into the nature of cross-cultural communication has been edited by Fersh (1989). Portraits of Americans abroad are available in several studies: Cleveland et al. (1960); Lambert (1966); Seelye (1969); Seelye and Brewer (1970); Thiagarajan (1973); Gorden (1974). For reports on overseas training programs, see Decaroli (1972), DeCrow (1969), Harrison and Hopkins (1966), and Althen (1970, 1983).

The two types of activities described below attempt to elicit an emotional as well as an intellectual grasp of one of the problems of cross-cultural communication—empathizing with the bearer of the other culture. The two techniques are the use of literary sources and classroom minidramas to create empathy.

Creating Empathy through Literature

A polyglot professor of English linguistics, the late William F. Marquardt, has described a method of sensitizing students to enable them to experience how it feels to be a member of another culture (Marquardt, 1969, 1970). Marquardt saw empathy, "the habit of trying in time of conflict to see things the other person's way," as the "most relevant magic in our day." He went on to say that empathy "is obviously a desired end-product of learning, but what is often overlooked is that it is also a starting point—particularly in the learning of communication skills."

Marquardt saw literature as ideally suited to developing empathy in the reader since creators of literature receive their basic motivation from a desire to explore the feelings of others and to communicate these feelings to their readership. Marquardt identified the following seven types of "communication situations" as the most useful for observing in literature the interplay between persons of different cultures.

Communication Situations

1. Works by mainstream-culture Americans primarily for mainstream readers showing interaction between mainstream- and minority-culture members in the minority culture setting.

2. Works by mainstream Americans primarily for mainstream readers focused on minority-culture and mainstream-culture members interacting in the mainstream-culture setting.

3. Works by minority-culture members primarily for mainstream readers focused on minority- and mainstream-culture members interacting in a mainstream-culture setting.

4. Works by minority-culture members primarily for mainstream readers focused on minority- and mainstream-culture members interacting in the minority-culture setting.

5. Works by mainstream-culture members focused on presenting some specific feature of the minority culture primarily to mainstream-culture readers.

6. Works by minority-culture members presenting or interpreting some specific feature of the minority culture to mainstream- and minority-culture readers.

7. Works by minority-culture members discussing some specific feature of the mainstream culture for mainstream- and minority-culture readers.

The main object of reading this type of literature is to increase awareness of the extent to which one's behavior is conditioned by one's culture. Marquardt provides a lengthy annotated list of titles falling within the range outlined above.

Some of my own favorites include the bestselling science fiction novel of all times, *Stranger in a Strange Land* by Robert Heinlein (1961); *White Dawn* by James Houston (1971); *The Woman Warrior: Memoirs of a Girlhood among Ghosts* by Maxine Hong Kingston (1976); *The Ancient Child* by N. Scott Momaday (1989); *Woman Hollering Creek and Other Stories* by Sandra Cisneros (1991); and *Wild Swans: Three Daughters of China* by Jung Chang (1991). I could go on and on.

Additional titles can be obtained easily by asking librarians, other teachers, and, best of all, your students for suggestions. To make it easier to "scoop up promising items at every cast," Marquardt proposes a grid wherein the horizontal rows represent the seven communication situations, and the vertical columns represent literary genres. (See table 5.1.)

FORM OR GENRE

	(a) Autobiog.	(b) Biography	(c) Novels	(d) Stories	(e) Plays	(f) Poems	(g) Essays
1	Griffin, Black Like Me (1961)	Kugelmass, Ralph J. Bunche: Fighter for Peace (1962)	Hentoff, Jazz Country (1965)	Dolch, Navajo Stories (1956)	Shulman, West Side Story (1961)	Rollins, ed. Christmas Gif (1963)	Durham & Jones, The Adventures of the Negro Cowboys (1965)
2	Buck, My Several Worlds (1954)	Shapiro, Jackie Robinson of the Brooklyn Dodgers (1957)	Archibald, Outfield Orphan (1961)	Faulkner "That Evening Sun"	O'Neill, All God's Chillun Got Wings (1932)	Culver, ed. Great American Negroes in Verse 1723-1965 (1966)	Henry, "White People's Time, Colored People's Time" (1966)
3	Davis, Yes, I Can (1965)	Bontemps, Famous Negro Athletes (1964)	Baldwin, Go Tell It on the Mountain (1953)	Hughes, ed. The Best Short Stories by Negro Writers (1965)	Baldwin, Blues for Mr. Charlie (1964)	Brooks, Bronzeville Boys and Girls (1956)	Baldwin, Nobody Knows My Name (1961)
4	Malcolm X, The Autobiography of Malcolm X (1965)	Bennett, What Manner of Man: A Biography of M. L. King	Hughes, Tambourines to Glory (1950)	Hughes, Simple Speaks His Mind (1950)	Couch, New Black Playwrights (1969)	Hughes, Selected Poems (1959)	J. Stands-in-Timber & M. Liberty, Cheyenne Memories (1969)
5	Sexton, Spanish Harlem (1965)	Plate, Palette and Tomahawk: The Story of George Catlin (1962)	Steinbeck, The Pearl (1962)	Porter, Collected Stories (1965)	Duberman, In White America (1964)	Rasmussen, Beyond the High Hills: A Book of Eskimo Poetry (1961)	Goldin, Straight Hair, Curly Hair (1966)
6	Thomas, Down These Mean Streets (1967)	Bontemps, Chariot in the Sky (1951)	Killens, And Then We Heard the Thunder (1963)	Harris, ed. Once Upon a Totem (1963)	Charles, Janus (1966)	Walker, For My People (1942)	Hughes, The First Book of Jazz (1954)
7	Baldwin, The Fire Next Time (1963)	Terkel, Giants of Jazz (1957)	Owens, Walking on Borrowed Time (1950)	Wright, Uncle Tom's Children (1940)	Richardson & Miller, eds. Negro History in Thirteen Plays (1935)	J.W. & J.R. Johnson, The Books of American Negro Spirituals (1940)	Samora, La Raza: Forgotten Americans (1966)

COMMUNICATION SITUATION

Reprinted with permission of the Florida FL Reporter and William F. Marquardt from the special anthology issue, Linguistic-Cultural Differences and American Education, 7, No. 1 (Spring/Summer 1969): 134-35. Alfred C. Aarons, Barbara Y. Gordon, and William A. Stewart, editors.

Table 5.1

Each grid contains one example. Many of the examples relate to African-Americans. This is because Marquardt's article was especially aimed at creating empathy between U.S. mainstream- and minority-culture bearers, and because there is a voluminous list of good titles in this area. The literary works do not, however, have to relate specifically to the target culture to be effective. The principle of cross-cultural empathy is, one hopes, transferable.

Since this technique revolves around our students' reading interesting literary works in a language they can easily enjoy—English—the ideal accommodation would be for the foreign language teacher to cooperate with the English teacher. Two concerns need to be worked out: the incentives to be offered by one or both teachers to encourage students to do the reading and the follow-up strategy to employ so that the students will have an opportunity to share their insights and to "sell" the reading selection to other students.

A complementary technique that goes one step further and establishes personal contact with a culture bearer of another society is described by Marquardt in a brief paper (1972). This article is contained in a two-volume collection of papers on intercultural communication that offers many insights of value to teachers of intercultural communication (Hoopes, 1971 and 1972).

Cultural Minidramas

Gorden has developed a prototype for sensitizing students to cross-cultural miscommunication through a "minidrama." A version of Gorden's minidrama, edited for junior high students, can be found in Fersh (1989). The use of skits and brief simulations is not new. They had been used previously at Wayne State, for example, by Behmer and Jenks (Behmer, 1972a,b). What Gorden brings to this tradition is a carefully developed format that carries the capability of evoking an emotional response in addition to providing cultural information.

The minidrama consists of three to five brief episodes, each of which contains one or more examples of miscommunication. Additional information is made available with each episode, but the precise cause of the misunderstanding does not become apparent until the last scene. Each episode is followed by a discussion led by the teacher.

The minidrama format exposes the student to a "process of self-confrontation." The student is led to experience the ambiguity of much cross-cultural communication in the dramatized misunderstanding, discomfort, confusion or embarrassment portrayed in the skit. Then, by identifying with the American youths in the drama, the student experiences the realization that "this could happen to me, too." Finally, by making the same incorrect assumptions as the Americans in the drama, the student has the chance to jump to false conclusions and thus recognize his or her own culturally determined "silent" assumptions.

To enhance the emotional effects of the "self-confrontation," any threatening interaction between the minidrama, the student, and the teacher must be avoided. The best way of doing this is for the teacher to establish a nonjudgmental atmosphere during the discussion periods that follow each episode.

Gorden admonishes the users of minidramas to "avoid any remark when introducing the mini-drama or in the discussion which would give any hint that the problem is basically one of communication. Let them discover this themselves!" To aid this personal expression of views, Gorden outlines two additional techniques for the teacher to use while asking questions during the discussion periods. Broad, open-ended questions should be used by the teacher, especially at the beginning of each discussion. The kind of question to avoid is the narrow-scope question that can be answered by yes or no. Gorden gives the following five examples of both kinds of questions:

Broad-scope	*Narrow-scope*
1. What are your impressions of this scene?	1. Is there conflict in this scene?
2. What is happening in this scene?	2. Is there any miscommunication in this scene?
3. What do you think about this scene?	3. Does this sound like the kind of thing that could really happen?
4. What are the feelings of the people interacting in this situation?	4. Do the Americans have a positive or negative feeling toward the Colombian in this situation?
5. Why does the Colombian customer do what he does?	5. Does the Colombian customer feel he has been wronged by the American?

Another reason to avoid narrowing the scope of inquiry is that the teacher might raise questions that have not yet occurred to the student—for the same reasons that they did not occur to the Americans in the minidrama.

The second technique is meant to supplement the open-ended questions just described. It involves using "neutral probes" to encourage the student to give more information, while at the same time it avoids leading the student to any specific area. Comments such as "Uh huh," "I see," "Very interesting," "Go on," "What else did you notice?" fall into this "neutral probe" area. Gorden also recommends that the discussion leader briefly summarize at the end of each discussion the reactions of the group.

Gorden's prototype minidrama (Gorden, 1970) is based on a true mundane event, cashing a check in a Colombian bank. In the first scene, two American Peace Corps volunteers stand in line in front of a teller and wait to take their turn. One of them hands the teller his check, then waits for his money. But before the money arrives, a Colombian cuts in front of him and hands the teller his check. The Americans are unhappy with the discourtesy of the local people. In the next scene a Colombian interviews the bank teller about how she regards Americans. "They are rude and don't let others take their turn," she says. In the last scene, the interviewer reports back that the Americans are discourteous. Upon probing it develops that (1) there is no "line" and (2) taking your turn consists of handing the teller your check (not waiting for your money). She then clears the check, sometimes having to get her supervisor's OK. Meanwhile, she takes checks from other patrons and clears them too.

Shortly after Gorden's minidrama became available through the ERIC system, I tried it on a graduate class of teachers—all of whom had resided abroad. The results were dramatic. At the end of the first scene the class strongly identified with the "wronged" American Peace Corps members. But by the end of the last scene the light had dawned, and the Colombians emerged clearly as the wronged parties. This changed perception drew mixed reactions. Several teachers who had served in the Peace Corps vehemently attacked the authenticity of the minidrama. Peace Corps members, they contended, were too smart to make mistakes in cross-cultural communication. By identifying with the Americans of the drama and by misinterpreting the same cultural cues, the teachers had almost to a person experienced the embarrassment of a cultural *faux pas*. The emotional sensitivity came from knowing that they were all vulnerable to lack of empathy. They shared the same barriers to communication. They also learned that knowing the vocabulary is not enough to avoid miscommunication.

The emotional sensation of self-confrontation that many experience through minidramas cannot be repeated often. Beyond the first or second, exposure to further minidramas becomes largely a cognitive experience. The affective potential of this approach depends on the novelty of the initial experience or so.

In presenting minidramas in class, each episode's dialogue can be given to the student actors a few minutes before that episode is enacted. Thus they too can experience self-confrontation.

A foreign language educator, Barbara Snyder, developed fifty-three minidramas for classroom use, all of which are written in the target language, Spanish (Snyder, 1975). Similar minidramas for foreign language classes have been prepared for French (Levno, 1977), German (Shirer, 1981), and ESL (Murphy, 1991). A compendium of 100 critical intercultural incidents, prepared in English by social psychologists (Brislin et al., 1986) is an outstanding tool for examining the underlying causes of culture fatigue.

Three Minidramas

Examples of the dialogue portion of a minidrama for French, English as a second language, and German are presented below. Teachers may want to try an appropriate one in their classes. Teachers interested in writing their own minidramas should model theirs on the one by Gorden (1968b; Fersh, 1989).

Les Achats: Un MiniDrame

(prepared by Emily Dewhirst, Jill Lohmann, Sam Russenburg, and Sister Christine Feagan)

Characters: Narrator, Cindy, Debbie, a fruit vendor, and a policeman.

Act I

NARRATOR: Two young American students, Cindy
and Debbie, are in Cannes for their
summer vacation. They pass an
expensive dress shop.

CINDY: Debbie, isn't that a beautiful dress?
Look, the price is 200 francs. I'd
love to buy it!

DEBBIE: The store won't be open for another
half-hour. Let's take a walk and
come back later.

NARRATOR: The girls pass an open-air market
where farmers are selling their fruits
and vegetables.

CINDY: It's so hot! I'm thirsty! Look at that
table of fruit over there . . . the one
where the fat woman is sitting.

DEBBIE: She has some beautiful peaches. Let's
go over and take a look at them.

CINDY: You're right, those are nice peaches.
(She starts to pick out the peaches
she wants to buy.) Let's take this one
and the one over there.

VENDOR: (sarcastically) *Eh bien, mesdemoiselles,*
you're planning to buy the whole
tableful?

DEBBIE: (whispers to Cindy) Is she ever rude!
I wonder what her problem is!
Probably had a fight with her
husband this morning.

(Class discussion)

Act II

DEBBIE: (handing peaches to the vendor)
We'll take these three peaches, please.
(The fruit vendor takes the peaches
and wraps them in a piece of
newspaper.)

CINDY: (whispers to her friend) She's too
cheap to even put them in a bag for
us! (Cindy takes the peaches from
the woman and bites into a peach as
Debbie asks . . .)

DEBBIE: How much do we owe you,
Madame?

VENDOR: 200 francs, Mademoiselle.

CINDY: (choking on the peach) I hope she's
kidding! I've heard of people being
cheated in France, but this is
ridiculous! The dress was only 200
francs!

VENDOR: (smiling) Nouveaux, Mademoiselle!

(Class discussion)

Act III

VENDOR: Give me my 200 francs!

CINDY: You're crazy, Madame! We're not
giving you 200 francs for three
peaches! That's ridiculous!

VENDOR: That's not too much for good
peaches! (talks to bystanders who are
watching the dispute) It's easy to see
that these girls are Americans! They
don't know what work is . . .
spraying trees, picking fruit, packing

it . . . everything is done by machine in their country! (to the girls) Give me my 200 francs!

DEBBIE: Not on your life. That's highway robbery!

VENDOR: Mon*sieur l'Agent*, come over here, please. These Americans owe me 200 francs for some peaches, and they refuse to pay.

POLICEMAN: Girls, what seems to be the problem? You have the peaches, so why not pay the lady?

DEBBIE: But 200 francs! How could they cost that much? You can buy a dress for that price!

POLICEMAN: Oh, I see what is troubling you, mesdemoiselles, but let me assure you that the price is just.

(Stop here for brief class discussion, then continue.)

It is a question of new francs and old francs. This woman wants you to pay her 200 old francs, which is the equivalent of 2 new francs. Some years ago the government changed our franc. 100 old francs became 1 new franc. However, many of the older people still count in old francs.

CINDY: I see. But tell me, why was the woman so upset when we picked out our fruit before we paid for it?

(Stop here for brief discussion, then continue.)

POLICEMAN: Mademoiselle, in France one does
              not touch the fruit in a display. The
              vendor selects the fruit for you.
              Much time is spent arranging a
              display of fruit. It is a shame to spoil
              it by pulling out a piece here and
              there.

ESL Minidrama: School

(prepared by Julia Estrada, Raymond Ellison, Chloe White, Gardenia Hung, and Margaret Durán)

Characters: José, Bruce, teacher, principal, José's father, community representative

Scene I

NARRATOR: Typical city school. José, a recent
             arrival from Mexico, and his
             American classmates are returning
             from recess and are lining up at the
             fountain.

JOSÉ: I want drink.

BRUCE: Ow! My chin!

JOSÉ: *¡Ay, perdón!*

BRUCE: Why did you push me? (begins to
          cry)

TEACHER: What's going on here?

BRUCE: He pushed me when I was drinking
          and I hit my chin.

TEACHER: José, did you push Bruce?

NARRATOR: José looks at the floor and says
             nothing.

(Class discussion)

Scene II

NARRATOR:	Teacher puts aide in charge of class and talks with José. Bruce is in the hall.
TEACHER:	All right, boys. What exactly happened?
BRUCE:	Well, we were lining up; we were thirsty after tag; it was my turn to drink at the fountain. Then José pushed me and I wasn't even finished.
TEACHER:	José, now you tell what happened. Was it like that?
NARRATOR:	José doesn't answer but begins to cry softly.
TEACHER:	Maybe we'd better talk to the principal. I've had this problem with you before.

(Class discussion)

Scene III

NARRATOR:	In the principal's office the boys are left in the outer office while the teacher discusses her problem.
PRINCIPAL:	Good morning, Mrs. Smith. What is it?
TEACHER:	Well, Mr. Brown, it's José Ramírez again. It seems he pushed a boy and bruised his chin at the water fountain. The main problem, though, is that I never can get him to answer a question. He does understand what I'm saying, I know he does; he just won't answer me. I'm getting tired of talking to a brick wall. The child lacks respect.

PRINCIPAL:	Let me talk to the boy. We'll get to the bottom of this or call on his parents through the community representative.

(Class discussion)

Scene IV

NARRATOR:	In the home of the Ramírez family, the community representative is talking the matter over with the parents.
COMMUNITY REPRESENTATIVE:	. . . so you see, Mr. Ramírez, José's teacher is concerned about his rudeness toward her and the principal.
SR. RAMÍREZ:	*No puedo creerlo.* My son has never shown lack of respect toward his elders. What could they say to him to make him talk back?
COMMUNITY REPRESENTATIVE:	But, Sr. Ramírez, that's precisely the problem. José never says anything, he won't even look the teacher squarely in the face.
SR. RAMÍREZ:	But of course not! What impudence!

(Class discussion)

Scene V

NARRATOR:	The principal's office where the community representative is discussing his visit with the principal.
PRINCIPAL:	Come in, Mr. Martínez.

COMMUNITY REPRESENTATIVE:	Well, Mr. Brown, the Ramírez family was quite upset about the school's treatment of José.
PRINCIPAL:	Pardon me?
COMMUNITY REPRESENTATIVE:	The parents are proud of the upbringing they've given their children. The problem seems to be that when the child is being castigated he is not to refute the teacher's comments but lower his head in respectful submission. I explained to the parents that in the United States the child is taught to look at the person speaking to him. Averting the eyes is taken as a sign of culpability.
PRINCIPAL:	I never realized that facet of the Mexican character. This will be taken up at our next inservice meeting.

The Noon Meal: A German Minidrama

(prepared by M. Cohen, Judy Moses, Anke Culver, and A. Bogucka)

Characters: Frank and Betty Harrison, Jack, their son, two German businessmen, a waiter, restaurant guests

Scene I

At about 1:00 p.m. on a pleasant spring afternoon two Americans arrive in Göttingen on a trip to visit their son Jack, who is spending the year studying chemistry in Göttingen on a Fulbright grant. They spot a restaurant, Zum Goldnen Adler, go in, and wait to be seated.

FRANK: I'm starved.

BETTY: I wonder how long we'll have to wait to be seated. Do you see the hostess anywhere?

FRANK: No, but there are a few empty tables. We shouldn't have to wait long.

(long pause)

BETTY: (greatly irritated) Just look at that, will you? Those people are just going right past us and sitting down.

FRANK: Well, why don't we just do the same? There's a table for four. Let's grab it before someone else does.

(Class discussion)

Scene II

Frank and Betty are seated at the table when the waiter gives them two menus on his way to serve another table. The waiter returns.

WAITER: What would you like?

BETTY: (pointing to the item Wienerschnitzel on the menu) I'd like that.

FRANK: I'll have the Sauerbraten. We'll both have beer to drink.

The waiter leaves. In the meantime the restaurant has filled up and two well-dressed German businessmen come to the table.

1ST GERMAN MAN: (with heavy accent) Is the place still free?

The Harrisons do not understand what he has said, but they smile. The men sit down and continue their animated conversation.

BETTY: (with a questioning look) Frank, do
         you know these people?

FRANK: No, I've never laid eyes on them.

BETTY: It's strange. I swear these are the
         same two men who were standing
         with us in line at the airport.

The waiter brings the meal and Betty and Frank eat in an uncomfortable silence.

(Class discussion)

Scene III

Later on that day the Harrisons discuss the incident with their son as they stroll through the park.

BETTY: It's peculiar, Jack, but I think we are
         being followed. The same two men
         who were behind us at Customs sat
         down at our table in the restaurant.

FRANK: The only thing they said to us was
         "Mahlzeit," and if I remember
         correctly the little high school
         German I had, I think it is a dirty
         word.

JACK: Oh, come on, both of you. This is
         ridiculous.

(Class discussion)

BETTY: What do you mean, ridiculous?

JACK: First of all, it was a coincidence that
         you ran into those two men again.
         Secondly, in Germany it is perfectly
         all right for any person to sit down
         at a table with unoccupied seats,
         even though there are other people
         already sitting at that table.

Other Simulations

The classic simulation of culture shock/fatigue is a 45-minute game (with a debriefing of an additional 30-40 minutes) called Bafá Bafá (or, in its permutation for grade school, Rafá Rafá). This was designed by Garry Shirts (1973). Participants are divided into two groups and each is given the rules of interaction. One group is patterned after a meritorious, achievement-oriented society; the other after a status-sensitive, socially interactive society. "Tourists," participants of each "society," individually visit the other group and are invited to participate with the host people. The game ends when all the participants have had the opportunity to be a "tourist." During the debriefing that follows, each society is described by the tourists. Participants also describe what they felt as they visited the other group. What they felt closely approximates culture shock and their sense of the other society's ground rules is usually way off the mark. Participants find this exercise a lot of fun (especially if there are at least eight participants—but less than twenty—in each group). It is during the debriefing, however, that the lights go on, metaphorically speaking. (Another game from the same source, Star Power [Shirts, 1969], simulates a three-tiered society with an unequal distribution of power and wealth.)

A card game that simulates culture shock/fatigue is *Barnga: A Simulation Game on Cultural Clashes* (Thiagarajan and Steinwachs, 1990). The debriefing is divided into three phases: affective (Would you like to share your feelings with the others?), cognitive (What do you think happened when a rule violation occurred?), and what-if questions (What if the players were permitted to talk with each other?). The game works with a minimum of nine players (no maximum) and takes about 45 minutes.

Another simulation of cross-culture contact was prepared by Abt Associates (Culture Contact, 1969). The Center for Teaching International Relations at the University of Denver has produced a number of interesting simulations (Lamy et al., 1991; Ulmer and Ulmer, 1990).

One happy result of suffering a bit of culture shock or fatigue is the perspective that it gives to our understanding of our own culture. In fact, the ACTFL committee on cultural competence, chaired by Howard Lee Nostrand, suggests several areas to test in this regard (Nostrand, 1991).

For example, the student can

- give an example of the problem of conforming to the norms of a foreign society while maintaining one's own values and identity
- present objectively some judgments that foreigners make concerning the home country
- show examples of how one's perceptions and judgments are patterned by one's home culture and are subject to temporary influences such as the phases of culture shock

Cultural fatigue, or worse, culture shock, can be discouraging. But cheer up! There are some books to perk you up as you find yourself returning to a fetal position in some dark, microbe-infested corner of an uncaring, alien world. Storti's brief book, titled *The Art of Crossing Cultures* (1990), deals with the travails of the traveler while drawing pertinent quotes from literature. Misery likes fellowship and it is a source of comfort to learn that illustrious people of letters have gone through the earnest rigors of Living Abroad. Storti's copious literary jewels sparkle with wit and relevancy. In a final chapter, Storti looks in on others' shock in discovering the United States. Isaac Weld, for example, is quoted as saying: "Civility cannot be purchased from Americans on any terms; they seem to think it is incompatible with freedom." Perhaps the definitive judgment is offered by Georges Clemenceau: "Americans have no capacity for abstract thought and make bad coffee."

Lewis and Jungman (1986) present short stories by well-known writers organized around the stages of adjustment to another culture. Yet another helpful book for students going abroad anywhere is Ladd's *Subject: India; A Semester Abroad* (1990). The author was particularly interested in "how people managed the 'doing' world and the 'being' world at the same time." A commendable design for learning from field experiences abroad has been prepared by Sikkema and Niyekawa (1987), and a very useful orientation for youth exchange programs is outlined by Grove (1989) and a design for study-abroad programs was prepared by Kauffmann et al. (1992).

The next chapter examines how social variables enable one to predict behavior in the target culture.

Suggested Activities_____

1. Identify ten recently published books suitable for creating cross-cultural empathy. They need not relate specifically to any one culture.

2. Develop a minidrama based on your own experience in another culture or subculture.

3. Describe an example of culture fatigue that you have experienced personally.

References Cited_____

Althen, Gary L. 1970. *Human Relations Training and Foreign Students.* Washington: National Association for Foreign Student Affairs. [EDRS: ED 048 084]

Althen, Gary L. 1983. *The Handbook of Foreign Student Advising.* Yarmouth, ME: Intercultural Press.

Austin, Clyde N., ed. 1986. *Cross-Cultural Reentry: A Book of Readings.* Abilene, TX: Abilene Christian Univ. Press.

Bache, Ellyn. 1990. *Cultural Clash.* 2d ed. Yarmouth, ME: Intercultural Press.

Behmer, Daniel E. 1972a. "Cultural Mini-Skits Evaluated." *American Foreign Language Teacher* 2, 3: 37, 43, 48.

Behmer, Daniel E. 1972b. "Teaching with Wayne State Cultural Mini-Skits." *American Foreign Language Teacher* 3, 1: 3, 38-39.

Brislin, Richard W., Kenneth Cushner, Craig Cherrie, and Mahealani Yong. 1986. *Intercultural Interactions: A Practical Guide.* Newbury Park, CA: Sage.

Chang, Jung. 1991. *Wild Swans: Three Daughters of China.* New York: Simon & Schuster.

Cisneros, Sandra. 1991. *Woman Hollering Creek and Other Stories.* New York: Random House.

Cleveland, Harlan, G. J. Mangone, and J. C. Adams. 1960. *The Overseas Americans.* New York: McGraw-Hill.

Culture Contact. 1969. Cambridge, MA: Abt Associates.

Decaroli, Joseph. 1972. "What Research Says to the Classroom Teacher: Simulation Games." *Social Education* 36: 541-43.

DeCrow, Roger. 1969. *Cross Cultural Interaction Skills: A Digest of Recent Training Literature.* Syracuse, NY: ERIC Clearinghouse on Adult Education.

Fersh, Seymour, ed. 1989. *Learning about Peoples and Cultures*. Evanston, IL: McDougal, Littell.

Finkelstein, Barbara, Joseph J. Tobin, and Anne E. Imamura, eds. 1991. *Transcending Stereotypes: Discovering Japanese Culture and Education*. Yarmouth, ME: Intercultural Press.

Furnham, Adrian, and Stephen Bochner. 1986. *Culture Shock*. New York: Routledge, Chapman & Hall.

Gorden, Raymond L. 1968a. *Contrastive Analysis of Cultural Differences Which Inhibit Communication between Americans and Colombians*. [EDRS: ED 023 337]

Gorden, Raymond L. 1968b. *Cross-Cultural Encounter in a Latin American Bank*. Yellow Springs, OH: Antioch College.

Gorden, Raymond L. 1968c. *Initial Immersion in the Foreign Culture*. Yellow Springs, OH: Antioch College. [EDRS: ED 023 339]

Gorden, Raymond L. 1974. *Living in Latin America: A Case Study in Cross-Cultural Communication*. Lincolnwood, IL: National Textbook.

Grove, Cornelius. 1989. *Orientation Handbook for Youth Exchange Programs*. Yarmouth, ME: Intercultural Press.

Harrison, Roger, and Richard L. Hopkins. 1966. *The Design of Cross-Cultural Training, with Examples from the Peace Corps*. Washington: National Training Laboratories, National Education Association [EDRS: ED 011 103]

Heinlein, Robert. 1961. *Stranger in a Strange Land*. New York: Putnam.

Hollo, Anselm. 1977. *Sojourner Microcosms: New and Selected Poems 1959–1977*. Berkeley, CA: Blue Wind.

Hoopes, David S., ed. 1971, 1972. *Readings in Inter-Cultural Communication*. 2 vols. Yarmouth, ME: Intercultural Press.

Houston, James. 1971. *White Dawn: An Eskimo Saga*. New York: Harcourt, Brace.

Hutchison, William, and Cynthia Poznanski, with Laura Todt-Stockman. 1987. *Living in Colombia: A Guide for Foreigners*. Yarmouth, ME: Intercultural Press.

Kauffman, Norma L., Judith N. Martin, and Henry Weaver, with Judy Weaver. 1992. *Students Abroad—Strangers at Home: Education for a Global Society*. Yarmouth, ME: Intercultural Press.

Kingston, Maxine Hong. 1976. *The Woman Warrior: Memoirs of a Girlhood among Ghosts*. New York: Knopf.

Kohls, L. Robert. 1984. *Survival Kit for Overseas Living: For Americans Planning to Live and Work Abroad*. 2d ed. Yarmouth, ME: Intercultural Press.

Ladd, Jennifer. 1990. *Subject: India; A Semester Abroad*. Yarmouth, ME: Intercultural Press.

Lambert, Richard D. 1966. *Americans Abroad*. A special issue of *The Annals* 368 (Nov.)

Lamy, Steven L., Roger B. Myers, Debbie Von Vihl, and Katherine Weeks. 1991. *Teaching Global Awareness with Simulations and Games*. Denver: Center for Teaching International Relations (CTIR), University of Denver.

LeVine, Robert A., and Donald T. Campbell. 1972. *Ethnocentrism: Theories of Conflict, Ethnic Attitudes and Group Behavior*. New York: Wiley.

Levno, Arley W. 1977. *Rencontres Culturelles: Cross-Cultural Mini-Dramas*. Lincolnwood, IL: National Textbook.

Lewis, Tom, and Robert Jungman. 1986. *On Being Foreign: Culture Shock in Short Fiction, An International Anthology*. Yarmouth, ME: Intercultural Press.

Marquardt, William F. 1969. "Creating Empathy through Literature between the Members of the Mainstream Culture and the Disadvantaged Learners of the Minority Cultures." *Florida FL Reporter* 7, 1 (Spring/Summer): 134-35. (Special anthology issue entitled *Linguistic-Cultural Differences and American Education*.)

Marquardt, William F. 1970. "Criteria for Selecting Literary Texts in Teaching Cross-Culture Communication, Especially in English as a Second Language," pp. 1919-27 in *Actes du Xe. congrès international des linguistes, 1967*. Bucharest: Editions de l'Académie de la République Socialiste de Roumanie.

Marquardt, William F. 1972. "Informant-Interaction as Training in the Foreign Language Classroom," pp. 36-40 in David S. Hoopes, ed., *Readings in Intercultural Communication*, Vol. 2. Pittsburgh: Regional Council for International Education, University of Pittsburgh.

Momaday, N. Scott. 1989. *The Ancient Child*. New York: Doubleday.

Murphy, Andrew. 1991. *Cultural Encounters in the USA: Cross-Cultural Mini-Dramas*. Lincolnwood, IL: National Textbook.

Nostrand, Howard L. 1991. "Basic Intercultural Education Needs Breadth and Depth: The Role of a Second Culture," pp. 131-159 in Ellen S. Siber, ed., *Critical Issues in Foreign Language Instruction*. New York: Garland.

Oberg, Kalervo. 1960. "Culture Shock: Adjustment to New Environments." *Practical Anthropology* 7: 177-82.

Seelye, H. Ned. 1969. "An Objective Measure of Biculturation: Americans in Guatemala, A Case Study." *Modern Language Journal* 53, 7 (Nov.): 503-14.

Seelye, H. Ned, and Marilynn B. Brewer. 1970. "Ethnocentrism and Acculturation of North Americans in Guatemala." *Journal of Social Psychology* 80 (April): 147-55.

Seelye, H. Ned and Alan Seelye-James. 1995. *Culture Clash: Managing Diversity in a Multicultural World*. Lincolnwood, IL: NTC Business Books.

Shirer, Robert K. 1981. *Kulturelle Begegnungen: Cross-Cultural Mini-Dramas*. Lincolnwood, IL: National Textbook.

Shirts, R. Garry. 1969. *Star Power*. La Jolla, CA: Simile II.

Shirts, R. Garry. 1973. *Bafá Bafá—A Cross Culture Simulation*. La Jolla, CA: Simile II.

Sikkema, Mildred, and Agnes Niyekawa. 1987. *Design for Cross-Cultural Learning*. Yarmouth, ME: Intercultural Press.

Snyder, Barbara. 1975. *Encuentros Culturales: Cross-Cultural Mini-Dramas*. Lincolnwood, IL: National Textbook.

Storti, Craig. 1990. *The Art of Crossing Cultures*. Yarmouth, ME: Intercultural Press.

Steinberg, Don. 1990. *PC Computing*, Nov., p. 179.

Sumner, W. G. 1906. *Folkways*. New York: Ginn.

Thiagarajan, Sivasailam, ed. 1973. *Current Trends in Simulation/Gaming*. Bloomington: Indiana University, School of Education. (Special edition of *Viewpoints* 49, 6.)

Thiagarajan, Sivasailam, and Barbara Steinwachs. 1990. *Barnga: A Simulation Game on Cultural Clashes*. Yarmouth, ME: Intercultural Press.

Triandis, Harry. 1983. "Essentials of Studying Cultures," in D. Landis and R. Brislin, eds., *Handbook of Intercultural Training* (vol. 1). New York: Pergamon.

Tyler, V. Lynn. 1987. *Intercultural Interacting*. Provo, UT: David M. Kennedy Center for International Studies, Brigham Young University.

Ulmer, Barby, and Vic Ulmer. 1990. *Starvation or Survival and Women and Development in Africa*. Center for Teaching International Relations (CTIR), University of Denver. [two simulations]

6 Who Does It? The Role of Social Variables in Predicting Behavior

This chapter provides a rationale for goal 2 and presents several classroom activities to illustrate how skill in predicting cross-cultural behavior can be developed.

Cultural Goal 2—Who: The student recognizes that role expectations and social variables such as age, sex, social class, religion, ethnicity, and place of residence affect the way people speak and behave.

The admonition that "they do things differently there" does not seem to prepare us adequately for interaction with all segments of another culture. Nor, alas, is goodwill enough.

An adventuresome pilot, wanting to take "the trip of a lifetime," advertised in a newspaper for a "venturesome, intrepid, athletic, unencumbered, Spanish-speaking lady" to accompany him on a two-year country-by-country tour of Latin America in his brand new red-and-white Maule M-5 aircraft. Bill Loveless and his intrepid companion, Ms. Susan Walls, quit their jobs, sublet their homes, and sold everything they owned. To the envy of their friends, the two sailed out into an October sunset. A little later, Ms. Walls, who had never been out of the United States before, faced a run-down motel in Baja California. She was home in Seattle the next day. "I've never seen poverty like that," she was quoted as saying. "I'm not rich, but I'm accustomed to a low-middle-class environment and this just blew me away."

This leads us intrepidly to another fact of life: all societies are stratified, and each societal segment exercises some behavioral options that are not available, for better or worse, to other strata of the same ethnicity or nationality. When Ms. Walls made the startling discovery that boondock accommodations lack many of the amenities of the hotels she was used to, she was responding to two important determinants of behavior: social class and place of residence.

Since the behavioral options available in any given society for the satisfaction of needs are not equally available to everyone in that society, the way people speak and behave is affected by role stratification variables. Some of these variables are age, sex, social class, religion, ethnicity, and place of residence. This is always so, and this fact provides us with a key question to ask of behavior: What stratum of society is involved in performing the observed behavior?

Many phrases are employed only in certain circumstances and are definitely avoided in others. Prompted by a perverse curiosity, I once asked a second-year Spanish class to translate "How is your mother?" The best student answered—using one of the worst vituperative epithets available in the Spanish of most Latin American countries—¿*Cómo está tu madre?*" (More acceptable would have been either ¿*Cómo está su madre?* or ¿*Cómo está tu mamá?*)

Illustrations of the interrelatedness of language and its cultural context are not confined to this kind of heavy-footed blunder. When do we learn the cues to social class? Some of these cues are embedded in language, others in "silent" behavior. Take the innocuous sentence "My little brother goes to school." With a little bit of context such as the social class of the family and place of residence, those who are culturally initiated can intuit a good deal of culturally pertinent information: What kind of school? Public? Private? Religious or secular? Coed? Half-day? Full-day? Is dress formal (coat and tie, uniform)?

No two people speak the same language. Voice prints are as personal as fingerprints. Individual differences are an important part of the personality a person projects, as any amateur mimic knows. Of much greater interest to a student of foreign cultures, however, are the systematic variations in the speech of large numbers of people that are caused by differences in age, sex, social class, and place of residence. An eight-year-old talks differently from an eighty-year-old. Speech regarded as appropriate for women might raise eyebrows if spoken in a men's locker room, and acceptable male locker-room speech would not go unnoticed at a church committee meeting. The speech of a dock worker is not often confused with that of a college professor, nor is the drawl of a Southerner (of any country) mistaken for that of a Northerner.

Students need to learn to expect dialect differences. This expectation in itself goes a long way toward psychologically equipping a student to cope with the inevitable range of speech he or she will encounter outside of the classroom. Jane Walmsley (1987), author of the humorous *Brit-Think, Ameri-Think*, dedicates her book to her daughter "who has an American mother and a British father, and is—as she puts it—'half and hawf.' "

We cannot, of course, teach students to speak different dialects, but just give them a taste for the wonderful diversity they will experience. For those among us who are Real Earnest Linguists, exposing language learners to a wide variety of speech forms is a realistic way of having students learn the target allophones. Allophonic differences usually are ignored in language classes because, although they present different ways to say the "same" sound, by definition they do not change the meaning of a word as a phonemic difference would. An example in English is *butter* pronounced with a definite *t* versus a sound closer to *d* (a sound called a "flap" that can occur when *t* is surrounded by certain other sounds).

Recognizing whether a sound is an allophonic variation of a phoneme requires more than knowledge of the phonemic speech range of some standard dialect. To be able to "ignore" allophonic variations one has to learn what is allophonic and what is phonemic.

Allophonic variations often convey considerable social information, such as the social class and place of residence of the speaker. *Pygmalion*, or *My Fair Lady* as the movie version was called, presents a clear dramatization of this linguistic fact. Following the butter example above, are there not geographic or perhaps social class differences implied in the way one pronounces 'aunt'? A very rich list of these "social markers" has been prepared by Scherer and Giles (1979). Drawing its examples from a wide range of languages, this anthology discusses speech markers of situations, age, sex, personality, social class, ethnicity, and social interaction.

Tape recordings provide a practical medium to bring these dialect differences to the students' attention. Students can be directed to identify which country the speaker comes from or whether the speaker is from an urban or rural area or whether the speaker is working-class or upper-class. It usually is best to use only the most obvious speech differences in these exercises.

Language can erect barriers to intercultural communication. First, language allows us to distinguish the status of a person by providing social markers. A few pairs of rough synonyms will illustrate this.

physique/figure

throw/toss

gulp/sip

swab/mop

buy/shop

In these examples, the first term is associated with males, the second with females.

Second, language often discriminates in systematic ways. A disproportionate share of words with negative connotations typically fall on certain sectors of the population. Again, pairs of near-synonyms will illustrate this.

roars/shrieks

complains/bitches

barks/snaps

Many people concerned with the ways popular perceptions of female roles have contributed to reduced workplace opportunities for women decry "sexist" language. Increasing awareness of how certain cultural connotations may diminish human potential adds an urgent rationale for looking carefully at the interface of language and culture.

A poem by Natasha Josefowitz (1983) illustrates contrasting gender expectations in an office setting.

Impressions from an Office
The family picture is on HIS desk.
Ah, a solid, responsible family man.
The family picture is on HER desk.
Hmmm, her family will come before her career.

HIS desk is cluttered.
He's obviously a hard worker and a busy man.
HER desk is cluttered.
She's obviously a disorganized scatterbrain.
HE is talking with his co-workers.
He must be discussing the latest deal.
SHE is talking with her co-workers.
She must be gossiping.
HE's not at his desk.
He must be at a meeting.
SHE's not at her desk.
She must be in the ladies' room.
HE's not in the office.
He's meeting customers.
SHE's not in the office.
She must be out shopping.
HE's having lunch with the boss.
He's on his way up.
SHE's having lunch with the boss.
They must be having an affair.
The boss criticized HIM.
He'll improve his performance.
The boss criticized HER.
She'll be very upset.
HE got an unfair deal.
Did he get angry?
SHE got an unfair deal.
Did she cry?
HE's getting married.
He'll get more settled.
SHE's getting married.
She'll get pregnant and leave.
HE's having a baby.
He'll need a raise.
SHE's having a baby.
She'll cost the company money in maternity benefits.
HE's going on a business trip.
It's good for his career.

SHE's going on a business trip.
What does her husband say?
HE's leaving for a better job.
He knows how to recognize a good opportunity.
SHE's leaving for a better job.
Women are not dependable.

(Reprinted with the kind permission of the publisher)

A bestseller by Deborah Tannen (1990) zeros in on communication difficulties across gender lines. A fascinating international overview of women has been prepared by Morgan (1984); for a statistical overview of women worldwide see Schmittroth (1991).

A communications specialist, Thomas Kochman (1981), has prepared a succinct study entitled *Black and White Styles in Conflict* that elucidates causes for some of the face-to-face misunderstanding that occurs between members of two major segments of U.S. society. Kochman examines topics such as classroom modalities, fighting words, boasting and bragging, male and female interaction, truth and consequences, information as property, and style. I have used this as one of a number of texts in intercultural communication courses, courses that contained a liberal mix of students with various racial, ethnic, and national origins. At first I assigned the whole book (less than 200 pages) for out-of-class reading and subsequent in-class discussion. I discovered that it hit close to home for many students, both black and white. Too close for some. The initial student reaction was negative. We worked through this during the discussion period, but many students retained a bad taste in their mouths. I solved this in subsequent courses by assigning the book one chapter at a time, with discussions following each chapter. The negativism was limited to the first chapter this way, with the other chapters affording very positive experiences. This is not because there is anything wrong with the first chapter. The same negative reaction typically accompanies any close look at one's own culturally conditioned values (Kraemer's cross-cultural videotapes [discussed in chapter 9], for example). We come to expect defensive reactions to personal challenges from "strangers," in this case a book by an author unfamiliar to the reader. Perhaps these are the dues we pay as we experience the shock of self-discovery?

In some situations such other variables as occupation, political persuasion, generation, schooling, time (i.e., era), or bilingualism strongly affect behavior. These variables are also within the scope of goal 2 (i.e., role expectations and social variables affect behavior).

One important variable is whether one is a "have" or a "have-not." All societies have three things that are too scarce to be shared equally by all societal segments: power, wealth, and influence. The perspectives of "dominant" peoples (the "haves") differ importantly from those of "subordinate" peoples (the "have-nots").

Another important variable in predicting behavior, circumstance, falls under goal 4 and is the subject of chapter 8.

An entirely different approach to giving students the experience they need to accomplish an end-of-course objective is the following activity for Spanish classes. This activity consists of a series of dialogues that are either acted out or taped and illustrated by filmstrips. The object is to show how language and gesture in greetings are influenced by the age, sex, social class, place of residence, and relationship of the speakers.

LEARNING ACTIVITIES FOR GOAL 2

After observing the four dialogues contained in this unit, the student will carry out activity A plus two of the remaining activities:

A. The student will be asked to recall what happened.

B. Given dialogue statements, he or she will identify the relationship of the speakers.

C. Given similar circumstances and a dialogue statement, the student will be able to vary appropriately the expressions and gestures used in greeting a friend of the same sex, a friend of the opposite sex, and various relatives.

D. Students write and present a similar skit of one or more circumstances portrayed in these dialogues.

E. Students research other social situations and other geographical places that would alter these greetings and procedures.

Saludos

(prepared by Pilar Aurensanz, Hildegard Bals, and E. S. Rife, under the supervision of Madeline A. Cooke)

Dialogue I

Personajes: Papá, María Rosa, Mamá, Abuelita (madre de papá), Juan, Tío

The Pérez family meets the uncle and grandmother in the park.

PAPÁ:	(besando a la abuelita en la mejilla) Buenas tardes, mamá. ¿Qué tal están todos?
ABUELITA:	Bien, hijo. ¿Y vosotros? ¿Cómo estáis?
PAPÁ:	Juan está con catarro. (dando un abrazo al tío) ¿Cómo van los negocios?
TÍO:	(acercándose) Así, así.
ABUELITA:	(besando a mamá) Ya sé que Juan está con catarro. ¿Tienes mucho trabajo?
MAMÁ:	María Rosa me ayuda mucho. Es muy buena ella.
ABUELITA:	(besando a María Rosa) ¿Trabajas mucho? ¿Sacas buenas notas?
MARIA ROSA:	Sí, abuelita. Ud. lo sabe, ¿verdad?
ABUELITA:	(besando a Juan en la frente) ¡Pobrecito! Vas al colegio, ¿verdad?
JUAN:	¡Claro!
TÍO:	(dándole la mano a mamá) María Pilar, ¡qué guapa estás!
MAMÁ:	(sonriendo ampliamente) Anda, anda, no seas mentiroso.

Dialogue II

Two teenage, middle-class, urban students

EDUARDO: ¡Hola, Daniel! (smile and wave)

DANIEL: ¿Qué hay de nuevo, Eduardo? (smile and wave)

EDUARDO: ¿Cómo te va?

DANIEL: Pasándola. ¿Adónde vas?

EDUARDO: Voy al cine. ¿Quieres venir?

Dialogue III

Two teenage, middle-class girls

CELIA: ¡Hola, Inés!

INÉS: ¡Hola, Celia! (They embrace and touch both cheeks.)

CELIA: ¡Cuánto tiempo sin verte!

INÉS: Sí, de veras. ¿Qué me cuentas?

CELIA: Pues, es el cumpleaños de mi prima Margarita y voy a su casa para felicitarla.

INÉS: Ah, qué bueno. Felicítala de mi parte. (They kiss again, touch cheeks, and embrace.)

CELIA: Entonces, ¡hasta luego!

INÉS: Chao.

Dialogue IV

A teenage girl and a teenage boy

MARIO: (walking toward the girl with an open hand) Hola, ¿qué tal? (shake hands)

BELITA: (greets him casually) ¡Hola! ¿Cómo te fue en el examen de matemáticas?

MARIO: No sé. Creo que bien. Regular, ¿y a ti?

> BELITA: Bastante mal. No lo terminé.
>
> MARIO: ¿No quieres tomar un helado?
>
> BELITA: Bueno. Encantada. (When Mario gestures his head toward the ice-cream vendor, Belita says: "Vamos." Mario pays for two ice cream Eskimo pies.)

The next chapter focuses on the cultural images we carry around in our heads and on how these affect communication.

Suggested Activities

1. Write a dialogue with three characters in which the speech demonstrates differences in the speaker's age, sex, social class, and place of residence.

2. Choose a word or phrase from another language and show how age, sex, social class, ethnicity, and place of residence affect its usage.

References Cited

Josefowitz, Natasha. 1983. *Is This Where I Was Going?* New York: Warner.

Kochman, Thomas. 1981. *Black and White Styles in Conflict.* Chicago: Univ. of Chicago Press.

Morgan, Robin, ed. 1984. *Sisterhood Is Global: The International Women's Movement Anthology.* New York: Anchor.

Scherer, Klaus R., and Howard Giles, eds. 1979. *Social Markers in Speech.* New York: Cambridge Univ. Press.

Schmittroth, Linda, ed. 1991. *Statistical Record of Women Worldwide.* Detroit: Gale Research.

Tannen, Deborah. 1990. *You Just Don't Understand: Women and Men in Conversation.* New York: Ballantine.

Walmsley, Jane. 1987. *Brit-Think, Ameri-Think: A Transatlantic Survival Guide.* New York: Penguin.

7 What Images Lurk Therein? Cultural Connotations of Words and Action

This chapter shows why communication requires sharing vital internal pictures each culture bearer carries (goal 3).

Cultural Goal 3—What: The student demonstrates an awareness that effective communication requires discovering the culturally conditioned images that are evoked in the minds of people when they think, act, and react to the world around them.

To a desert Arab the thought of a beautiful woman might conjure up sensuous images of a 250-pound lovely, while to an American lexically equivalent words in English might connote a slim but disproportionately big-busted lass. One Italian neighbor of mine complains that in Italy men did not pay much attention to her because she was too skinny at 110 pounds, while in the United States the same fate has befallen her now that her weight has risen to 170 pounds. If only she could be "fat" in Italy and "skinny" in the United States, she would be "beautiful" everywhere. The cultural connotations of words can make the difference between an active social life and staying home.

How can an understanding of the relation between culture and semantics be developed? One way is for students to experience directly the cultural connotations of common words such as "man," "house," "standing," and "walking" by observing these objects and activities as they occur in the target culture. This experience need not be limited to students studying abroad. The graphics of magazines, newspapers, and movies are well suited to conveying these objects and activities in the target culture.

A simple classroom activity to help students gain a perspective of culturally formed images begins by having them select a word that intrigues them. This word can come from any number of sources: a list provided by the teacher of the hundred most common words in the language or a word appearing in the glossary of the textbook or in a foreign newspaper. The task of the student is to compile authentic visual examples of his or her chosen word from newspaper and magazine clippings or from his or her own photography. One student of mine illustrated through a collage of thirty magazine photos of *mujeres* (women) how social class, age, and Indian, European, and African backgrounds affected the appearance of women in Latin America.

Since it happened so long ago I thought it had been forgotten, but I was not to escape so easily. Just last month my wife was visiting relatives in Central America when one of them said something to the effect that Americans were intelligent. "Let me tell you about these so-called intelligent Americans," my wife chimed in. She then told her enthralled audience about the time we had visited a remote town on the coast thirty years before. The bathhouse adjoined the boarding house. I went for my morning bath and discovered the largest bathtub I had ever seen. A porcelain-coated structure resting on large lion paws, it was filled to the top with clear water. I looked around the room and, except for a sink, a wooden stool, and some pots and pans strewn around the floor, there was nothing else there. I took off my bathrobe and was about to get into the tub when my wife knocked on the door. She wanted to brush her teeth. After letting her in, I returned to the issue at hand. I tested the water with my foot.

"What are you doing!" my wife demanded.

"I'm going to take a bath," I replied.

"Get your foot out of that water!" she said with chilling directness.

"Well, how am I supposed to take a bath if I don't get wet," I responded with infallible logic. (We Americans are so smart.)

"That's what the pans are for."

I looked at her blankly. She looked at me as though I were retarded. Then she showed me how to dip the pan into the tub and then pour the water over me. The water in the tub, she explained, was for the whole boarding house.

As her relatives roared with laughter, my wife said, "And this is the intelligence of Americans. Imagine, they would have run us out of town for ruining all the water!"

In a first-grade textbook written in Kiché for rural Mayan children in Guatemala—and published thirty years too late to help me—a lesson on hygiene shows four ways to take a bath. I've reproduced the pages (see figure 7.1). Do you see a tub or shower?

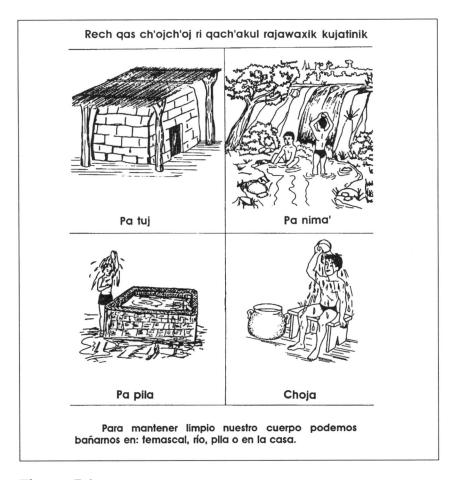

Figure 7.1
"The Bath"

One of the many requisites to "thinking like a native," besides fluency in the target language, is the conditioned ability to visualize culturally appropriate images that language evokes. Whether we are bantering with an Italian coquette or relaxing in the pleasantly cool mud home of the Masai, communion with a native of another language demands sharing meanings that go beyond listless dictionary definitions. This is amply illustrated in Coupland, Giles, and Wiemann (1991).

Nonverbal Behavior

Many—some communication specialists say most—of the cues to inward meaning are not verbal at all. They are the gestures and other physical signals people use to communicate.

There are excellent overviews that present many aspects of nonverbal behavior: Birdwhistell (1952, 1970), D. Morris (1977), Weitz (1979). Birdwhistell's 1970 work is the classic in the field. Morris's oversized book (8½" × 11") is replete with eye-catching photographs and illustrations and is written for the adult lay person. It treats 71 different manifestations of nonverbal behavior. One of its strengths is that Morris, an anthropologist, makes many cross-cultural comparisons. Weitz (1979) edits twenty-six chapters prepared by experts in the field. She divides the anthology into five sections: facial expression and visual interaction, body movement and gesture, paralanguage, proximity behaviors, and multichannel communication.

A brief overview of kinesics by a leading foreign language educator was prepared by Morain (1978). Other overviews include Fleming (1971a, 1971b, 1971c). Two illustrated books deal with the gestures of Spain (Green, 1968; see also Green, 1973) and Latin America (Saitz and Cervenka, 1972), respectively. Brault (1963) and Tsoutsos (1970) focus on French gestures.

LEARNING ACTIVITIES FOR GOAL 3

One intriguing activity for probing cultural images was prepared by Gwen Shimono for students of Japanese culture. This activity can be experienced in two ways: through listening to the teacher's illustrated classroom presentation or by reading the illustrated presentation after class. There is much to gain by having a teacher personally present a lesson that inspires many fruitful tangents for subsequent exploration. After hearing Shimono present this lesson in one of my classes, I was convinced that it could well serve to introduce the student to everything Japanese. For example: Why do Japanese sit on the floor? How is this reflected in architecture? How are radishes prepared and eaten? What puns use the words radish or actor in them? What other forms of word plays do Japanese use?

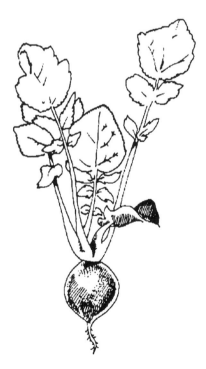

Figure 7.2
The European Variety of Radish

Futoi Daikon Monogatari (Saga of the Fat Radishes)

Daikon literally means "big root" and does not refer to radishes with small round red roots. The European variety has shorter leaves and a smaller root, and is mainly used to feed cattle in Japan. The larger ones, which originated in southern China, are consumed daily by Japanese in many diverse ways. There is no land where *daikon* is grown in greater variety and in a larger quantity than in Japan. *Daikon* is so important in Japan that its price is quoted in reporting rising prices in general. There are some thirty-four varieties of *daikon*; the *Sakurajima daikon* can weigh as much as 23 kilograms and the *Moriguchi daikon* reaches a length of up to two meters.

Daikon is a very important source of nourishment in the Japanese diet because it provides diastase, vitamin C, and lysine, which are not found in rice. It also helps digestion, and no matter how old it is, it never causes food poisoning, or *ataru* (attack or hit). Because of this, Japanese refer to poor actors as *daikon*-actors because neither the *daikon* nor the actors make a "hit" (*ataru*).

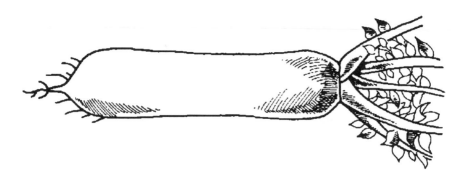

Figure 7.3
The Larger *Daikon*

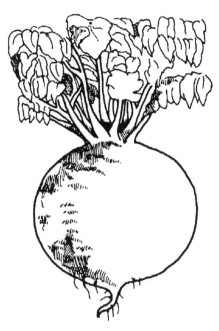

Figure 7.4
The *Sakurajima Daikon*

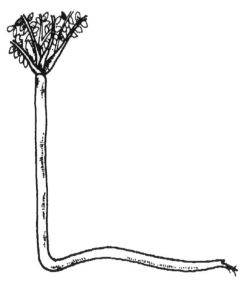

Figure 7.5
The *Moriguchi Daikon*

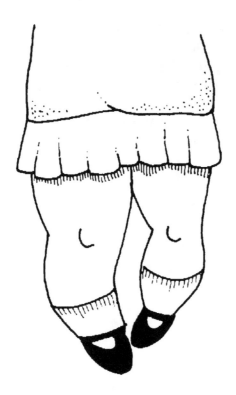

Figure 7.6
A Lady with *Daikon-Ashi*

Another idiomatic expression that uses the word *daikon* is *daikon-ashi* (heavy fat legs). *Daikon* connotes a long, thick radish that resembles a thick leg. There is no such term as "radish-legs" in English because the connotation of radish is entirely different.

Heavy legs are the result of sitting on tatami mats. When one sits on the floor Japanese-style, with one's legs tucked neatly under oneself, most of one's body weight is redistributed below the waist. So it is no wonder that many Japanese have *daikon-ashi*.

Cultural Connotations of *Daikon*

Compare the lady with *daikon-ashi* (see figure 7.6) with the *daikon* commonly eaten in Japan (see figure 7.3).

Japanese kimonos nicely cover this kind of legs, but most Japanese girls now wear dresses. To shed the excess flesh on their legs, many have given up sitting on the floor in favor of sitting on chairs. Naturally, Japanese men have such legs, too. Not much is made of this fact, however, because their legs are usually covered and women don't take interest in men's legs, with the exception, perhaps, of the legs of Mr. Takamiyama.

Takamiyama, the huge Hawaiian sumo wrestler who was a former football player, had the reputation of having "weak" legs. This, and the fact that he has to do certain exercises to build up strength in his legs—exercises that most other sumo players would not find necessary—has been much publicized. Being an American, he never sat on the floor Japanese-style before he went to Japan and took up sumo.

Another approach to cultural connotations is illustrated by the following French unit.

Say "Cheese"

(prepared by Carol Larson, Joyce Lopas, Dorann Klein, Carolyn Amelung, and Madeleine Kent)

Students will indicate the cultural meanings associated with the word *cheese* in the target culture by doing all of the following student activities:

A. Students will be able to give a popular saying that exemplifies the role of cheese in French culture.

B. Students will be able to cite an example from French literature in which cheese plays an important role (La Fontaine, "Le corbeau et le renard").

C. Students will be able to point out examples in French advertisements and cartoons of the interrelationship of cheese and the culture.

D. Students will be able to list [some number of] examples of the relationship between cheese and the culture upon witnessing a short skit.

E. Students will be able to identify [some number of] cheeses by sight and taste.

Teacher Activities

A. Present a popular saying (e.g., "There is no complete meal without cheese.")

   1. Show students French menus to substantiate the saying.

   2. Have students memorize the saying.

B. Present fable (La Fontaine, "The Crow and the Fox")

   1. Explain

   2. Have students dramatize

C. Present French advertisements

   1. Point out the frequency of cheese advertisements.

   2. Point out varieties of advertised cheeses.

   3. Point out prices of French cheeses (expensive, but even relatively poor families treat themselves to delicious food when they can).

   4. Aid the students in perceiving the appeal to cultural themes in the advertising of cheese (the family, *savoir vivre*, intellectualism).

D. Find a French political cartoon that contains a reference to cheese. Discuss the relevance of cheese.

E. Present a short skit.

   1. Prepare a short skit in which the importance of cheese is revealed.

2. The personification of cheese. (Holes in Swiss cheese [*gruyère*] are called *les yeux*. The point of a wedge is called *le nez*.)

3. A popular saying related to cheese *ça se passe entre la poire et le fromage*. (Save important discussion for between the fruit and cheese course.)

4. Have some students practice and present the skit for the class, including information on how to eat cheese. (Cut with knife. Put onto bread with knife, or in formal situation, eat with fork.) Never eat with fingers.

F. Provide for an assortment of French cheeses in the class.

1. Purchase or have some students purchase cheeses.

2. Introduce and allow the students to sample the various cheeses.

3. Introduce a game in which students must recognize cheeses by sight and taste.

The next chapter examines some of the ways that circumstance prescribes behavior.

Suggested Activities

1. Choose something (anything) in the target culture that interests you and illustrate the range of its occurrence through photographs clipped from newspapers and magazines.

2. Choose a word in the target language and interview a native speaker about what he or she visualizes when he or she hears the word.

3. Select a book cited in this chapter and report on it.

References Cited

Birdwhistell, Ray L. 1952. *Introduction to Kinesics*. Washington: Foreign Service Institute, Department of State.

Birdwhistell, Ray L. 1970. *Kinesics and Context: Essays on Body Motion Communication*. Philadelphia: Univ. of Pennsylvania Press.

Brault, Gerard. 1963. "Kinesics and the Classroom: Some Typical French Gestures." *French Review* 36: 374-82.

Coupland, Nikolas, Howard Giles, and John M. Wiemann, eds., 1991. *'Miscommunication' and Problematic Talk*. Newbury Park, CA: Sage.

Fleming, Gerald. 1971a. "Gesture Significances Then and Now: In Honor of Albrecht Dürer's 500th Anniversary." *Lebendiges Wort* 2, 3: 26-30.

Fleming, Gerald. 1971b. "Gestures and Body Movement as Mediators of Meaning in Our New Language Teaching Systems." *Contact* 16: 15-22.

Fleming, Gerald. 1971c. "The Role of Gesture in Language Teaching." *Pensiero e linguaggio* 2, 5: 31-43.

Green, Jerald R. 1968. *A Gesture Inventory for the Teaching of Spanish*. Skokie, IL: Rand McNally.

Green, Jerald R. 1973. "Kinesics in the Foreign Language Classroom." *Foreign Language Annals* 5 (1971): 62-68. Reprinted in Jerald R. Green, ed., *Foreign Language Education Research: A Book of Readings*. Skokie, IL: Rand McNally.

Morain, Genelle G. 1978. *Language in Education: Theory and Practice*. Washington, DC: Center for Applied Linguistics.

Morris, Desmond. 1977. *Manwatching: A Field Guide to Human Behavior*. New York: Harry N. Abrams.

Saitz, Robert L., and Edward J. Cervenka. 1972. *Handbook of Gestures: Colombia and the United States*. The Hague: Mouton.

Tsoutsos, Theodora M. 1970. "A Tentative Gesture Inventory for the Teaching of French." Master's thesis, Queens College, Brooklyn, New York.

Weitz, Shirley. 1979. *Nonverbal Communication. Readings with Commentary*. New York: Oxford Univ. Press.

8 Fitting the Where of Behavior to the When of Circumstance

The situation itself shapes one's response to it, and many situations cue conventional responses. This chapter describes goal 4 and presents a number of illustrations of how to develop skill in reacting appropriately.

Cultural Goal 4—*Where and When*: The student recognizes that situational variables and convention shape behavior in important ways.

Custom resolves the awkwardness of responding spontaneously to the same situation over and over again by conventionalizing the response. When you meet someone new, in English you say "How do you do" or, in informal settings, simply "Hi." Some cultures provide conventionalized linguistic responses where others do not. For example, the dilemma of what to write to a friend or acquaintance upon the death of his mother is simplified in Spanish by the convention *mi más sentido pésame*, whereas the English, of my dialect at least, does not provide a conventionalized linguistic response. In the Hispanic world *mi más sentido pésame* affords both parties satisfaction in a difficult encounter; in the Anglo world the same function is performed by mailing commercial sympathy cards to the bereaved.

All conventional responses share several characteristics: (1) They are cued by common social situations; (2) Both verbal and kinesic responses are limited to a prescribed few; (3) While utterance of the expected response may be mildly rewarding to the involved persons, absence of an expected response causes the would-be recipient to feel slighted. This is as true of conventional responses to a mundane occurrence, such as wishing someone a happy birthday, as it is of responses to a crisis situation, such as consoling someone who has suffered a divorce or serious illness.

The sociological foundation for analyzing conventional behavior is elaborated by Erving Goffman (1959, 1961, 1980, 1982). Goffman says that "Talk is socially organized, not merely in terms of who speaks to whom in what language, but as a little system of mutually ratified and ritually governed face-to-face action, a social encounter" (1964). Goffman goes on to say that face-to-face interaction has its own regulations, its own processes, its own structure, and "these don't seem to be intrinsically linguistic in character, however often expressed through a linguistic medium."

Elementary language texts always contain a number of low-key conventional responses, such as "good morning" or "thank you," which students learn to replicate when given the proper sociolinguistic setting. Teachers and students can prepare a shoe box full (well, maybe not really *full*) of these settings, then dip into the box as the occasion requires. Using the major headings from Nostrand or Murdock (see chapter 9), or the episodes from culture assimilators (see chapter 11), or imaginary circumstances suggested by students, teachers prepare brief scenarios on index cards. For example, one scene could be someone looking for work, another could be visiting a friend at the hospital.

To exploit further the cultural aspect of conventional responses, the teacher can manipulate social variables such as age, sex, social class, and country of origin. (See chapter 6 for a discussion of how role and other social variables affect behavior.) A simple way to do this is to prepare poster boards adorned with a visual of the social variable; underneath is the word in the target language that best describes the visual (e.g., old banker, young farmer). A bit of string attached to the poster so it can be hung from the student's neck completes the picture. Either the students or the instructor then invents a "when and where" scenario, posters (i.e., social variables) are then assigned to specific students, and they are told what their task is (e.g., cash a check). The instructor acts as movie director, supplying lines and critiques as needed.

Besides the role and social variables listed above, there are other variables that affect behavior. For example, the mission or role that one assumes when one goes to another culture is critically important. How do the host people see you? Are you a missionary or a diplomat or student or CIA agent? One common role is that of a businessperson.

Role Etiquette

Business men and women from industrial societies often find themselves—like Marco Polo before them—in exotic environs, and they too have to survive. To the rescue come many books: See references under Business in end-of-book resources.

And so it goes for many roles. There are books aimed at students (e.g., Gorden, 1974; Ladd, 1990), diplomats (e.g., Fisher, 1988), and many other niches in the host country. One library assignment (to engender skill in goal 6; see chapter 10) would be to identify as many books as possible that offer information and maybe advice for people in a specific role. The student chooses a role that interests him or her.

LEARNING ACTIVITY FOR GOAL 4

Students can develop skits that are useful in learning about conventional responses to common situations by getting the necessary background information from native informants, books, or the teacher.

The following German unit is an example of how this might be done in the classroom. The activity limits itself to street encounters, which the students experience through slides, skits, and role playing.

Begrüßung

(as developed in a German unit by Adele Farger, David K. Aacladan, Dzidra Schllaku, Cecilia C. Baumann, and Richard O. Whitcomb, under the supervision of James Hammers)

Dialogue I

A. View first slide plus tape recording of dialogue (street scene, two boys greeting each other with a handshake).

B. Two boys or girls from class are called upon to imitate the slide. Teacher gives points about handshake (i.e., firm grip, one shake).

C. Boys and girls demonstrate handshake again while the teacher models linguistic greeting. She stands behind the appropriate student supposedly speaking.

> HANS: Guten Tag, Klaus!
>
> KLAUS: Guten Tag, Hans! (boys release hands)

D. Students pair off with someone of the same sex, imitate the procedure for handshake, and imitate the dialogue lines after teacher model.

E. Teacher calls upon several pairs of students to demonstrate the ability to greet each other. If 90 percent of pairs respond accurately, proceed to dialogue II. If not, repeat D and E.

Dialogue II

A. View slide (boy meets girl on street) and hear tape recording.

B. A boy and girl imitate the slide. Teacher explains proper procedure (i.e., girl offers her hand first, boy bows slightly when shaking her hand).

C. The boy-girl couple repeats steps while the teacher again models the dialogue lines.

> JONATHAN: Tag, Heidi!
>
> HEIDI: Tag, Klaus! Wie geht's? Was gibt's zu Hause?

D. Students pair off with someone of opposite sex, imitate the handshaking pattern, and imitate simultaneously the dialogue lines.

E. Teacher calls upon several pairs of students to demonstrate ability to greet one another. If 90 percent of couples respond accurately, go on to dialogue III. If not, repeat steps D and E.

Dialogue III

A. View slide and hear tape recording. (A student meets an adult friend of his father on the street.)

B. Teacher takes the role of a friend of the student's father and calls upon a student to demonstrate the proper procedure. The adult offers his hand first, the boy bows slightly when shaking hands.

C. Teacher and student repeat handshaking patterns while teacher models dialogue lines.

> FRIEND: Guten Tag, Hans. Wie geht es dir?
>
> HANS: Guten Tag, Herr Schulz. Es geht mir gut, danke. Und Ihnen?
>
> FRIEND: Danke, auch gut.

D. Students pair off, one of them assuming the role of the adult. They imitate the handshaking procedure and also the dialogue lines.

E. Several of the students are called upon to greet the teacher. If 90 percent of them respond correctly, go on to test. If not, repeat steps D and E.

Test procedure

A. Several students are called upon to:

 1. Greet a student of same sex

 2. Greet a student of opposite sex

 3. Greet the teacher

    Each greeting must include the appropriate handshaking pattern, a greeting, and an inquiry about health.

B. If more than 90 percent of the students respond to all three situations accurately, the unit is finished. If not, repeat steps D and E of the inaccurately portrayed situation. Repeat the test.

The next chapter examines why people act the way they do.

Suggested Activities_____

1. List five situations in which people of the target culture are expected to act in a conventional way.

2. Choose a common situation with conventional behavioral patterns and discuss how role variables affect the way people respond to it.

3. Do one of the activities suggested in this chapter.

References Cited_____

Goffman, Erving. 1959. *The Presentation of Self in Everyday Life*. New York: Doubleday.

Goffman, Erving. 1961. *Encounters*. Indianapolis: Bobbs-Merrill.

Goffman, Erving. 1964. "The Neglected Situation." *American Anthropologist* 66, 6: 133-3.

Goffman, Erving. 1980. *Behavior in Public Places*. Westport, CT: Greenwood.

Goffman, Erving. 1982. *Interaction Ritual*. New York: Pantheon.

9 Why Do People Do That? The Rationale behind Behavior

People act the way they do to satisfy universal physical and psychological needs. This chapter examines several approaches (national character studies, basic postulates, and main themes) to understanding how societies evolve different ways to satisfy their basic needs. These "cosmic" approaches provide an interpretive framework for helping students explain the reason people of the studied culture act the way they do.

Cultural Goal 5—Why: The student understands that people generally act the way they do because they are using options the society allows for satisfying basic physical and psychological needs, and that cultural patterns tend mutually to support this.

A daily newspaper featured a front-page photo of the state department's leading international diplomat holding hands with an Arab diplomat of the same sex (male). Our international expert was using, appropriately, an Arab gesture to express friendship with an Arab. The intent of goal 5 is to see the logic behind any example of cross-cultural behavior—however bizarre or perplexing the behavior initially may appear to culture-bound eyes.

When an individual attempts to satisfy a basic need he or she usually has to employ many interacting cultural patterns that form a relatively cohesive structure. Some of these patterns are linguistic; others are not. For example, maintaining the respect of male peers in upper-class Guatemala City might involve skill in telling jokes and discussing literature, knowledge of English and of wines and liqueurs, having a resort home in which to entertain guests away from the city, and dressing conservatively.

The Motive behind Human Behavior

We hear "people are the same all over the world." Yet there are obvious differences. How can we reconcile this universality of the species with the uniqueness of its many cultures?

People everywhere are impelled to satisfy certain basic needs such as for food and shelter, for love and affection, and for self-respect. People have banded together to meet these needs. Predictably, different bands of people have developed different ways of doing so. An Eskimo might convey love and thoughtfulness to an elderly person by helping the person's friends and relatives hang him or her when he or she wishes to die; an American might manifest the same sentiment by attempting to prolong the life of an incurably sick elder in constant pain from cancer. The question students of intercultural communication can ask of any observed or reported behavior in the target culture is: What universal need is the individual trying to satisfy? (See Maslow, 1954; Aronoff, 1967.)

Maslow's sense of what motivates humans (he calls it "a holistic-dynamic theory") begins with satisfying fundamental physiological drives. "A person who is lacking food, safety, love, and esteem would most probably hunger for food more strongly than for anything else." When physiological needs are relatively well gratified, a new set of needs emerges. Maslow calls these "safety needs": Security; stability; dependency; protection; freedom from fear, anxiety, and chaos; need for structure, order, law, limits; strength in the protector; etc. If both physiological and safety needs are fairly well gratified, "belongingness and love needs" will emerge. These needs evidence themselves as a "hunger for affectionate relations" within the individual's group or family. This individual will "feel sharply the pangs of loneliness, of ostracism, or rejection, or friendlessness, or rootlessness."

Maslow maintains that in addition to physiological, safety, and belongingness and love needs, every healthy person also has "esteem" needs. There are two types of esteem needs: (1) the desire for strength, for achievement, for adequacy, for mastery and competence, and for independence and freedom, and (2) the desire for reputation, prestige, status, fame, and glory. Finally, Maslow says that even if all of these needs are satisfied, one will still experience a "new discontent and restlessness," unless the individual is doing what he, individually, is fitted for (Maslow, 1971, p. 37).

One universal need is to eat. The World Relief Corporation sent forty tons of Canadian cheddar cheese to refugee camps in Thailand in 1975. The Thai response: "Thank you for the soap, but it doesn't wash clothes very well." A doctor at the site got them to eat a little cheese by letting them think it was medicine. Not only didn't they like the taste, they complained that when they perspired it made them smell like white people.

The attempts of some Southeast Asian refugees to feed themselves in the United States have met cultural resistance on the part of some segments of U.S. society. Reports that the refugees were trapping domestic animals in San Francisco city parks and eating them has outraged animal lovers in those parts. Animal lovers who, it might be noted, are not themselves vegetarians, have been vehemently unsympathetic to the practical suggestion by the city's Catholic Charities that the refugees be allowed to get—and eat—unwanted pets from the humane society.

One poll taken in Korea indicated that 61 percent of Korean men reported that they ate dog meat. Dog, generally eaten in summer, is held to contain magic ingredients, including boosting virility—which makes it a favorite among men of the older generation. The euphemism for dog meat, *poshitang*, literally translates "healthy stew." This dietary custom posed a public relations problem for the government as it prepared to host the Seoul Olympics in 1988. The government launched a campaign to clear out sellers of dog meat from the downtown area. The government's ban had some effect. According to the *London Daily Telegraph*, large signs advertising *poshitang* were replaced by smaller ones.

Similarly, in Chicago there was an outcry of revulsion when "foreign speaking" individuals were asked what they were going to do with the pigeons they were trapping in Grant Park. Through graphic pantomime they conveyed that they were going to eat them. This response provoked an extended outcry in the city's newspaper columns.

Five hundred years before the birth of Christ, Confucius observed that "By nature people are nearly alike; by practice they get to be wide apart." We are by nature alike because we share the same basic needs. We all need to eat and to make friends, for instance. The different ways we go about doing this frequently puzzle and sometimes alienate people who are looking in from the outside.

To satisfy universal needs we have to employ behavioral patterns that will enable us to "bring home the bacon." For some Southeast Asians, trapping dogs is an accepted behavioral option for getting food. In certain societies, dogs are eaten only on prescribed ritual occasions, while in others they taste good all year round. Here in Disneyland we slaughter domesticated bovines for daily food but shun the ingestion of domesticated canines on even the most sacred of ritual occasions.

It takes us years to become socialized in the do's and don'ts of need gratification, and it takes even longer to develop skill levels that allow us success in satisfying these needs. A lot of options, or patterns of behavior, are available in any society for the satisfaction of basic needs. In technologically complex societies, the role of "hunter of food" can be discharged through any one of 40,000 or more occupations. (Technologically "simple" societies tend to have between a dozen and a hundred work-related roles.)

The satisfaction of psychological needs, on the other hand, is less affected by technological complexity than it is by two other issues: the amount of *interpersonal confidence* we feel in the presence of those with whom we must interact to satisfy a given need; and the extent to which the behavior we have to exhibit to satisfy our needs supports our *sense of continuity* of identity. (In some situations, our salient identity is 'self'; in other cases it is 'group.') Experiencing interpersonal confidence and maintaining a sense of continuity are both the outgrowth of a predictable and respectful cultural setting.

Even the simplest of choices can plunge one into anxieties about self-identity. The importance of maintaining a sense of self-determination and historical continuity in the face of culture change is illustrated by the successful experience of one upper–Amazon tribe, the Shuar. These people, better known to the outside world as the Jívaro of shrunken-head fame, have very recently changed from making their own clothes from fibers beat from trees to wearing blue jeans imported from abroad. This fiercely nationalistic group has effected a drastic sartorial change without any sense of historical loss or cultural diminution because they consciously made a choice for themselves that was not imposed from without, even though the presence of choice in this instance was dependent on an event (i.e., the manufacture of jeans) outside their own culture.

In addition to asking what basic human need the observed behavior helps people in that society to satisfy, there are important auxiliary questions to ask also: Is the observed behavior a frequently used behavioral option or is its occurrence rare in that society? What substitute behavioral patterns does the society allow for the satisfaction of that need? What complementary behavioral patterns are commonly associated with the observed behavior?

By itself, a behavior pattern is usually just a piece or fragment from one's repertoire of options designed for the gratification of any given universal need. When an observer of the human scene sees how a given behavior fits into the larger cultural context to enable the actor to satisfy a need everyone can identify with, the behavior makes sense and no longer seems quite as bizarre. It is at this point that understanding of another way of life begins to achieve significance.

Stewart and Bennett (1991) put it this way: "Statements such as 'Deep down, everyone in the world is really just the same,' betray the peculiarly American mix of individualism and egalitarianism that pervades American cultural self-perception. While these values and their attendant behavior may function well within American culture, their application . . . is not universal."

How do we help students develop skill in perceiving the functionality of "weird" behavior patterns encountered in "foreign" societies? Let me give two examples. The first example uses imagination as a catalyst to understanding; the second draws upon textual materials for its source of understanding.

Imagination as Source: Dial-a-Soap [Opera]

Activity A

The objective of this classroom activity is to get students thinking about the different forms of human behavior. The students clip photos from some handy source such as a target-language magazine that portrays the target people in the midst of action. A student draws a clipping at random. The student projects an imaginary scenario to "explain" why the person is doing the observed action, that is, what basic need has motivated the behavior. This activity is done without any pretense to even a semblance of authenticity. Rival scenarios are elicited from other students to "explain" the motivation behind the portrayed action. Again, the whole objective of this activity is to get the students to begin looking for the reasons behind human behavior; the classroom activity is not at this point concerned with ascertaining the "correct" explanation.

Activity B

Students select one of the scenarios produced in Activity A for refinement of the cultural content. The assistance of one or more natives of the target culture is elicited to help make the scenario "more plausible" for its cultural setting. The student(s) report on the modifications that were suggested and the reasons behind them. Again, one should not expect this activity to produce an authentic rationale for the observed behavior, but it does reinforce the desirability of inquiry and serves to refine student skill in making culturally appropriate attributions.

The objective of this activity is to help students begin to gain insight into "the fallacy of projected cognitive similarity" (Alfred J. Kraemer's wording). This fallacy underlines the difficulty, if not the impossibility, of getting inside another person's mind. We all project the logic of our own reasoning to explain the actions of others. The result often makes the observed action appear childish, not because the logic of the target people is primitive but because of the inappropriateness of our own projected logic to explain causal patterns in another cultural system. Classroom activities are needed to provide cathartic companions to activities such as Activity A above, which, if left undisturbed, would lead students into a false sense of understanding.

Textual Materials as Source: The Kapauku Papuans of West New Guinea

An excellent series of anthropological case studies were edited by George and Louise Spindler and published by Holt. One case study, written by Leopold Pospisil (1963), focuses on the Kapauku Papuans. Briefly, in this society wealth and prestige depend on the cost-effective harvesting of yams. Harvesting is done by wives. Obtaining and maintaining a wife is, as everybody knows, expensive. The trick is to make sure one's wives are neither too idle because there isn't enough land to tend, nor too busy to exploit the yam harvest because there are not enough wives to help. Adding wives at the right critical time, then, is essential for the accumulation of wealth (seashells).

To demonstrate how the custom of plural wives among the Kapauku Papuans enables families to gratify both social and economic needs in a way that would not be possible in that society through monogamy, the student elects to do one of the following four activities:

Activity A: Present an oral or written report on "What limits the number of wives any one man in Kapauku society can have?"

Activity B: Act out a game or skit of his/her own making that shows how wealth and prestige are achieved in Kapauku society.

Activity C: Participate in a panel that discusses what changes might occur in other areas of Kapauku life if polygyny were outlawed.

Activity D: Take a brief quiz that tests how women relate to social, economic, and political life in Kapauku society.

The satisfaction of basic human needs is not necessarily the reason people see for doing what they do. The conscious rationale for action more often speaks of love, God, motherhood, and other lofty concerns. Inquiry into the reasons people give for their behavior provides the lexicology of euphemisms we need to communicate inoffensively with people from the target culture.

Each culture imposes needs upon its members to some extent through societal values that require a person to behave in a given way in given situations. Even the goals a person works toward are culturally influenced. Consequently, while physical and psychological needs are universal, the individual aspirations that give direction to these needs arise out of the basic values of a particular culture.

A productive approach to understanding another society involves ascertaining the way culture has influenced basic needs, both in terms of the relative importance assigned by that society to a particular need and the ways provided by the society to satisfy the need. While all cultural patterns relate to a need with which people from any society can identify, the patterns themselves may seem peculiar. A red-blooded American student can understand trying to win the respect of others, but he or she may not immediately identify with those upper-Amazon Jívaros (i.e., Shuar) who used to shrink heads as a means to this end (among others).

Not only do different societies satisfy universal needs through patterns that may be unique to that society, but the priority with which they rank a need may differ substantially from one society to another. An American might indicate the priority he or she places on the need for shelter by buying an opulent house in an affluent suburb and by equipping it with the latest electrical wonders, while a Buddhist from Laos might indicate a lower priority for the same need through satisfaction with a simple hut with a thatched roof and earthen floor. The Laotian Buddhist value of disassociation from all worldly passions and interests and the American value of conspicuous consumption born of "capitalism and the spirit of Protestantism" affect the way "adequate" housing is seen.

Each culture offers its people a number of options for satisfying any particular human need. Many of these options are widely shared across cultures; the cross-cultural occurrence of other options is rare. Except in highly conventional circumstances, one can rarely predict with precision exactly what a person will do. But one can, with great precision, indicate the range of options within which a person will act to gratify a particular need in order to be considered "normal" by his or her neighbors. No matter how badly a U.S. politician may want to grow in wisdom, proclaim his or her bravery, or vent anger, he or she will not shrink heads.

Much of the individuality of a person's actions is the result of the relatively different set of options that person has chosen to satisfy needs. When regarded as an individual a person is relatively unpredictable. But when viewed as a collection of individuals who share the same society (i.e., the same cultural ground rules), individual behavior becomes relatively predictable. When faced with a particularly laudable or a particularly reprehensible act of an individual, we attempt to "explain" the act through the causal relationships that occur in the psychological recesses of a mind. When faced with a societal behavior, such as higher (or lower) frequency of divorce, war, mental breakdowns, suicide, or crime, we look to an explanation not within the recesses of an individual mind but within the values of the society at large.

The exceptionally broad potential range of human action is dramatically highlighted by Murdock's anthropological inventory of behavior (Murdock et al., 1983). Murdock outlines almost 100 general areas of behavior, with these further broken down into 900 subcategories. One utility of this outline is to alert us to many types of relationships we might want to explore as we pursue some special topic of interest.

One way to test a student's understanding of the inter-relatedness of human need and cultural patterns is to ask the student for the ramifications of a certain action. The more ramifications that occur to a student the broader his or her understanding.

National Character Studies

Just as many linguists maintain that an explicit knowledge of "rules of grammar" will assist students in learning to speak, so too do many social scientists hold that a knowledge of "codes of behavior" will help a student understand how people from different societies act.

If we do what we do because of our values and if values are widely shared within a culture but substantially disparate across cultures, knowledge of the few basic tenets of a culture should greatly aid one in predicting the behavior of any one culture-bearer.

The late Margaret Mead observed that national character studies "attempt to delineate how the innate properties of human beings, the idiosyncratic elements in each human being, and the general and individual patterns of human maturation are integrated within a shared social tradition in such a way that certain regularities appear in the behavior of all members of the culture which can be described as a culturally regular character" (Mead, 1953). Kaplan (1961, 1968) argues that while there is evidence of national variations of behavior, there is great variability within national groups and much overlap between the groups. Kaplan concludes by saying "the key to the diversity of behavior was seen to lie in the existence of any one of a small number of motivational tendencies which could be found in any society in the world."

Another review of national character studies by an anthropologist (Hsu, 1969, chapter 5) acknowledges that most of these studies were done in the 1940s and 1950s, but says that "a temporary drop of enthusiasm for national character studies among anthropologists is no reason to presume their total demise." An impressive social psychological study of the characteristic way members of similar subgroups in six countries (Greece, India, Japan, Peru, Taiwan, United States) perceive their social environment was conducted by Harry Triandis (Triandis et al., 1972). Triandis sees enough cross-cultural variance of behavior ascertainable through statistical analyses to amply justify continued research into national character studies.

Osgood, May, and Miron (1975) applied tests of semantic differential across twenty-seven countries in an attempt to identify cross-cultural universals of affective meaning for selected noncontextual terms (e.g., "good," "bad"). In looking for universals of affect, this ambitious study identifies interesting national variations.

A study of the international differences in work-related values (Hofstede, 1984) examines elements such as power distance, uncertainty avoidance, individualism, and masculinity as they appear in 40 industrialized nations. On the individualism scale, for instance, Hofstede finds the United States, Australia, and Great Britain to have the most individualistic workers, and Venezuela, Colombia, and Pakistan to have the least individualistic. Hofstede (1991) examines the implications of cultural differences on a multi-cultural workforce and international negotiations. Donald Brown (1991) lists some 400 characteristics said to describe all peoples.

Harold R. Isaacs's (1975) provocative book on group identity makes the point that "no mind, no personality, no individual or group identity ever looks like a set of neat boxes." Isaacs goes on to say that he pictures group identity as "looking more like a cell of living matter with a sprawlingly irregular shape." Still, at least with regard to some dimensions, ethnic or national groups do have recognizable, if irregular, shapes. If we look for "fractal" shapes, rather than traditional, pre-Mandelbrot geometric shapes, we will be closer to the mark. (An example of a fractal is the shape of a coastline or a galaxy.)

Cultural Values of Americans

Three books that describe American culture deserve special recommendation to teachers. *Meet the U.S.A.* by the historian Henry Steele Commager (1970) was written primarily for foreign visitors to the United States; *American Society: A Sociological Interpretation*, by Williams (1970), contains 100 pages on American values. A description of American values for visitors to the United States is available in Althen (1988).

A major work, first published in 1972 by Edward Stewart, and recently revised, expanded, and updated (Stewart and Bennett, 1991), is *American Cultural Patterns: A Cross-Cultural Perspective*. This highly recommended book contrasts basic Western and non-Western societies, then presents a set of core U.S. middle-class (mostly male and white) assumptions and values. These are organized around four areas: form of activity, form of social relations, perception of the world, and perception of self and the individual. In the course of a probing analysis of U.S. cultural values, the authors provide many gems of wisdom for the transcultural pilgrim that will help overcome the obstacles of intercultural communication. For example: "Americans who believe that 'deep down' everyone appreciates honest directness will continue to exact a heavy toll of tolerance from their more indirect foreign associates." Or, "If Americans (and others) seek sure answers that will eliminate all ambiguity from communication, the result is likely to be stereotyping."

An intriguing attempt to reduce the basic working philosophy of Americans to a series of postulates and their corollaries was written by Francis Hsu in his excellent little book *The Study of Literate Civilizations* (1969). Hsu is an anthropologist who has lived half his life in China and half in the United States. Before stating his nine postulates (and many corollaries) of life in the United States, Hsu describes pre-Communist China in terms of its own nine postulates. The raw material for identification of these postulates comes from personal experience, both literary and popular prose, social science studies, and studies of crime and other forms of societal breakdown.

Hsu's Postulates of Basic American Values

1. An individual's most important concern is self-interest: self-expression, self-improvement, self-gratification, and independence. This takes precedence over all group interests.

2. The privacy of the individual is the individual's inalienable right. Intrusion into it by others is permitted only by invitation.

3. Because the government exists for the benefit of the individual and not vice-versa, all forms of authority, including government, are suspect. But the government and its symbols should be respected. Patriotism is good.

4. An individual's success in life depends upon acceptance among his or her peers.

5. An individual should believe in or acknowledge God and should belong to an organized church or other religious

institution. Religion is good. Any religion is better than no religion.

6. Men and women are equal.

7. All human beings are equal.

8. Progress is good and inevitable. An individual must improve himself or herself (minimize efforts and maximize returns); the government must be more efficient to tackle new problems; institutions such as churches must modernize to make themselves more attractive.

9. Being American is synonymous with being progressive, and America is the utmost symbol of progress.

Besides providing insight into U.S. culture patterns, Hsu's postulates illustrate a principle of observation that anthropologists slowly have come to accept. Namely, that no matter how well trained one is in objective social observation one can never leave the influence of one's own culture completely behind. How much of Hsu's selection of U.S. cultural items was provoked by the particular way the items contrasted to the Chinese norm that Hsu expected to find in the United States? For example, Hsu finds that privacy is very important to Americans (postulate 2). Would a French observer of U.S. life, noticing office doors left open and residential windows facing the street like store windows, conclude that Americans do not value privacy? The more our concepts are challenged by people of different cultural frameworks, the more chance we have to understand them apart from the unconscious assumptions we make because of cultural conditioning. Hsu's postulates and corollaries for the United States are further elaborated in another book (Hsu, 1970).

Another useful book aimed at Americans who interact with Chinese is Hu and Grove (1991). A superb guide to Americans interacting with Japanese was prepared by John Condon (1984); the same author has prepared a guide for interactions between Americans and Mexicans (Condon, 1985). Gochenour (1990) describes the dynamics of American–Filipino interactions. A comparison of Brazilian and American behavior is available in Phyllis Harrison (1983). A guide for Westerners to understanding Arabs was done by Nydell (1987). Renwick, Smart, and Henderson (1991) discuss cultural

differences between Americans and Australians. Fieg (1989) highlights interaction between Americans and Thais. Raymond Cohen
(1990) examines cultural conflict between Egyptians and Israelis.

One irreverent essay on the effect of television on U.S. consumer
choices, *Snap, Crackle, and Popular Taste: The Illusion of Free Choice
in America* (Schrank, 1977), illustrates in example after example how
Americans are conditioned to behave in predictable—if rather as-
tonishing—ways. Much of this conditioning is accomplished by
aiming a consumer product to fill a psychological need (e.g., the
youthful "Pepsi generation" or the sensual "Oil of Olay"). Grocers
keep their shelves full because researchers have discovered that partially
empty supermarket shelves can cut sales by as much as 20 percent—
shoppers have the feeling of being able to choose only from remnants
or rejects of previous shoppers. Schrank reports that Campbell's
recommends that grocers stack their soups more vertically than
horizontally. Cans that are stacked higher and more narrowly sell
5 percent to 26 percent more than cans stacked lower but more
horizontally extended!

As a spinoff product of a training course for U.S. government
personnel stationed abroad, Alfred J. Kraemer (1973) identified
twenty-one values of mainstream U.S. culture that influence behavior in Americans, behavior that is often rather "inscrutable" from
the perspective of people from another culture.

Kraemer's Postulates of Mainstream American Values

1. Individualism—the belief that each person is a distinct
   entity and ought to assert and achieve independence from
   others
2. Egalitarianism—the belief that all human beings are equal in
   their intrinsic worth
3. Action orientation
4. Perception of interpersonal encounters primarily in terms of
   their immediate utility, and downgrading of the social
   significance of such encounters

5. Universalism—the value attached to being guided in one's actions in certain situations primarily by an obligation to society, i.e., by general standards of conduct—laws, regulations, rules, established procedures, etc. (In other situations, the value of individualism prevails.)

6. Definition of persons (including oneself) in terms of their work and achievements

7. The belief that the collective wisdom of the group is superior to that of any individual

8. The idea that the process of decision-making requires evaluation of the consequences of alternative courses of action, and selection of the one that, on balance, seems most advantageous

9. The belief that competition is a good way of motivating people

10. The idea that there is usually a best way of doing something, which should be determined and then followed

11. The belief that knowledge gained through observation is superior to knowledge gained in other ways

12. The belief that quantifying aspects of experience with numerical precision increases credibility (e.g., We moved 1243 desks and 2182 chairs in seven hours and fifteen minutes today.)

13. Placing a higher value on utilitarian aspects of experience than on aesthetic ones

14. Problem orientation—the tendency to perceive "problems" in the world, and in one's existence in it, and to look for "solutions"

15. The belief that thoughts cannot directly influence events

16. Reasoning in terms of probability

17. Impatience—the tendency to be annoyed by the pace of activities, if it is slow by one's own standards

18. The tendency to make comparative judgments

19. The willingness to offer one's services for the benefit of "the common good"

20. The belief in the existence of a behavior pattern called "self-help"

21. The belief that the use of absurd suppositions (arguing by *reductio ad absurdum*) will help communicate ideas or elicit ideas from other persons

Kraemer selected the above as illustrative of the values commonly held by U.S. government personnel, values that may provoke misunderstandings as Americans interact with host nationals.

Cultural Themes

A leading advocate of an analytic approach to cross-cultural rules of behavior is Howard Lee Nostrand. Nostrand (1967) has sought the "main themes" of French culture in particular, and teachers of French will want to obtain his four-volume *Background Data for the Teaching of French*. As an aid in identifying main themes, he has adapted Murdock's *Outline of World Cultures* (1983; originally published in 1964) into a structured inventory that he calls the "Emergent Model" (Nostrand, 1978). Emergent because, while still an inventory, it is organized so as to favor its conversion to a model that will show the interaction of the parts. In it some thirty topics are grouped under six large headings.

Nostrand's Emergent Model

1. *The Culture.* Value system, habits of thought, assumptions about reality, verifiable knowledge, art forms, language, paralanguage, and kinesics

2. *The Society.* Organized under institutions: familial, religious, economic-occupational, political and judicial, educational, intellectual-aesthetic, recreational, the mass media, stratification and mobility, social properties (*le savoir-vivre*), status by age group and sex, ethnic/religious and other minorities

3. *Conflicts.* Interpersonal and intergroup conflict, intrapersonal conflict

4. *The Ecology and Technology.* Exploitation of physical resources, exploitation of plants and animals, demographic control, health care and accident prevention, settlement and territorial organization, travel and transportation

5. *The Individual.* Integration at the organismic level, intrapersonal variability, interpersonal variation

6. *The Cross-Cultural Environment.* Attitudes toward other cultures and toward international and supranational organizations

Nostrand suggests that this organization of human behavior into six component relationships can best be taught by organizing the actions of a given lifestyle under its main theme—a theme being a value that is more fully defined in terms of its underlying assumptions and applications in human relations, personality structure, and interaction with the physical and subhuman environment. A theme, Nostrand explains, is "an emotionally charged concern, which motivates or strongly influences the culture bearer's conduct in a wide variety of situations" (Nostrand, 1974).

An essay by Nostrand (1973) elaborates on one manifestation of a main theme of French culture—intellectuality—within a historically evolutionary model. This manifestation is the French tendency "to seek understanding of any object of attention by looking for relationships within and surrounding the phenomenon one seeks to understand." Nostrand sees this characteristic in Frenchmen of various social classes. His essay superbly illustrates the thematic approach to understanding the behavior of a national group. Nostrand has incorporated this approach to understanding French culture in an intermediate language text (Nostrand et al., 1988).

Applying Nostrand's Emergent Model to French and Hispanic cultures, Ladu et al. (1968) developed a commendable booklet for teachers. It describes and interprets many of the cultural aspects of French and Hispanic life under the four major categories of an earlier version of Nostrand's Emergent Model. (For a discussion of Hispanic themes as illustrated in some Spanish plays of the 1960s, see Ruple, 1965.)

An informative discussion of the thematic approach to cultural understanding, along with an analysis of the major themes of North India, is supplied by the sociologist Morris Opler (1968). Mathiot

(1967) draws a distinction between those aspects of the cognitive system that are reflected in language and those reflected in nonlinguistic behavior. Consequently, she separates themes of the language from themes of the culture.

A detailed description of how songs may provide the basis for illustrating the main themes of a culture is presented by Damoiseau and Marc (1967). The authors pass over the two most frequent uses to which songs are subjected in language classes (as a literary text for linguistic analysis or as a vehicle for the study of the target culture as illustrated in song). Musical compositions, according to these authors, should be selected from writers who are involved with the daily life of the target society as seen through their thesis songs of social commentary.

The main social problem treated in the song would be the first concern of the class. The authors suggest a linguistic analysis of the coexistence of both urban and more traditional vocabulary with a view to illustrating the direction of social change. They further suggest that each thematic point could itself be carefully illustrated by a series of slides that show, for instance, the effect of urbanization on life in the target culture. Damoiseau and Marc also illustrate in considerable detail how lesson plans can be developed from this principle. The examples are French, as is the language of the article.

In addition to the ability to detect the themes of values of a culture, Frances and Howard Nostrand (1970) identify eight other skills, or abilities, that the foreign language student can develop:

1. The ability to describe a pattern or to ascribe it to a subculture of which it is typical
2. The ability to recognize a pattern in an instance of behavior
3. The ability to "explain" a pattern, whether in terms of its functional relation to other patterns or in causal terms
4. The ability to predict a probable reaction to a given situation
5. The ability to select an approved attitude
6. The ability to evaluate the evidence given for a descriptive generalization

7. The ability to describe or demonstrate a method of analysis or of synthesis

8. The ability to select descriptive knowledge significant for a common human purpose

Summing Up

The kaleidoscopic variety of human actions can be perceived as expressions of a few basic physical and psychological needs. The means for gratifying these needs are the behavioral options offered by one's culture.

The behavioral options available in any one society are the product of its past history, its world view, its geographical setting, its technological advances, and its contemporary crises. These options are influenced by the central postulates and corollaries accepted by the society. Societal postulates are fiction in the same sense that rules of grammar are fiction. Both are attempts at explanation after the fact. It is daily usage in both language and nonlinguistic behavior that the "rules" have to accommodate. The interaction of these central assumptions, or their more detailed main themes, with the ecological and historical realities of a society is what gives each society its distinctive character. It is this mix that gives a society its flavor.

Nelson Brooks (1968) suggests that as teachers of intercultural communication our approach to a culture should "never lose sight of the individual." Our inquiry should focus on how societal values, institutions, language, and the land affect the thought and lifestyle of someone living in the culture we are studying. While an economist might study how a bumper crop of peanuts affects the price of soybeans, the intercultural communication student asks how price fluctuations in corn affect the way Juan Pedro García lives.

Motivation for behavior relating to food, for example, is obviously prompted by the most critical of basic physical needs. Yet the behavior associated with the collection, domestication, processing, marketing, and consumption of food can also be viewed as a response to psychological needs. Hsu's first postulate of United States culture is that an American's most important concern is self-interest.

A corollary is that "an individual should seek the good life and pursue happiness." According to Hsu, in the United States the good life consists "primarily of the maximization of bodily comforts, food, and sexual enjoyment."

Students of U.S. culture can be directed to explore the psychologically motivated behavior of Americans as they cultivate the good life through food. Students of other cultures can ascertain which foods have ritual significance (e.g., afternoon tea to express friendship; evening *crêpes suzette* and champagne to convey the hope of intimacy; raw termite queens to extend a red-carpet welcome). Both the nutritional and social aspects of food can become objects of student inquiry.

The broad perspective advocated in this chapter is that any behavior can be viewed as an outgrowth of physical and psychological needs. These needs are codified in the attitudes, adages, and advice on any given topic, such as food, that a student can elicit from natives and other sources of information about the target culture.

This perspective has two implications for teachers. First, it is intellectually satisfying to approach an understanding of complex phenomena (human actions) by the process of deduction from a few major postulates or themes. This method affords the student at the onset of their inquiry the key (i.e., the explanatory postulate) to understanding any frequently recurring human action.

If, however, one approaches culture inductively, where the given is a perplexing action rather than an explanatory assumption, it is certainly helpful to have the vision that while the behavior of other people may look ridiculous, it is hardly absurd. Behavior occurs in largely patterned modes that can be characterized by a few basic assumptions. Whether these assumptions cause the behavior we see or whether they are accommodating rationalizations of behavior provoked by less lofty exigencies may be a chicken-or-egg dilemma. The best likelihood is that they are interactive. That is, assumptions and actions influence each other. As Nostrand (1974) says, "There is no need for agreement on ultimate beliefs, but rather for agreement on working principles and modes of action."

Nostrand (1974), a strong proponent of the thematic approach, says this about inductive techniques: "The Socratic technique has two great advantages over any other: that the learner values his hard-won knowledge and that meanwhile he gains experience in the skills of observation, creative imagination, and inferential reasoning."

After the student has identified a basic need and "translated" it into the form of the target culture, questions can be directed toward perceiving the relationship among different patterns.

A learning activity may be quite simple. To acquire the knowledge needed to do the four "Religion in San Pedro" activities outlined in chapter 12 relating to perceiving the rationale behind culturally conditioned behavior, one of the following out-of-class activities may suffice.

LEARNING ACTIVITIES FOR GOAL 5

A. Seek to determine how religion fits into the tapestry of rural Latin American culture by interviewing someone from that background; or

B. Read pages 72-78 in *San Pedro, Colombia: Small Town in a Developing Society*, by Miles Richardson (1970).

The next chapter features intercultural research skills.

Suggested Activities

1. List key questions you would ask to elicit how people of your target culture satisfy the need for food and shelter, for love and affection, for pride in oneself.

2. How has culture influenced satisfaction of the basic need for food in your target culture? What is the range of options?

3. Choose one of Hsu's postulates and redefine or rework it to be appropriate for your culture area.

4. Identify those American values that both Hsu and Kraemer identify and those where there appears to be a difference of interpretation.

5. Choose an everyday occurrence within the target society
   that is rare in your own, and show how it helps satisfy a
   basic need. What other options does that society provide to
   enable its people to satisfy the same need?

References Cited

Althen, Gary. 1988. *American Ways: A Guide for Foreigners*. Yarmouth, ME: Intercultural Press.

Aronoff, Joel. 1967. *Psychological Needs and Cultural Systems: A Case Study*. Princeton, NJ: Van Nostrand.

Brooks, Nelson D. 1968. *Language and Language Learning: Theory and Practice*. New York: Harcourt, Brace.

Brown, Donald E. 1991. *Human Universals*. Philadelphia: Temple Univ. Press.

Cohen, Raymond. 1990. *Culture and Conflict in Egyptian-Israeli Relations: A Dialogue of the Deaf*. Bloomington: Indiana Univ. Press.

Commager, Henry Steele. 1970. *Meet the U.S.A.* Rev. ed. New York: Institute of International Education.

Condon, John C. 1984. *With Respect to the Japanese: A Guide for Americans*. Yarmouth, ME: Intercultural Press.

Condon, John C. 1985. *Good Neighbors: Communicating with the Mexicans*. Yarmouth, ME: Intercultural Press.

Damoiseau, R., and E. Marc. 1967. "La Chanson moderne: Étude de civilisation et de langue." *Le Français dans le monde* 47: 40-44.

Fieg, John Paul. 1989. *A Common Core: Thais and Americans*. Rev. Elizabeth Mortlock. Yarmouth, ME: Intercultural Press.

Gochenour, Theodore. 1990. *Considering Filipinos*. Yarmouth, ME: Intercultural Press.

Harrison, Phyllis A. 1983. *Behaving Brazilian: A Comparison of Brazilian and North American Social Behavior*. New York: Harper & Row.

Hofstede, Geert. 1984. *Culture's Consequences: International Differences in Work-Related Values*. Newbury Park, CA: Sage.

Hofstede, Geert. 1991. *Culture and Organizations: Software of the Mind*. New York: McGraw-Hill.

Hsu, Francis L. K. 1969. *The Study of Literate Civilizations*. New York: Holt, Rinehart and Winston.

Hsu, Francis L. K. 1970. *Americans and Chinese: Reflections on Two Cultures and Their People*. Garden City, NY: Doubleday.

Hu, Wenzhong, and Cornelius Grove. 1991. *Encountering the Chinese: A Guide for Americans*. Yarmouth, ME: Intercultural Press.

Isaacs, Harold R. 1975. *Idols of the Tribe: Group Identity and Political Change*. New York: Harper & Row.

Kaplan, Bert, ed. 1961. *Studying Personality Cross-Culturally*. New York: Harper & Row.

Kaplan, Bert. 1968. "Personality and Social Structure," in R. A. Manners and D. Kaplan, eds., *Theory in Anthropology: A Sourcebook*. Chicago: Aldine.

Kraemer, Alfred J. 1973. *Development of a Cultural Self-Awareness Approach to Instruction in Intercultural Communication*. Alexandria, VA: Human Resources Research Organization.

Ladu, Tora T., et al. 1968. *Teaching for Cross-Cultural Understanding*. Raleigh, NC: Department of Public Instruction.

Maslow, A. H. 1954. *Motivation and Personality*. New York: Harper.

Maslow, A. H. 1971. *The Farther Reaches of Human Nature*. New York: Viking.

Mathiot, Madeleine. 1967. "An Approach to the Study of Language-in-Culture Relations." *Dissertation Abstracts* 27, 3765B, Catholic University of America, Washington, DC.

Mead, Margaret. 1953. "National Character," pp. 642-67 in A. L. Kroeber, ed., *Anthropology Today: An Encyclopedic Inventory*. Chicago: Univ. of Chicago Press.

Murdock, George P., et al. 1983. *Outline of World Cultures*. 5th ed. New Haven, CT: Human Relations Area File.

Nostrand, Frances, and Howard L. Nostrand. 1970. "Testing Understanding of the Foreign Culture," pp. 161-70 in H. Ned Seelye, ed., *Perspectives for Teachers of Latin American Culture*. Springfield, IL: Superintendent of Public Instruction.

Nostrand, Howard L., ed. 1967. *Background Data for the Teaching of French*. Seattle: Univ. of Washington Press. Part A, *La Culture et la société française au XXe siècle*; Part B, *Exemples littéraires*; Part C, *Contemporary Culture and Society in the United States*. [EDRS: ED 031 964; ED 031 989; ED 031 990]

Nostrand, Howard L. 1973. "French Culture's Concern for Relationships: Relationism." *Foreign Language Annals* 6: 469-80.

Nostrand, Howard L. 1974. "Empathy for a Second Culture: Motivations and Techniques," pp. 263-327 in Gilbert A. Jarvis, ed., *Responding to New Realities*. ACTFL Review of Foreign Language Education, Vol. 5. Lincolnwood, IL: National Textbook.

Nostrand, Howard L. 1978. "The 'Emergent Model' (Structured Inventory of a Sociocultural System) Applied to Contemporary France." *Contemporary French Civilization* 2, 2 (Winter): 277-94.

Nostrand, Howard L., Frances B. Nostrand, and Claudette Imberton-Hunt. 1988. *Savoir vivre en français: Culture et communication.* New York: John Wiley.

Nydell, Margaret Kleffner. 1987. *Understanding Arabs: A Guide for Westerners.* Yarmouth, ME: Intercultural Press.

Opler, Morris E. 1968. "The Themal Approach in Cultural Anthropology and Its Application to North Indian Data." *Southwestern Journal of Anthropology* 24, 3: 215-27.

Osgood, Charles E., William H. May, and Murray S. Miron. 1975. *Cross-Cultural Universals of Affective Meaning.* Urbana: Univ. of Illinois Press.

Pospisil, Leopold. 1963. *The Kapauku Papuans of West New Guinea.* New York: Holt.

Renwick, George W., Reginald Smart, and Don L. Henderson, eds. 1991. *A Fair Go for All: A Guide for Australians and Americans.* Yarmouth, ME: Intercultural Press.

Ruple, Joelyn. 1965. "Teaching Cultural Themes Using the Spanish Theatre." *Hispania* 48: 511-16.

Schrank, Jeffrey. 1977. *Snap, Crackle, and Popular Taste: The Illusion of Free Choice in America.* New York: Dell.

Stewart, Edward C., and Milton J. Bennett. 1991. *American Cultural Patterns: A Cross-Cultural Perspective.* Yarmouth, ME: Intercultural Press.

Triandis, Harry C., et al. 1972. *The Analysis of Subjective Culture.* New York: Wiley-Interscience.

Williams, Robin M. 1970. *American Culture: A Sociological Interpretation.* 3rd rev. ed. New York: Knopf.

10 There's Gold in Them Thar Hills: Exploring the Target Culture

This description of goal 6 focuses on three research skills: evaluating the relative truth of cultural generalizations; developing library skills; and refining interviewing skills.

Cultural Goal 6—Exploration: The student demonstrates (a) the ability to evaluate a generalization about the target culture in terms of the amount of evidence substantiating it, and (b) shows that she or he has developed the skills needed to locate and organize information about the target culture from the library, the mass media, people, and personal observation.

Evaluating Statements about a Society

All our lives we hear things about other cultures. The challenge is to learn to differentiate judgments that serve the ethnocentric bias of national politics from judgments that have an adequate empirical base. There are many prerequisite skills for sorting through the pronouncements of our species. Among these are skill in balancing the evidence with the generalization, in separating speculation from objective observation, and in discerning vested interest.

LEARNING ACTIVITY FOR GOAL 6A:
IS IT TRUE THAT ...?

Statements about a culture for subsequent evaluation can be taken from a number of sources, including a textbook, foreign visitors, and even the classroom teacher. The following ten statements were fabricated for the occasion.

In class the student will be given ten statements about Hispanic culture. After reading the statements, mark each statement either (A) probably true, (B) probably false, or (C) I don't know. For those statements you marked A or B, indicate briefly what evidence supports your judgment; for those you marked C, indicate what specific additional information you need to make a judgment. The list will be given in class. You have the whole period to answer. You will not be graded on the basis of whether you answered A, B, or C, but on the strength of your supporting comments. Each statement is worth up to three points; you need 20 or more to pass.

1. Most Spanish-speaking people take siestas at noon.
2. Most religions are allowed in Spain, although Catholicism is dominant.
3. The Latin American's concept of space is such that among friends there is a fair amount of touching involved (e.g., embracing, patting on the shoulder, handshaking).
4. Flamenco is the music most popular in Spain.
5. Spanish is spoken everywhere in Latin America.
6. Shopping for groceries in Latin America is accomplished by going to a supermarket once weekly and getting all that is needed.
7. If one were to go to a bank in a Spanish-speaking country, he would have no trouble cashing a check since the banking system there is the same as that in the United States.

8. The tradition of girls being chaperoned when they go out at night is slowly dying out.

9. The gaucho of Argentina has been highly idealized through literature.

10. The appropriate response of a woman to a *piropo* would be to ignore it.

(The compilers assumed that 1, 4, 5, 6, and 7 were false and the rest of the items true. Do you agree? What is the status of religious freedom in Spain? Has the women's movement in any of the Spanish-speaking countries altered the status of the *piropo*?)

Generating Cultural Hypotheses

Facts are the fuel we use to propel our thoughts; as such they are used, used up, and discarded by the growing mind. Schools often unwittingly reinforce greater respect for teacher authority than for the value of student intellectual discovery. Yet there is a practical opportunity to demonstrate respect for individual intellectual inquiry in the teaching of culture. A teacher's lack of training in cultural concepts need not be a crippling disadvantage in activities where the focus is on developing in students the ability to hazard productive guesses about the target culture.

This approach to guessing, or hypothesis refinement, helps us avoid what Alfred North Whitehead (1929) has called the Fallacy of Dogmatic Finality.

There are many sources for these guesses. Books are a great source of information about a culture, but they are not, of course, the only source. Magazines, newspapers, radio, television, movies, records, comic books, and other people offer much up-to-date data for cultural analysis.

Generalizations can be drawn from even the bits of authentic cultural information contained in foreign language newspapers, even by students with little or no fluency in the target language.

Simple facts can be used as building blocks to develop skill in extracting meaning from fragments. This is the same technique an archaeologist uses when examining pottery shards. What is important is not the acquisition of a broader base of arbitrary and pointless facts, but the ability to gather facts from a variety of sources—and then to do something with the facts! It is the human mind that organizes and assigns importance to facts. Many great insights are formed by people who are puttering around with data in an attempt to tease out something that makes sense.

Minimedia units can begin with a simple question or two to help focus attention on the "document"—the newspaper or magazine clipping. The next several questions zero in on aspects of the everyday life of some target people. The student is then asked to generalize beyond the specific information contained in the clippings. The student should not feel under much pressure to generate a "correct" hypothesis, or even a well-educated guess. No hypothesis starts by being correct. Some are more useful than others. One often does not discover which are useful until a lot of time has been spent on a problem and one belatedly realizes that understanding of the problem is still where it was at the beginning. Such is the reward of scientists.

A second concept these minimedia units develop is that hypotheses (or guesses or insights or generalizations or whatever) must *always* be refined. If x is true, under what circumstances is it true? For the purpose of minimedia units, it is much more important to begin identifying what additional knowledge is necessary to check the soundness of your generalization than it is to get the information needed to refine it. The easiest way to begin refining a hypothesis about human behavior is to ask how the generalization is affected by variables such as age, sex, social class, and place of residence.

The cultural generalization that results from the guess or hypothesis in a minimedia unit can and perhaps should be based on empirical evidence. The advertising illustrations in foreign language newspapers and magazines are an ideal source of authentic empirical evidence. What help can teachers and trainers get in their efforts to develop in their students the reading skills needed to penetrate the mass media? A sample of available materials in Spanish includes units to develop skill in reading newspaper headlines (Seelye and Day, 1971, 1982) and newspaper content in general (Smith, 1981). Other newspaper units are presented for Spanish (Day, 1977), French (Schulz, 1982; Jorstad, 1976), Italian (Rallo, 1976), and German

(Culver, 1982) cultures to sensitize students to the potential of these "documents" in developing cultural insights. For French print media, one publication aims at presenting the feminine view (Steele and Bourlon, 1980), another looks at cross sections of *la vie quotidienne* (Paoletti and Steele, 1981).

The example below is a brief exercise to develop student skill in making and refining hypotheses and it is taken from the first of a series of these minimedia units published by National Textbook Company. It deals with Hispanic culture (Seelye and Day, 1982). The unit is entitled "George?"

This ad ran in an Argentine newspaper. The word George, which appears three times in the ad, is an English proper noun and has no other meaning in Spanish.

Figure 10.1
An Argentine Ad for George

Check the best response.

1. What kind of business establishment is George?

    ___ (a) a general notions store for men and women

    ___ (b) a men's store

    ___ (c) a women's store

    ___ (d) a children's store

    ___ (e) not enough information to determine

2. The ad implies that the reader should buy gifts for _____.

    ___ (a) children

    ___ (b) parents

    ___ (c) mothers

    ___ (d) fathers

    ___ (e) not enough information to determine

3. Why do you think the advertiser chose to use children in the picture?

4. Why do you think English was mixed with Spanish in this ad?

Another, somewhat longer, unit from the same source uses physicians' ads as the cultural "documents" to be scrutinized.

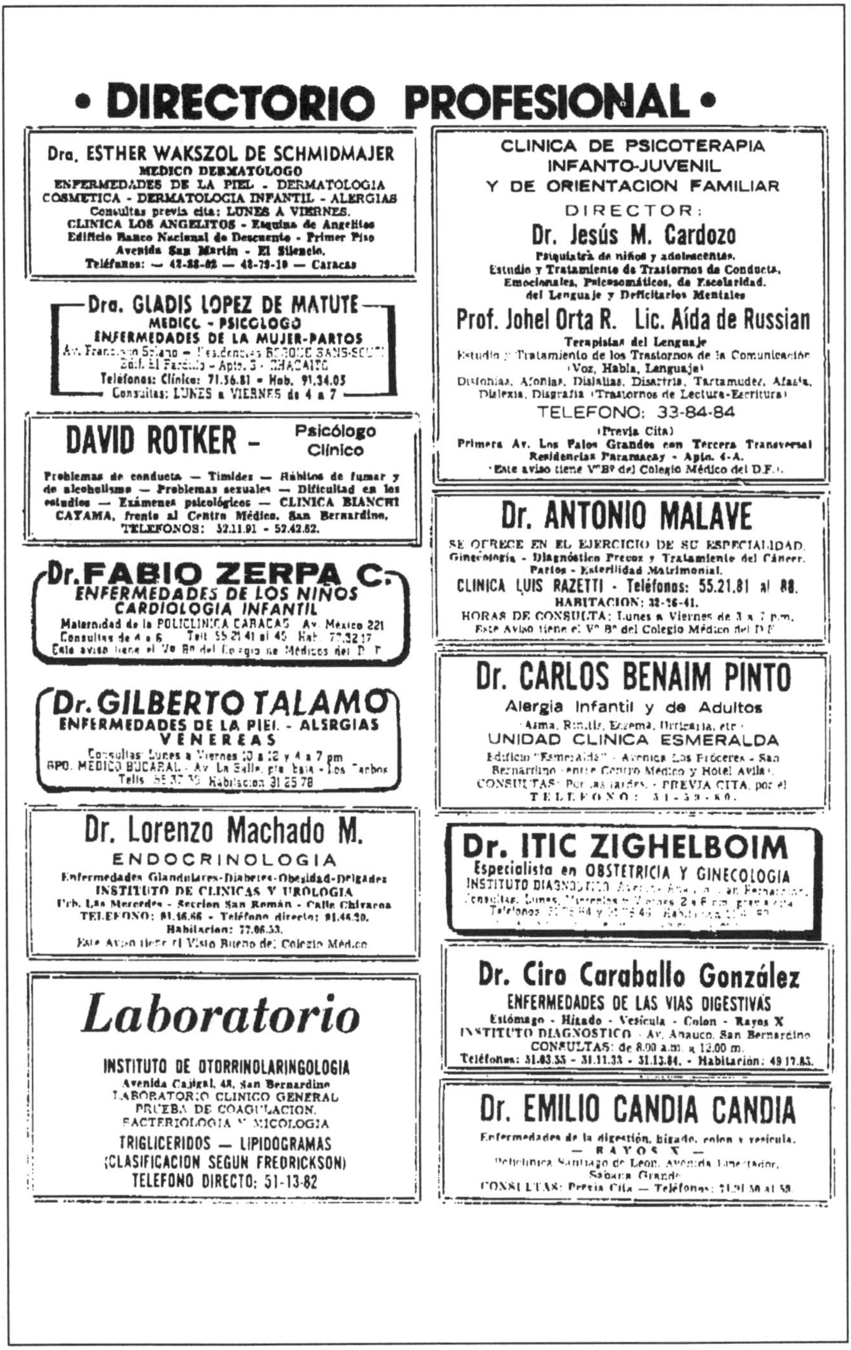

Figure 10.2
Is there a doctor in the ad?

The training required of a medical doctor in Spain or Latin America is about the same as that required in the United States. Mexico, for example, has some of the world's most distinguished specialists in heart disorders. The authors of this booklet, or their families, have received medical treatment, some of which required surgery, in five different countries of Latin America. For us, the competency of Latin American physicians is well established. One of the best of these was a neighborhood doctor who made house calls for fifty cents in an urban slum area where one of the authors was living. Latin America may be one of the few places in the hemisphere where doctors still make house calls.

As you can see from the ads shown in this unit, medical doctors (as well as other professionals) advertise. Based on these ads, all of which appeared on one newspaper page, answer the following questions.

Check the best response, or answer in the space provided.

1. How many women doctors appear in the ads?

   _____ (a) one   _____ (b) two   _____(c) four

2. Which doctors are advertising treatment for disorders?

3. Which ads are advertising treatment for children?

4. Which ads are advertising treatment for allergies?

5. How many doctors have one or more "last" names that seem to be of non-Spanish origin (e.g., German, North American)?

   _____ (a) less than 5 _____(b) 6-9 _____(c) 10-13

6. What does the initial stand for in a name such as Dr. Lorenzo Machado M.?

   ____ (a) indicates his medical specialty

   ____ (b) indicates his mother's surname

   ____ (c) none of the above

   ____ (d) not enough information to determine

7. What is an otorrinolaringólogo?

   ____ (a) an ear specialist

   ____ (b) a throat specialist

   ____ (c) a nose specialist

   ____ (d) all of the above

8. List at least one characteristic of the language of the ads.

9. What is the significance of the name Matute in Dra. Gladis López de Matute?

_____ (a) It's her mother's surname.

_____ (b) It's her father's surname.

_____ (c) It's her husband's surname.

_____ (d) none of the above.

10. What does V.° B.° stand for?

_____ (a) Visto Bueno

_____ (b) Vías Bateriológicas

_____ (c) Venas Buenas

11. List as many hypotheses about life in Latin America as you can (for some future refinement, perhaps), based on your analysis of the documents in this unit.

Researching Another Culture

Of utmost import are the classroom or workshop skills that stay with a student during all the years after he or she leaves our tutelage. Many students forget all the facts and lose their hard-earned linguistic fluency, but none loses the need for continuing his or her education. Despite historic precedents replete with isolationism and anti-intellectualism, we have been made painfully aware that even distant small countries importantly influence our daily options. Understanding other cultures is frequently a matter of life or death. In the best of times, knowledge of another culture is tantamount to moving out of a dark dank corner of the cave into greater illumination.

The average college graduate nowadays has been the recipient of an education costing more than $50,000—and the cost keeps rising! Most of the content of this education soon becomes obsolete. This is not a criticism of the education; it is a tribute to our commitment to pushing back the frontiers of knowledge. Still, education is difficult to justify on the basis of the "facts" learned. Alfred North Whitehead (1929) utterly rejects this notion. The learning of facts, he writes, has not justified education since the

establishment of libraries and the availability of inexpensive paperbacks. If the actual content of education has little currency, what
is of inestimable value is learning how to learn. Practically all learning
of any value is learned outside of a formal classroom. Learning,
however, can be greatly enhanced by an educational system that
develops skill in pursuing knowledge.

Developing research skills is easily accomplished. There are only
so many founts of knowledge subject to rational inquiry—books,
newspapers, magazines, other printed materials, films, recordings,
pictures, other people, and personal experience. In its simplest form,
an elementary school child can be taught to ask of any statement
of "fact" about a foreign culture: "Who says so?"

Bibliographic and interview techniques are well developed and
lend themselves to practice within a school setting. For help with
the former, consult any librarian; for help with the latter, see Gorden
(1987). Svobodny (1973) has written an excellent article outlining
the techniques of retrieval of print data for foreign language educators.

Research into another culture can involve mass media sources
such as movies and comic books. Wendell Hall, a professor at Brigham
Young University, developed highly innovative learning activities to
accompany a popular Latin American comic book, *Condorito*. A
rationale for using comic books in the foreign language classroom
appears in Hall and Lafourcade (1970). In 1990, Vaughan P. Simmons
began editing an illustrated periodical, *Mangajin*, which wonderfully
combines language and culture studies of Japanese (Mangajin, P.O.
Box 10443, Atlanta, GA 30319). *Mangajin* includes comic book art,
a form popular with highly literate Japanese readers—both young
and old. Visits to the exhibitors' booths at professional conferences
will turn up many more sources for penetrating the mass media.

The Intercultural Press (P.O. Box 768, Yarmouth, Maine 04096)
is run by people such as Margaret D. Pusch, David S. Hoopes, and
George W. Renwick, who really know the field of intercultural
communication; they put out a useful catalog.

A stickier matter is the organization of information culled through
standard retrieval techniques. Each academic discipline has many
theoretical constructs that compete for attention. Some hold promise
for getting an answer to certain questions, others for answering other
questions. For the purposes of students of intercultural communication, the simple framework offered by the six goals described in

chapter 3 provides enough organization to begin earnest cultural inquiry.

LEARNING ACTIVITIES FOR GOAL 6A AND B, EXPLORING THE CULTURE

The sample end-of-course performance objective on researching another culture presented in chapter 12 requires the student to do eight exercises leading up to a report on a topic.

A classroom activity done with the assistance of a librarian has as its object getting students accustomed to searching for print sources. This activity takes the same statements contained in the activity listed at the beginning of this chapter under Goal 6a but changes the performance objective to read:

The student is given a list consisting of ten statements on Hispanic culture. After reading the statements, he or she will list two or three sources he or she would consult either to verify what the statement says or to render the statement implausible. He or she must respond to all statements with two or three appropriate sources.

The following stab at writing an end-of-year performance objective that might apply to many minimedia units helps let students know what is expected of them.

Terminal behavior

To demonstrate skill in generating and refining cultural hypotheses, the student will

1. Observe a cultural pattern from a picture, cartoon, drawing, or news fragment
2. Make one generalization about the culture drawn from examination of the picture, etc.

3. Indicate five sources of information to which one might refer in order to further refine the generalization

Conditions

The illustrations will be given in class. You will be allowed to choose one from among five; all will be taken from target newspapers or magazines that have been available in class for at least one month. You will be given 30 minutes to complete the three terminal behaviors.

Criterion

At least four of the five chosen sources must be valid choices.

Key Ideas

How to develop students' skill in identifying sources to answer their questions?

One approach (Seelye, 1968) took twenty-three "key ideas" of a culture area, Latin America, and had students prepare an annotated bibliography of relevant sources from forty books that were available to the classroom. The key ideas in this case had been identified previously by a group of historians and social scientists (Gill and Conroy, 1967a,b,c; Gill and Conroy, 1968) and were organized under six headings (Gill, Conroy, and Cornbleth, 1967):

1. The physical environment
2. Historical backgrounds
3. Contemporary society and the family
4. Contemporary culture values, ideals, and creative expression
5. Contemporary economics
6. Contemporary politics, government, and international relations

The following example of how one key idea was indexed illustrates the process. The titles referred to are listed in the bibliography in Seelye (1968, 1972).

Key Idea 3. C. Relations among the many ethnic groups vary from nation to nation, although in general there tends to be less overt racial discrimination and hostility than in the United States.

Adams (1960); Alexander (1962:29-56, the people); Arciniegas (1967:215-33, Africans and Europeans in Haiti); Hand (1967b, new Latin American nationalism); Heath (1965:342-60, social stratification in Latin America; 475-556, world-views); Keen (1967:456-89, society in transition); Loprete (1965:206-26, social life); Mörner (1967); Schurz (1964:51-87, the people); Wagley (1968:155-74, concept of social race); Wagley (1958:93-118, Africans in Martinique).

This type of exercise combines development of basic bibliographic skills with the spinoff effect of teaching key ideas. Excellent sources for learning how to learn in cross-cultural situations are available in Wight et al. (1970). Their bibliography at the end of this book identifies many specific sources of specific cultural data.

Topical Performance Objectives

An effective approach to teaching cross-cultural research skills in elementary school social studies classes has been prepared by Ernest L. Rock (1973). Rock is an exceptionally creative person who took his doctorate in foreign language education. Even though these instructional materials are aimed at the later elementary school social studies student, many teachers report success with them on the junior high and tenth-grade levels.

The materials include 100 performance objectives ("I can name at least three ways by which a _____ person entertains himself in his home") contained in a series of booklets (e.g., What's to Eat, What the People Wear, It Happens Every Day). Students are not given information on the topics; rather, they are guided through a series of "prerequisite activities" to finding the information themselves. A number of creative activities are suggested for each topic to interest students in using their newfound information.

The following examples illustrate how Rock's technique was adapted by foreign language teachers. Three examples, developed in workshops conducted by Seelye, are for French classes, one for Spanish. (A recommendable book dealing with cultural misunderstandings between the French and Americans is provided by Raymonde Carroll, 1987.)

The French Telephone

(prepared by Blossom Adler)

Performance objectives

1. I will be able to describe at least one feature of a French telephone that differs from ours.
2. I will be able to use the telephone in the French manner of composing the number using good French pronunciation.
3. I will begin a conversation with a friend using the French pattern of *politesse,* with good pronunciation.

Prerequisite activities

1. In the library, consult the *Encyclopaedia Britannica* and the *World Book.* Look up "France, communication."
2. Look into the stack of back copies of *Bonjour* on the table at the back of the French classroom. Look for pictures of telephones and skits about the use of telephones. Practice reading the words and phrases aloud. Ask your teacher for help with pronunciation.
3. Look into the stacks of other French magazines on the reserve shelf in the school library. Look for pictures of people using phones or of phones alone. Study them to see if the French phones are different from ours.
4. Ask your teacher or audiovisual department to help you locate filmstrips, slides, etc., on the telephone in France.

Creative activity

1. From pictures available, enlarged (line) drawings may be done by willing/artistic members of the class.

2. Constructively creative students may add an *écouteur* to a toy telephone so that there are two "French" phones to use for role playing.

3. Each student will perform in front of the class in pairs, using the phone, composing the number orally as he or she reaches the number (after dialing), and with French *politesse,* begin a conversation with a friend.

Breton

(prepared by Emily Dewhirst)

Performance objectives

1. The student will list four Breton customs and write a paragraph in French on each with no more than five errors. Each paragraph is to explain the significance of the custom.

2. The student will name and tell how four Breton customs (including any distinctive language usage among the elderly) represent values that differ from those held by French people in general.

Prerequisite activities

1. In the library, consult the card catalog, encyclopedias, and the *Reader's Guide to Periodical Literature.*

2. Consult the books on French civilization and culture in the foreign language learning center.

3. Check the list of filmstrips, slides, and other visual materials in the language center.

4. Consult the card box for French people in the area who have knowledge of Bretagne and are willing to be interviewed.

5. Look up recent articles on Bretagne in the *National Geographic.*

6. Write to the French National Tourist Office for information on Bretagne.

7. Write or phone airline companies or travel bureaus for information and brochures.

8. Check the record collection of French music (learning center).

9. Listen to the tapes of people from Bretagne (see instructor).

Creative activities

1. Decorate a bulletin board illustrating Bretagne and its customs.

2. Draw a traditional Breton costume, describe it to the class in French, and explain when it is still worn.

3. Compile a scrapbook of information, pictures, and sketches concerning one of the following topics: a Breton church, a pardon (a religious ceremony unique to Bretons).

4. Correspond with a French student in Bretagne. Exchange at least three letters.

5. Build a model of a Breton cemetery, explaining to the class in French the significance of the different parts.

6. Look through copies of *Réalités, Paris Match, National Geographic,* etc., for pictures to illustrate a five-minute talk in French contrasting *l'Arcoat* and *l'Armor.*

7. In a five-minute talk in French, explain the history of the Breton language and the furor in present-day France over the use of the language today.

8. In a written paper of not less 500 words or in a five-minute speech in French, give examples of five famous Breton sailors and their exploits.

9. Draw a *menhir* and a *dolmen* and explain what they are to the class in a five-minute talk in French.

The French University

(prepared by Connie Layton and Sister Clare Eileen Craddock)

Performance objectives

1. I will be able to discuss at least four social activities of a French university student.
2. I will be able to discuss at least five academic activities of a French university student.

Prerequisite activities

1. Consult French magazines and periodicals in the library or in the French language room.
2. Interview French exchange students.
3. Contact a member of a French student organization.
4. Write to a French university for copies of schedules and curricula.
5. Contact the French embassy for posters, flyers, etc., relating to French student life.
6. Write to the Services Culturels Français, 972 Fifth Ave., New York 10021, for their series of brochures on French education.
7. Consult the *International Index to Periodicals* for articles on French education.
8. Consult reference works (e.g., civilization books) containing information on French education.

Creative activities

1. Write a paper contrasting requirements for a university degree in France and in the United States.
2. Present a skit of a classroom situation in French university life.
3. Make a notebook of newspaper articles on French academic life.
4. Prepare a discussion on student organizations at French universities.

La Comida

(prepared by Jerome Carvajal)

Performance objective

I can identify appropriate Mexican foods eaten at the four meals: *desayuno, comida, merienda (refacción),* and *cena.*

Prerequisite activities

1. Study the menus from several Mexican restaurants.
2. Study the food ads in Mexican newspapers.
3. Refer to lesson 36, pages 189-91 in textbook *Primera Vista.*
4. Refer to lesson 28 in textbook *Bienvenidos.*
5. Refer to menu, pages 352-54, in *Usted y Yo.*
6. Ask native speakers to describe what they eat.
7. Go to a Mexican restaurant.
8. View the filmstrip "Skimpy come un buen desayuno."
9. Refer to the Time-Life series *Mexican Cookbook.*
10. Talk with the home economics teacher.
11. Write letters to the Del Monte Company, asking for menus and recipes.

Creative activities

1. Cut out pictures of food and people in restaurants from Mexican newspapers and magazines and make a notebook.
2. Draw your own conclusion from the data you have collected and incorporate them into writing your own menu for one of the four meals.
3. Make a bulletin board.
4. Illustrate a menu for a Mexican restaurant using art media of your choice.
5. Learn how to make one of the foods and offer it to the class.

6. Take the information you have gathered about Mexican food and hypothesize that the same food is eaten in all Hispanic cultures. How would you refine (test) this hypothesis to see to what extent it is true?

The next chapter lists two techniques (culture assimilators and culture capsules) that can be employed during workshops or the first-semester course, and a third technique (culture clusters) that may be more appropriate for second- or third-semester students. These techniques can be used to enhance skill in any of the six goals of cultural instruction outlined in chapter 3.

Suggested Activities

1. Clip a display ad from a foreign language newspaper or magazine. Do the following four activities: (1) Observe a cultural pattern from a picture, cartoon, drawing, or news fragment; (2) Make one generalization about the culture drawn from examination of the picture, etc.; (3) Indicate how you would go about probing the soundness of your generalization. (How widespread is the observed pattern in terms of age, sex, social class, and place of residence?); (4) Identify five specific sources of information to which one might refer in order to further refine the generalization.

2. Prepare a learning activity based on your chosen topic to teach cross-cultural research skills. (Use as many media as are available to you.)

References Cited

Carroll, Raymonde. 1987. *Cultural Misunderstandings: The French-American Experience* tr. Carol Volk. Chicago: Univ. of Chicago Press.

Culver, Anke I. 1982. *The Magazine: A Reflection of Life-Styles in the German-Speaking World*. Lincolnwood, IL: National Textbook.

Day, J. Laurence. 1977. *The Sports Page: Based on Selections from Major Newspapers from the Spanish-Speaking World*. Lincolnwood, IL: National Textbook.

Gill, Clark C., and William B. Conroy. 1967a. *Teaching about Latin America in Social Studies Instructional Materials. Latin American Curriculum Project, Bulletin 1.* Austin: University of Texas. [EDRS: ED 012 832]

Gill, Clark C., and William B. Conroy. 1967b. *Teaching about Latin America in the Secondary School: An Annotated Guide to Instructional Resources. Latin American Curriculum Project, Bulletin 2.* Austin: University of Texas. [EDRS: ED 012 833]

Gill, Clark C., and William B. Conroy. 1967c. *The Social Scientists Look at Latin America: Six Position Papers. Latin American Curriculum Project, Bulletin 3.* Austin: University of Texas. [EDRS: ED 012 365]

Gill, Clark C., and William B. Conroy, eds. 1968. *The Treatment of Latin America in Social Studies Instruction Materials. Latin American Curriculum Project, Bulletin 5.* Austin: University of Texas.

Gill, Clark C., William B. Conroy, and Catherine Cornbleth. 1967. *Key Ideas about Latin America. Latin American Curriculum Project, Bulletin 4.* Austin: University of Texas.

Gorden, Raymond L. 1987. *Interviewing: Strategy, Techniques, and Tactics.* Homewood, IL: Dorsey.

Hall, Wendell, and Enrique Lafourcade. 1970. "Teaching Aspects of the Foreign Culture through Comic Strips," in H. Ned Seelye, ed., *Perspectives for Teachers of Latin American Culture.* Springfield, IL: State Superintendent of Public Instruction.

Jorstad, Helen L. 1976. *The Magazine: French Mini-Culture Unit.* Lincolnwood, IL: National Textbook.

Nostrand, Howard L., Frances B. Nostrand, and Claudette Imberton-Hunt. 1988. *Savoir vivre en français: Culture et communication.* New York: Wiley.

Paoletti, Michel, and Ross Steele. 1981. *Civilisation française quotidienne.* Paris: Hatier.

Rallo, John A. 1976. *The Newspaper: Based on Selections from Major Newspapers from Italy.* Lincolnwood, IL: National Textbook.

Rock, Ernest. 1973. *An Individualized Program for Cultural Understanding.* Dayton, OH: Educaids.

Schulz, Renate A. 1982. *The Newspaper: French Mini-Culture Unit.* Lincolnwood, IL: National Textbook.

Seelye, H. Ned, ed. 1968. *A Handbook on Latin America for Teachers: Methodology and Annotated Bibliography.* Springfield: Illinois Office of Education. [EDRS: ED 027 797]

Seelye, H. Ned, ed. 1972. *Teaching Cultural Concepts in Spanish Classes.* Springfield, IL: Illinois Office of Education. [EDRS: ED 108 454]

Seelye, H. Ned, and J. Laurence Day. 1971. "Penetrating the Mass Media: A Unit to Develop Skill in Reading Spanish Newspaper Headlines," pp. 69–81 in *Foreign Language Annals* 5 (Oct.).

Seelye, H. Ned, and J. Laurence Day. 1982. *The Newspaper: A Reflection of Life-Styles in the Spanish-Speaking World.* Rev. ed. Lincolnwood, IL: National Textbook.

Smith, William Flint. 1981. *Noticiario: Primer Nivel.* Rowley, MA: Newbury.

Steele, Ross, and Annie Deville Bourlon. 1980. *Elle.* Paris: Didier.

Svobodny, Dolly D. 1973. "Information Sources for the Foreign-Language Teacher-Researcher," pp. 37-50 in Jerald R. Green, ed., *Foreign-Language Education Research: A Book of Readings.* Skokie, IL: Rand McNally.

Whitehead, Alfred North. 1929. *The Aims of Education, and Other Essays.* New York: Macmillan.

Wight, Albert R., and Mary Anne Hammons. 1970. *Guidelines for Peace Corps Cross-Cultural Training, Part II. Specific Methods and Techniques.* Washington, DC: Peace Corps, Department of State. [EDRS: ED 059 938]

Wight, Albert R., et al. 1970. *Guidelines for Peace Corps Cross-Cultural Training, Part III. Supplementary Readings.* Washington, DC: Peace Corps, Department of State. [EDRS: ED 059 939]

11 Culture Assimilators, Culture Capsules, Culture Clusters

This chapter illustrates three techniques for teaching cultural concepts. Through culture assimilators (six examples are given), students have interesting programed readings that they do outside class. Culture capsules (four examples are given) are presented in class in a five-minute talk illustrated by visuals. Culture clusters (one example is given) build upon two or three related culture capsules to simulate in class an event from everyday life in the target society.

The three techniques described in this chapter have proven popular with teachers in culture workshops across the country. The first two techniques, culture assimilators and culture capsules, deal with "miniexposés" of a small unit of target behavior that often is confusing to an American. The third technique, culture clusters, sketches broader relationships among several cultural fragments.

Culture Assimilators

Several social psychologists have developed a programed out-of-class technique to facilitate adjustment to another culture (Fiedler et al. 1971). This technique, called the culture assimilator, provides the student with as many as seventy-five or one hundred episodes of target cultural behavior. Each episode describes a "critical incident" of cross-cultural interaction that is usually a common occurrence in which an American and a host national interact, a situation one or both find puzzling or conflictful or that they are likely to misinterpret, and a situation that can be interpreted in a fairly unequivocal manner, given sufficient knowledge about the other's culture.

After reading the episode, the student chooses the correct response from four plausible explanations of the behavior described in the episode. The student is provided with feedback that, if the student has erred in his choice, redirects the student and asks him or her to make another selection. The whole process takes about three minutes for each episode. In a variation of this, Brislin et al. (1986) engineers the responses so that more than one may be correct to one degree or another. Brislin et al. have produced 100 episodes that are commendably suited for use in intercultural communication workshops and courses.

Culture assimilators have three advantages over the more common procedure of presenting information via books. Assimilators are more fun to read; they actively involve the student with a cross-cultural problem; and they have been shown to be more effective in controlled experiments.

The content of the assimilators can be varied to suit the instructor's purpose. For example, within the organizational framework argued in this book, about twenty episodes that pertain to each of the six cultural goals could constitute an assimilator. The validity of the episode and the correct response are ascertained by pretesting with host nationals.

Rosita Albert (1983), a social psychologist who herself has developed a culture assimilator under rigorous research conditions, has identified extant assimilators. Culture assimilators have been constructed for the Arab countries, Iran, Thailand, Central America, Greece, Mexican-Americans and Latinos, and for black-white interaction in the urban United States.

The following two illustrative episodes are taken from the *Honduras Culture Assimilator* (Symonds et al., 1967). Each response to each episode appears, in the original, on a different page.

Culture Assimilator Episode 1: Honduras

George was involved in a serious conversation with the schoolteacher. He was trying to find out why the educational standards were so low and why the teachers did not unite in an endeavor to better their working conditions and improve the educational standards. He told the teacher that back home in Chicago the teachers had gone on strike and refused to teach until their working conditions were improved. He also stated that since the teacher is a professional, the teacher must promote new and better methods of teaching and not wait for the school board or the government to initiate changes. The teacher merely smiled wanly, shrugged, and changed the subject.

Why do think the teacher did not seem to be interested in what George had to say?

A. Teachers, like all Hondurans, are lazy. As long as they get paid, they do not really care about educational standards.

B. Unions are illegal in Honduras.

C. Teachers in the villages are appointed by the government and have very little to say about what or how they teach.

D. The teacher himself was poorly educated and did not feel competent to discuss the matter.

You chose A

It is unlikely that a person would voluntarily become a teacher if he or she did not have some interest in helping to educate people. You have made two assumptions here that are not warranted by what you have read in this and past episodes. The assumptions are that Hondurans are lazy and that Hondurans have a strong affinity for money at the expense of other values. Do not make assumptions like this unless you have good reasons for doing so.

Reread the episode and make another choice.

You chose B

This answer might explain the teacher's behavior, if it were the case. Have we given you any indications that unions are illegal?

Do not make assumptions like this when you are going through the assimilator. Try to apply information you have already learned.

Reread the episode and make another choice.

You chose C

Right! Even if you had not been aware that teachers are appointed by the government, you were able to apply the information you learned in the last episode, about the situation of the mayor, to this episode and the situation of the teacher. Their situations are somewhat similar. Teachers are required to conform rigidly to the curriculum laid down by the Honduran Board of Education, a department of the government. Not only that, but the teacher's position as teacher is dependent upon the government. Quite often when there is a change in government a teacher is out of a job and is replaced by another teacher. Under conditions of such instability, the teacher is not in a position to exert much pressure upon the central government.

You chose D

There may be some truth in this, but on what evidence are you basing your choice of this alternative? Use information you have already learned and try to apply it from one situation to another.

Reread the episode and make another choice.

Culture Assimilator Episode 2: Honduras

George and his friend had made plans to visit some of the surrounding *aldeas* (very small villages, or hamlets). They intended to travel quite a considerable distance, so they decided to rent some burros. They went to the mayor of their village who promised to have two burros ready for them the following morning. The boys were up early and ready to leave by 8:00. When the burros had not arrived by 8:30, they went in search of the mayor. He told them the man with the burros was up in the hills and would be back about 10:00. The boys waited and finally the man arrived at 11:00. He told

them that he had some burros, but that he would not be able
to get them that day since someone else had them. He said
that if they wanted to leave the next day, he would have
them for them by 8:00 the next morning. The boys were
annoyed and told the man that since they were paying for the
use of the burros, they expected that he would have them
ready for them. The man just shrugged. The boys realized
there was nothing else for them to do, so they agreed to wait
till tomorrow. After searching for the man the next morning,
they finally found him at 9:30. He told them he had forgotten
about the burros but would have them for them in a few
minutes. At 11:00 he finally showed up with only one burro,
stating that the other one was still away and the boys would
have to take turns riding and walking.

Which alternative best describes the reason for the behavior
in the episode?

A. Hondurans are inconsiderate.

B. Neither the mayor nor the other man really believed the
North Americans would pay for the burros, so they were
not putting themselves out.

C. Hondurans have many different values from North
Americans. One of them is very little concern for the
passage of time.

D. The man with the burros and the mayor both felt that the
North Americans should not visit the aldea. They felt the
boys should spend all their time in the village, so they
were making it difficult for them to make the trip.

You chose A

By now you should have realized that this just is not so.
Hondurans are very hospitable and easy to get along with.
They would not consciously be inconsiderate to a visitor.

Think this over more carefully. Reread the episode and
make another choice.

You chose B

This choice is not consistent with what you have already learned about the hospitality and friendliness of the Honduran.

Reread the episode and make another choice.

You chose C

Right! Were you able to choose this alternative by a process of elimination? The other alternatives are either inconsistent with the idea of Honduran hospitality or emphasize only individual personality differences of one or two people.

An incident such as the one described in this passage could occur, and does, many times in Honduras. By North American standards, Hondurans are unreliable. However, you cannot use North American standards when you are interacting with people of another culture.

The Honduran conception of time is somewhat different from that of the North American. The villager is not at all concerned with what we would call procrastination. He does things if and when it pleases him and cannot easily be pushed. It is not so much that he is stubborn or inconsiderate; it is just that he cannot understand why anyone else should be in a hurry when he is not. This is, by and large, a general aspect of village life. It is slow and easy. What does not get done today can just as easily wait till tomorrow, or next week. You will encounter this and have to contend with it in all your dealings with Hondurans.

You chose D

It might be possible that this explanation could account for an isolated incident, but the assimilator is not concerned with isolated incidents. An attitude on the part of the mayor and the other man as described in D is not really consistent with what you already know about the hospitality of the Hondurans. While there might be one or two Hondurans who feel this way, it would certainly not be a general attitude.

Reread the episode and make another choice.

A practical forum for writing assimilator episodes is a workshop where each participant suggests some. The most promising of these episodes can be validated by trying them on natives of the target culture. Four unvalidated episodes appear here—one for German, one for Spanish, and two for French. These episodes were prepared by experienced teachers (many of them experts in the target culture) in courses or workshops I directed. Several were written under the direct supervision of Harry Triandis.

Culture Assimilator Episode 3:
On a Train in Germany

(prepared by Ildiko Bodoni)

Susan was traveling from Hamburg to Frankfurt. The train ride was rather long, so she decided to buy a ticket for a Liegewagen. It was only slightly more expensive than the regular ticket and she would be able to get a good night's sleep. When she entered the compartment, she was surprised to see four men and a lady already seated there. Since she could see no beds, she assumed that later on they would go to another compartment, with the men separate from the women. Imagine her astonishment when the porter came, folded down the seats so that they formed six bunk beds, and gave everyone a pillow and a blanket! She sat upright on her bunk bed, not sleeping all night, afraid of the men.

Why was Susan upset?

A. The German ticket agent had cheated her and sold her the wrong ticket.

B. She thought that she should have moved to the correct compartment and was angry at herself for not doing so.

C. She had confused the concept of a Liegewagen with that of a Schlafwagen.

D. Germans have very loose morals and she might have been the object of "improper" behavior.

Your answer was A

This answer is incorrect because Susan had received the correct ticket for the amount of money paid and for what she had requested.

Go back and reread the article carefully.

Your answer was B

This answer is incorrect; all the compartments in that car were alike, and her ticket had specified this compartment.

Go back and reread the article carefully.

Your answer was C

This is the correct answer, because Susan had confused a Liegewagen with a Schlafwagen. In a Liegewagen one does not have a private compartment with a made-up bed, and strangers ignore each other. Susan was thinking of a Schlafwagen, which is similar to the American Pullman car, when she had bought the ticket.

Your answer was D

This answer is incorrect, because it is a false generalization.

Go back and reread the article carefully.

Culture Assimilator Episode 4: Colombia

(prepared by Diane Pretzer)

Bob and Mary Jones, recent arrivals in Bogotá, have been invited to the home of a Colombian coworker for a dinner party. Their host mentioned 9 P.M. Bob was surprised at the late hour of starting, but he and Mary made it a point to arrive right on time so as not to delay dinner.

Arriving at the door, they rang the bell. After a long pause, they rang again. Finally a servant appeared and ushered them into the living room, which was dark until that moment, when the lamps were lighted. Rather puzzled looks passed between them as they sat silently for a while, and they finally began to talk, almost in whispers. "Do you suppose we got the wrong house or the wrong night?" Anxiously they watched the door. At 9:45 their host appeared, greeted them cordially, and said he and his wife would be with them shortly. At 10:30, host and hostess appeared, followed by servants with drinks, and soon, other guests arrived. Still puzzled, the Joneses relaxed, but were certainly glad when dinner was finally served at 11:30.

What best explains the delay?

A. Bob and Mary did have the wrong night, but their host and hostess were graciously and valiantly trying to make the best of it. They hurriedly dressed, got some neighbors to come in, and gave a pretty good impromptu party.

B. Bob and Mary hadn't discovered yet that, regardless of time mentioned, no host would expect his guests to arrive until at least one or one and one-half hours later.

C. Bob was mistaken when he thought they were told the party was at 9:00. His friend had said there would be nine guests.

D. Bob and Mary forgot to change their watches when they arrived in Bogotá.

You chose A

This is not the right choice. Latins may be known for hospitality, but not that much!

You chose B

This is the appropriate choice. Few nonnatives would know it until they had such an experience, or were especially cautioned by those in the know. The party would proceed at a very leisurely pace, and it might be after midnight when dinner is served. The party might last till 3 A.M., even on a weeknight.

You chose C

If Bob's Spanish was adequate for work in Bogotá, he isn't too likely to mix up *a las nueve* and *habré nueve invitados*. This is not a good choice.

You chose D

Since they probably have been there at least a few days, this choice is extremely unlikely.

Culture Assimilator Episode 5: France

(prepared by Genelle Morain)

As a young American tourist in Tours, France, you have been invited to dinner at the home of a French business associate of your father. You know that under such circumstances it is considered polite to bring a bouquet of flowers to the hostess. Accordingly, you arrive at the door of the apartment with a handsome bouquet of white chrysanthemums. As your hostess greets you, you offer the bouquet to her. You notice a look of surprise and distaste cross her countenance before she masters herself and accepts your offering graciously.

All evening you are haunted by the feeling that you have done something wrong. You would like to apologize—but you are at a loss to know what for.

What could explain your hostess's reaction?

A. A bouquet of chrysanthemums is considered an apology for a serious blunder in French culture.
B. A bouquet of chrysanthemums is considered a proposal of marriage in French culture.
C. Chrysanthemums are considered the flower of death in French culture.
D. The hostess was allergic to chrysanthemums.

You chose A

Although this symbolic use of flowers would be valid in some cultures, the French do not consider the chrysanthemum as a flower of apology.

You chose B

This would seem to be a logical possibility, but in French culture the symbolism of the chrysanthemum is allied to an aspect of life other than romance. The French consider the rose the flower of love.

You chose C

Your choice is the correct one. The chrysanthemum is considered *la fleur de mort* because it is traditionally used in conjunction with funerals and interments in France.

You chose D

To the allergy-conscious American, this would seem a logical assumption. The French, however, are not so obsessed with allergies, preferring to blame most physical troubles on the liver.

Culture Assimilator Episode 6: France

(prepared by Jane Wright)

Mary Jones, an American coed majoring in French, was spending her junior year abroad in Paris. She was extremely eager to improve her language skills and to gain deeper insights into the workings of the French culture. Shortly after Mary's arrival in Paris, she made the acquaintance of Jeanne Dupont, a French girl in one of her classes. Jeanne, her parents, and her brother live in an apartment building about four blocks from Mary's dormitory. The two girls sat together in class and often went to a nearby café after class with a couple of other students for coffee.

Mary has been hopeful that Jeanne would invite her to her home some evening, perhaps for dinner, so that she could meet Jeanne's family, learn more about the French family structure, and see a "real French home." Mary considers Jeanne a friend and can't understand why she hasn't been invited to her home for a casual evening. Finally, Mary decided to drop a subtle hint. In a group one day, she commented that it was difficult to understand much of French culture while living in a dormitory and never really getting on the "inside." Jeanne displayed no reaction to Mary's "hint" and still did not extend such an invitation to her. Mary wondered why.

Which of the following "explanations" most accurately describes why Jeanne has not invited Mary into her home?

A. Mary's hint was rather "brazen," and the French are disdainful of such forward behavior.

B. French people tend to invite only very good friends into their home. Jeanne and Mary simply do not know each other well enough to be "friends," as Jeanne sees it.

C. Jeanne probably does not like Mary very much. Mary should take the hint and not pursue the relationship.

D. Most French people have negative feelings toward Americans visiting in France. Mary must understand that fact and realize that she will probably never be permitted by Jeanne's parents to visit in their home.

You chose A

It is understandable that you have chosen this explanation because neither Americans nor the French value forward and brazen behavior. However, in this case, Mary was subtle and tactful in dropping her "hint." There must be a different reason for not being invited into Jeanne's home. Think about characteristics typical of the French culture and try again.

You chose B

Correct. It is true that French people tend to invite only very good friends into their homes. Such a tendency does contrast with the American custom of opening homes to casual friends as well as to very close friends. For the French family, the "home" is one's very personal and private domain—not to be invaded by just anyone. Rather, only very close friends are invited to share an evening with the family. Mary must understand how the French value the home and the concept of friendship. She must be patient and continue to nurture her relationship with Jeanne. If their friendship continues to mature, perhaps she will someday be invited into Jeanne's home.

You chose C

To us Americans it would, indeed, seem plausible that Jeanne simply does not like Mary. However, if we try to step outside of our own culture for a moment and examine the situation more objectively, we see no other indications that Jeanne dislikes Mary. Rather, they seem friendly. Our only indication of any "problem," according to Mary, is that she has not been invited to Jeanne's home. Go back and try again.

You chose D

It is true that we hear many negative things about the "ugly Americans" in France. But to believe that most Frenchmen dislike most Americans on the basis of exposure to a few bungling tourists alone would indeed be a misconception. Certainly if Mary is considerate of her French friends and is a friendly person, she will be accepted.

Culture Capsules

Culture capsules are generally prepared outside of class by a student but presented during class time in 5 or 10 minutes at the end of a period.

The concept was developed by a foreign language teacher, the late Darrel Taylor, in collaboration with an anthropologist, John Sorenson. A succinct description of the technique appeared in *The Modern Language Journal* (Taylor and Sorenson, 1961). Briefly, a culture capsule consists of a paragraph or so of explanation of one minimal difference between an American and a target custom, along with several illustrative photos or relevant realia. Taylor and Sorenson offer the example of a Mexican bullfight to illustrate a cross-cultural difference.

The minimal cultural difference to be highlighted in the capsule can be selected in much the same way as the episodes in culture assimilators are selected. So that culture capsules are not merely disassociated fragments of the life of a society, the capsules' content can be chosen to represent the various relationships outlined in Nostrand's Emergent Model (see chapter 9).

Like culture assimilators, the subject matter of culture capsules can be quite varied. There are several differences between the two techniques. In assimilators the student has to identify culturally appropriate explanations for the described situation; in culture capsules the explanation of the cross-cultural difference is presented to the student in both the textual description and in the accompanying multimedia razzle-dazzle. Teacher-made assimilators represent essentially out-of-class activities, whereas capsules can be prepared by students for oral delivery during class.

Many well-defined culture capsules have been developed into a series of classroom activities by J. Dale Miller. Under his direction, 100-page units have been developed that examine U.S.-Hispanic and U.S.-South American cultural differences (Miller et al., 1979), U.S.-French cultural differences (Miller and Loiseau, 1974), and U.S.-Mexican cultural differences (Miller and Bishop, 1979).

Grant Skabelund and Susan Simms edit a series of four-page briefings called "culturgrams" for 100 countries. These are periodically updated; all 100 country "culturgrams" were revised in 1992; individual titles are updated regularly. Many ideas for culture capsules can be derived from each "culturgram." (These are available from Publications Services, David M. Kennedy Center for International Studies, 280 HRCB, Brigham Young University, Provo, Utah 84602). The same organization also publishes "infograms," which cut across cultures with topics such as travel stress, keeping the law, and how the family unit adjusts to international living.

Culture Capsule: French Bread

(prepared by Blossom Adler)

We speak of a thing being as good as gold, but the French people speak of a thing as being as good as bread. The French love and value bread as an important element of life. The French eat bread at every meal. It comes in various shapes and sizes.

The urban French housewife does not bake her own bread. She goes to the bakery daily to buy fresh bread. If bread is left over from the evening meal, it will not be wasted. It will be used in cooking or will be toasted for breakfast to be eaten with butter and/or jam. Bread and butter is called *une tartine.*

Except in Normandy and Brittany, butter is served only at breakfast or with certain foods (e.g., radishes, Roquefort cheese, on dark bread [*pain bis*] with oysters).

In rural areas, families often make their own delicious dark bread, *pain de campagne* (country bread), which keeps well. Traditionally, a person of honor in the household, perhaps the grandfather, makes a cross on the loaf with a large knife, then cuts slices for all, holding the loaf against his chest and drawing the knife toward himself. Nowadays, this custom is rare, especially in urban areas. Taking a slice of bread, each person places it on the tablecloth above the fork. To eat it one will break off a bite-sized piece and hold it in the left hand as one eats. The bread is used as a "pusher." When it is full of sauce or meat gravy, one will pop it into one's mouth and break off another piece. One will use bread as a pusher for sauces, salads, and between courses to "clear the palate."

French bread is made without shortening or preservatives. Therefore, it dries quickly and a fresh supply must be purchased for each meal.

Questions

1. How often do the French eat bread?
2. How do they indicate the importance of bread?
3. Why is bread often purchased just before the meal?
4. What happens to any leftover bread?
5. What is a *tartine?*
6. Is butter always served with the bread?
7. How is the bread traditionally sliced in rural France?
8. How does each person eat his slice?
9. Is it polite to use bread as a "pusher" in France?
10. Have you tasted French bread? Do you like it?

Material and instructions to be included with capsule

Title of capsule:

Bread

Visual equipment:

Slide projector

Recommended use:

Junior high students studying a unit on food

Materials:

Enough French bread for each student to have a slice; enough chunky chocolate bars, broken into pieces, for each student to have a piece; one napkin for each student.

Reusable materials:

Slides: Street view of a boulangerie, inside view of a boulangerie, people carrying bread, several baguettes, boy or girl eating their snack of *pain au chocolat* (a roll with chocolate bar baked inside), family table scene.

Chart showing various shapes of bread and their names (taken from volume 2 of Julia Child's *Mastering the Art of French Cooking*).

When each student is served with a napkin, bread, and chocolate, the teacher tells them that they are about to experience not only French bread but what French boys and girls eat at snack time (*le goûter*).

Vocabulary to be stressed:

le pain, la boulangerie, la tartine, le goûter, la baguette.

Culture Clusters

Culture clusters consist of about three illustrated culture capsules that develop related topics, plus one 30-minute classroom simulation that integrates the information contained in the capsules. In the culminating simulation, or skit, practically all of a classroom can be actively involved in dramatizing one or another of the roles. This active integrating skit is accomplished by having the teacher act as narrator to guide the students (through stage directions) to the appropriate actions and speech.

The concept of culture clusters was developed at the University of Georgia by two teachers, Betsy Meade and Genelle Morain. The technique is succinctly described in English and well illustrated in French with an example of a French country wedding (Meade and Morain, 1973).

The easiest way to develop culture clusters is to begin by thinking of a slice of target life that leads itself to a half-hour skit, then work backward by identifying three or four component segments that can be explained through culture capsules. Assignments for preparation of the capsules can be delegated to students.

Besides the excellent illustration of this exciting technique contained in the article by Meade and Morain, another example is given below.

Culture Cluster: Un Repas familial

(prepared by Marsha Rybski)

Cultural goal

The student will demonstrate awareness of French behavior in a conventional situation in the target culture: a family meal in a French home.

Performance Objective 1

Terminal behavior

The student will place the following items of table service correctly on the table in the position in which they would be placed by a French housewife: tablecloth, plate, glass, silverware/knife rest, napkin, loaf of bread.

Conditions

The student will place the items on the table in the presence of the teacher. The student may have as much time as necessary to place all the items on the table.

Criterion

The student must correctly place five of the items from the above list. The silverware items will, as shown on the list, be considered as one. (They are in relatively the same positions on the table as in an American home.)

Performance Objective 2
Terminal behavior

The student will demonstrate proper French table manners in eating the following foods: soup, bread, an apple, meat.

Conditions

The teacher will provide the student with a slice of bread and an apple. (These are difficult to pantomime.) The student will pantomime appropriate manner for eating soup and meat. The student will be seated at a table and provided with a French place setting.

Criterion

The student will correctly demonstrate French etiquette while eating three of the four items mentioned above.

Culture capsule 1

How to set the table

Culture capsule 2

How to act at the table

Culture capsule 3

The family at the table

Simulation

A family meal

Discussion

(Time—15 minutes for each cluster, over three days; 30 minutes for simulation and discussion, final day)

Culture Capsule 1: How to set the table

Objectives

1. The student will be able to set a table in the French manner.

2. Identify and pronounce correctly in French the words for the various parts of the table service.

Procedure

1. Teacher holds up objects, one at a time, that belong on table; pronounces their label in French; and asks the students to repeat. As each item is labeled, a flash card for that item is displayed on a flannel board in the front of the class.

   Visual 1: Table-service items and table

   Visual 2: Vocabulary cards and flannel board

   Cards

la cuiller	*le porte-couteau*
le couteau	*le plat*
la fourchette	*le verre*
la cuiller à soupe	*l'assiette creuse (à soupe)*
la serviette	*mettre le couvert*
la nappe	

2. Teacher then gives capsule information, placing items correctly on the table as each is described.

   Alternate: Student may place items on the table as teacher gives the following narrative:

   In a French home, the table is set for a meal in this way: A tablecloth, *la nappe*, is nearly always used. The plate, *l'assiette*, is put at each place, and the glass, *le verre*, is placed to the right and above the plate. The knife, *le couteau*, and the large soup spoon, *la cuiller à soupe*, go to the right of the plate. The spoon, *la cuiller*, is usually placed above the dinner plate, facing bowl down on the tablecloth, rather than at the right beside the knife as is the American custom. The forks, *les fourchettes*, are placed on the left. You may notice, however, that the spoons and forks are turned over and placed on the table. When soup is being served, *l'assiette creuse* is put on the plate. The French bread is placed directly on the tablecloth. Bread and butter plates are not used at each place. A napkin made of cloth, *la serviette*, is put at each plate, usually on the plate. In its position at the right of the plate, the knife is rested on a knife holder, *le porte-couteau*.

3. Evaluation: Teacher holds up items again, eliciting answers to where the object is placed.

Culture Capsule 2: How to act at the table

Teacher may review vocabulary items from the previous day with flashcards.

Objective

The student will be able to pantomime dining in a French home using the appropriate table manners.

Procedure

Visual 1: Set table and chairs
Visual 2: Loaf of bread and bottle of "wine"

1. The teacher gives capsule information while acting out the described behaviors.

   Alternate: Student may act out behaviors described in the following narrative:

   Table manners in France are somewhat different from ours. First, you place the napkin on your lap; the men might tuck them into their belt. The wine is then served. (While most French adults drink wine at lunch and/or dinner, a bottle of mineral water and a carafe of tap water are always served as well. Many adolescents prefer soft drinks and fruit juices. In some families, especially those in rural areas, children drink wine mixed with half water.) As you may have guessed, when soup is eaten, the large *cuiller à soupe* is used. However, the French spoon the soup toward themselves and eat from the end of the spoon, not the side. While eating, it is proper to keep your free hand on the table, not in your lap. Also, the bread is quite handily used to scoop up vegetables or sauces and clean up the plate at the end of the meal. To cut food, the knife is used in the right hand and the fork in the left. Food is then put directly into the mouth with the left hand and the fork. The knife is held in the right hand while chewing or returned to the *porte-couteau* while not being used. This protects the tablecloth from getting dirty. When whole fruits (such as apples or pears) are served, they are not eaten with the hands. The fork is again used in the left hand to hold the fruit and the knife is used to cut and peel the fruit. The pieces of fruit are then eaten with the fork in the left hand. It is important that the plate be empty at the end of the meal since this shows you have enjoyed the meal. At the end of the meal, in some French families, children thank their mother for the food she prepared.

2. Evaluations:

   A. Teacher asks for volunteers to come up to table to demonstrate correct manners for eating bread, cutting and eating meats and vegetables, eating soup.

   Visual 3: (student furnished) apple or pear, knife and fork.

   B. Each student demonstrates ability to eat a piece of fruit in the French manner.

Culture Capsule 3: The family at the table

Objective

The student will be able to state three reasons why the family meal is so important to the French.

Procedure

Visual 1: Slide—family seated at table
Visual 2: Picture of French woman at work in kitchen

The teacher explains the following attitudes and customs:

The French family meal is considered an important time of togetherness. Problems and ideas are discussed as a family while everyone enjoys the meal. Since this is an important part of the day for each member of the family, each makes a point of allowing time for this meal, which may last two hours or more. During this time the family may talk together about the day's events, vacation plans, events in the news, and so on. Most French families have this large meal at noon. However, in cases where the father or children do not come home during the middle of the day, the family dines together in the evening. Food is a very important part of the French way of life. The average French family spends about a quarter of the budget on food, economizing to save for occasional treats. The family meal is especially important to the mother since she has spent much of her day shopping for and preparing the food with care.

Evaluations

1. Teacher asks students for three reasons why the family meal is important to the French.

2. Discussion, led by the teacher, may deal with differences between American and French attitudes toward eating together as a family.

Simulation: A family meal

Objectives

1. Demonstrate ability of students to set the table in the correct French manner.

2. Demonstrate proper French table manners.

3. Demonstrate understanding of the rapport within family and importance of the meal by enacting roles of the family members.

4. Contribute to class discussion of French attitudes such as importance of food, importance of family, role of mother as cook, respect for traditional formalities, and the importance of "receiving" guests with proper consideration. (Except in the case of intimate friends, guests are usually entertained at cafés and restaurants.)

Procedure

(The teacher may wish to provide a narrative by which the students can tell what food they are eating to demonstrate correct manners. In this case the teacher has chosen to circulate around the room, observing behaviors, including discussion, as they would more naturally occur since everyone at the table would not necessarily be eating the same food at the same time.)

Realia: Desks arranged as tables. Table service items, "wine," fruit, bread.

1. Teacher divides students into groups of four and assigns roles as family members.
2. Students arrange themselves at tables as "families."
3. Teacher names items to be placed on table in French as students place them correctly on their family table.
4. Students playing roles of mother and father begin serving on instruction from the teacher.
5. Students simulate a family meal together, simulating behaviors learned in culture capsules.

Discussion

1. Teacher leads discussion on attitudes illustrated in simulation.
2. Teacher asks students to discuss differences and similarities in the behavior they just exhibited and the behavior they exhibit at their table at home.

Evaluations

1. Post-simulation discussion.

2. Students may be asked to name items from table service in French.

3. Students may be asked to draw diagram of a properly set table in France.

4. Role-playing:

   a. Students might perform a short dramatization showing the French reaction to Americans eating in a French café.

   b. Students might dramatize the visit of a French exchange student to an American home for dinner.

5. Students may be asked to discuss their personal reactions to the attitudes expressed in the simulation.

The next chapter shows how the six rather general goals illustrated in chapters 3 to 10 can be broken down into measurable bites.

Suggested Activities

1. Write a culture assimilator on a topic of your choosing.

2. Prepare a culture capsule related to your chosen topic.

3. Prepare a culture cluster composed of three culture capsules including the culture capsule you have prepared.

References Cited

Albert, Rosita. 1983. "The Intercultural Sensitizer or Culture Assimilator: A Cognitive Approach," in D. Landis and R. Brislin, eds., *Handbook of Intercultural Training*, vol 2. New York: Pergamon.

Brislin, Richard W., Kenneth Cushner, Craig Cherrie, and Mahealani Yong. 1986. *Intercultural Interactions: A Practical Guide*. Newbury Park, CA: Sage.

Fiedler, Fred E., Terence Mitchell, and Harry C. Triandis. 1971. "The Culture Assimilator: An Approach to Cross-Cultural Training." *Journal of Applied Psychology* 55: 95-102. [EDRS: ED 042 343]

Meade, Betsy, and Genelle Morain. 1973. "The Culture Cluster." *Foreign Language Annals* 6, 3 (March): 331-38.

Miller, J. Dale, and Russell H. Bishop. 1979. *USA-Mexico Culture Capsules.* Rowley, MA: Newbury House.

Miller, J. Dale, John Drayton, and Ted Lyon. 1979. *USA-Hispanic South America Culture Capsules.* Rowley, MA: Newbury House.

Miller, J. Dale, and Maurice Loiseau. 1974. *USA-France Culture Capsules.* Rowley, MA: Newbury House.

Symonds, John, Gordon O'Brien, Marvi Vidmar, and John Hornik. 1967. *Honduras Culture Assimilator.* Urbana: University of Illinois, Department of Psychology.

Taylor, H. Darrel, and John L. Sorenson. 1961. "Culture Capsules." *Modern Language Journal* 45 (Dec.): 350-54.

12 Setting Student Performance Objectives

To determine whether students are moving toward achievement of the six cultural goals illustrated in chapters 3-10, precise and measurable end-of-course objectives are necessary. This chapter illustrates the process of goal refinement by giving sample student performance objectives organized under each of the six goals of intercultural communication.

Writing End-of-Course Objectives

Once the instructor has a purposeful rationale for introducing various facets of culture into his or her classroom or workshop and after he or she decides how many different cultural purposes (i.e., goals) to include in the course, the next task is to identify a limited number of specific competencies that encapsulate the intent of each of the selected purposes. These competencies will be used as end-of-course indicators of student achievement.

The first time around, end-of-course objectives should be limited to one or two for each cultural purpose. Ask what one or two things you would want students to be able to do to show they had developed the amount of skill or understanding you were looking for in each purpose. The instructional techniques available to help a teacher reach these purposes can be modified to suit the interests and maturity of one's students. Because maturity levels generally correspond to the traditional designations of primary school, middle school, high school, college, and graduate school, some sort of cooperative division of labor with a view to minimizing costly duplication of effort and to maximizing an intelligent articulation from course level to course level obviously is desirable.

Previous Attempts to Define Cultural Competencies

The way one divides and distinguishes cultural competencies depends upon one's understanding of the learning process. If we accept Jerome Bruner's theory that any concept can be taught in an academically honest way at any age level, the methodological task becomes one of identifying examples and exercises to illustrate the concept at a level readily understandable by a given age group. If, on the other hand, one believes that effective teaching of a concept depends on assessing its difficulty and then presenting it to an age group that has reached the requisite level of maturity to comprehend it, the problem becomes one of arranging cultural concepts into a hierarchy of relative complexity. Certainly how a concept is presented will depend on the student's maturity, educational background, and experience.

An eclectic scheme that suggests which cultural items might be presented at which sequential levels was developed by a 1968 committee of the Pacific Northwest Conference on Foreign Language Teaching (Nostrand, 1968). The committee, chaired by Nostrand, based its efforts on the previous work of Ladu (1967). The Pacific Northwest Conference committee report was done a quarter of a century ago. The direction the report took was promising, and fortunately the intervening years have seen further advances in defining end-of-year student behaviors relating to cultural understanding by levels.

An ACTFL committee on cultural competence refined these earlier efforts with a set of new cultural competencies appropriate for the various levels of language proficiency (ACTFL, 1982). However, the cultural component was suspended from the revised edition of the proficiency guidelines published in 1986 because it had not been defined sharply enough to test. ACTFL acknowledges that the cultural context is essential to language teaching and awaits a more refined list of cultural competencies. Nostrand and an able AATF committee continue to work on this. A draft of the cultural competencies, organized into the categories of sociolinguistic ability, knowledge of the culture area, knowledge of cultural analysis, and attitudes, appears as an appendix to a thoughtful article on cultural competencies (Nostrand, 1991). The competencies are arranged by an ILR-type scale, with 0 being "novice" and 5 being "native or near-native."

Social studies teachers have an easier go of it. Good basal texts have clearly stated goals and objectives that can be illustrated by examples from virtually any culture area. Many of the activities suggested by this book can fit comfortably within a given text's organization. Other goals that are advanced here can be added to the scope of the text.

Goal-Oriented End-of-Course Performance Objectives

Teachers are paid to change behavior. There would be little point in attending school if people who were "schooled" did not behave differently from those who were not. The assumption most commonly made, but not by any means uncontested, is that behavior changed by school is changed for the better. That is, school is seen as a catalyst for positive behavior that will benefit both the individual and society. The worth of the school can and should be measured by the nature of the lifestyle it inspires. A teacher or a taxpayer can legitimately ask at any point in the long obligatory sequence of education just what the student can do now that he or she could not do before interacting with the teacher.

The current emphasis on measurable units of student accomplishment, usually called student performance or behavioral objectives, is based on two different kinds of logic. First, to change behavior effectively, the teacher (the change agent) must be able to recognize the desired behavior when he or she sees it and have a plan for getting students to perform in the desired way. In other words, if you don't know where you're going it is hard to get there—or know you're there when you are! Second, the operation of our school system is entirely dependent on money. To help convince taxpayers, most of whom have been through our school system, that students do learn something positive there, learning must be stated in a documentable fashion.

A performance objective is designed to provide answers to four questions: (1) Why teach a given aspect of the culture? This is the purpose, or goal. (2) What should the student be able to do or say after learning the aspect? This is the terminal behavior that is the desired outcome of the learning. (3) What are the circumstances under which the student will be expected to do or say what he or she has learned? This clarifies the conditions or constraints associated with observance of the student's performance. (4) How well does the student have to perform under the stated conditions? This specifies the criterion of acceptable performance.

Simple, vague, ambiguous statements of intent gradually develop into full-fledged performance objectives. Good objectives are written in an ongoing process, continually stating the objectives with greater detail and precision. A performance objective is "strong" when several different teachers can agree that it has been accomplished by a student. It is "mature" when the performance objective is accepted by both students and teachers as a reasonable reflection of its avowed purpose.

To illustrate the kind of end-of-course performances I am describing, I'll list a number of them and organize them under appropriate goals. The most common activities for teaching culture are omitted in favor of activities that are not widely used.

In chapter 3, I specifically recommend six goals, or purposes, as the basic ingredient for organizing classroom instruction. The following seven end-of-course performance objectives are meant to illustrate the process of goal refinement. They are not especially recommended in their present state of specificity to the teacher. For these end-of-course objectives to be relevant to any specific classroom, the age, interests, and language fluency of the students and the nature of the course must be taken into account.

Goal 1. Interest in Other Societies. The student shows intellectual curiosity about the target culture and empathy toward its people.

Performance Objective 1: Curiosity about the target culture

One hopes each student develops a very positive attitude toward people who live in the target culture. As an indication of a positive attitude, carry out the following activities.

Terminal behavior

Demonstrate intellectual curiosity by

1. Giving evidence of having read 300 or more pages about the target culture from any journal or book in the general bibliography the teacher gave you or from any other publication that meets the teacher's approval
2. Asking ten or more questions of a classroom visitor from the target culture
3. Traveling, for any duration, in the target culture
4. Attending five or more films in the target language

Terminal behavior

Demonstrate empathy toward target peoples by

1. Inviting a foreign exchange student home for dinner
2. Making contact with at least one person in your community who speaks the target language at home

Conditions

These activities are to be carried out on a volunteer basis at the student's convenience.

Criterion

The instructor will grant extra credit upon being presented with evidence of the student's having completed the activity.

Goal 2. Who Does It? The student recognizes that social variables such as age, sex, social class, and place of residence affect the way people speak and behave.

Performance Objective 2: Hispanic dialects

To demonstrate some ways in which language and other behavior are affected by social variables, carry out two of the following five activities.

Terminal behavior

Identify the places of origin of speakers from four different regions of Hispanic culture (Spain, Caribbean, Mexico, Argentina).

Conditions

A one- to two-minute taped speech sample of five different speakers will be played twice during class time.

Criterion

The national origin of three of the five speakers must be correctly identified.

Terminal behavior

Prepare a two- to four-minute oral presentation in Spanish, based on one written source and on interviews with at least two native speakers, about five words or expressions that are associated with one sex or age group.

Conditions

For classroom presentation with at least two weeks advance notice.

Criterion

70 percent of the class must be able to follow the exposition clearly.

Terminal behavior

Associate five sample dialogs, which will be given you in English and in writing, with the following social levels: urban working class, urban middle class, urban upper class, rural common people.

Conditions

Each dialogue will be one page in length. Determination will be made within a 20-minute period during class time.

Criterion

Four of the five dialogues must be correctly identified.

Terminal behavior

Indicate on a blank map of the target culture the geographic range and variant linguistic forms of one word or expression of the student's choosing.

Conditions

The student will have six weeks to prepare this map, which will be turned in to the teacher.

Criterion

The map must show how the linguistic form is employed in at least twenty-five different locations within Hispanic culture.

Terminal behavior

Identify one or more qualities or beliefs (e.g., carrots for better vision, aphrodisiac effect of powdered ram's horn) associated with ten different foods or drinks in one specific subculture of the target society (e.g., one's age, sex, social class, or regional group). Compare your findings to the responses from another subculture.

Conditions

Four weeks will be allowed for completion of this task. The teacher will write the information in the target language and type it on a stencil to be distributed to each class member.

Criterion

Each quality or belief must be conveyed in the target language as a direct quote from a specific source. The sources must be fully identified. The information should clearly contrast the data from the two compared subcultures.

Goal 3. What? The student realizes that effective communication requires discovering what is imaged in the minds of target people when they think, act, and react to the world around them.

Performance Objective 3: Nuances of a French word

To demonstrate an understanding that what one associates with an object or concept is to a considerable extent culturally determined, carry out the following two activities.

Terminal behavior

Identify photos of French cultures where the clues are clothing styles, physical types of people, and topology.

Conditions

The teacher will display in the classroom fifty numbered photos from diverse sources; twenty-five portray authentically French scenes with people. The display will be shown for one week, after which the student will hand in to the teacher a list of the photo numbers that correspond to French culture anywhere in the world.

Criterion

The student must score at least eighteen correct responses.

Terminal behavior

Identify the most likely images associated with five nouns and five verbs selected by the teacher from a first-semester vocabulary list.

Conditions

The list will be given two days in advance of the required identification. The identification will take place during 30 minutes in class. During the examination the teacher will present 25 pictures or characterizations (walking, sitting, pantomime "talking") from which the student chooses those that relate to French culture.

Criterion

The student must make correct identifications for at least seven of the ten words.

Goal 4. Where and When? The student recognizes that situational variables and convention play a role in shaping behavior.

Performance Objective 4: The Respectful Russian

(prepared by Judy Ratas)

To demonstrate how Russians show respect and affection through the conventional ways they address each other, complete two of the following three activities.

Terminal behavior

The student will use the appropriate form of address, Tbl or Bbl, in the following social situations:

Two young people who are strangers converse.

Two friends converse.

A young person converses with an older person.

An older person converses with a young person.

Two adults who are strangers converse.

Conditions

During a class period the teacher will assign to students the role of friend, stranger, or older person. The student will give three oral responses in simple phrases such as "How are you?" This conversation should take two to three minutes, with each participant responding to the other participant or participants.

Criterion

The student has to choose the correct form, either Tbl or Bbl, in each of his or her three responses. Pronunciation has to be good enough for the teacher to identify which form the student used.

Terminal behavior

The student will use the appropriate form of address—Russian first names and surnames—in the following social situations:

Two Russian teenage friends address each other.

A young Russian addresses an older Russian.

An older Russian addresses a young person (1) when the young person is of high social status; (2) when the young person is of no special prestige.

Adult members of the same extended family address each other (1) when two close members of the family are alone; (2) when two close members of the family are in the company of other members of the family.

Conditions

The teacher will assign to each student in class a complete complement of Russian names, such as Ivan Ivanovich Vania Dolgich, and will assign him one of the following roles: young person of high social status or of no special prestige, adult, relative. The student will then be assigned to one of the above six social situations. The student will ask the other participants three simple questions such as "Dostoyevsky, are you hungry?" The conversation should not take more than two or three minutes, with each participant responding at least once to the other participant(s).

Criterion

The student must use the appropriate form of a person's name in each of his or her three responses.

Terminal behavior

Demonstrate the appropriate oral and kinesic response in five of the following six situations:

Someone compliments your new dress or suit.

You bump into someone.

Someone bumps into you and apologizes.

You congratulate an individual on the occasion of his birthday.

You are passing through the reception line at a friend's wedding and congratulate her.

You are introduced to someone of your own age and to a schoolteacher.

Conditions

These activities will be performed in class in Russian, with the teacher or another student playing the role of the other person. Each activity should take less than one minute to complete.

Criterion

At least one Russian gesture should accompany each activity. The oral response should be said well enough to be easily understood by a native and should be without grammatical error. The response must be situationally appropriate in each instance.

Goal 5: Why? The student understands that people generally act the way they do because they are using options society allows for satisfying basic physical and psychological needs, and that cultural patterns tend mutually to support this.

A common international social phenomenon is that rural people, especially in lesser developed countries, are leaving their towns to seek their fortunes in the city. The performance objective that follows invites students to look at one aspect of the lives of most rural people—religious celebration—and to relate it to need gratification. (This particular objective was written to tempt some students into reading an exceptionally well-presented ethnography—*San Pedro, Colombia: Small Town in a Developing Society* [M. Richardson, 1970].)

Performance Objective 5: Religion in San Pedro

To demonstrate how religious ritual provides a model for rural Latin Americans that helps them face the exigencies of everyday life, engage in one of the following four activities (terminal behaviors).

Terminal behavior

Present an oral or written report on "Why Good Friday is considered by the people of San Pedro to be more important than Easter Sunday."

Conditions

Oral reports should be about five minutes in duration and can be delivered in either English or Spanish. Written reports should be about 500 words, typed double-spaced, in either English or Spanish. Both reports are to be presented to the whole class; written reports are to be duplicated and distributed.

Criterion

The reports should make clear to most of the class the way suffering, resignation, and religious processions are related to everyday life. Mistakes in grammar, pronunciation, or spelling will not count against the student. To determine whether most of the class understood the relationships, a five-item, multiple-choice, teacher-made quiz will be given; 70 percent of the class are expected to score at least four correct answers.

Terminal behavior

Act out or portray via drawings or clay figures of your own making, or via collages assembled from magazine or newspaper clippings, how religious processions might look in rural Latin America.

Conditions

The presentation can be done in pantomime, in English or Spanish, and can last anywhere from 5 to 20 minutes. In the case of artistic presentations, the portrayal will be exhibited in the classroom.

Criterion

The reports should make clear to most of the class the way suffering, resignation, and religious processions are related to everyday life. Mistakes in grammar, pronunciation, or spelling will not count against the student. To determine whether most of the class understood the relationships, a five-item, multiple-choice, teacher-made quiz will be given; 70 percent of the class are expected to score at least four correct answers.

Terminal behavior

Be a member of a panel that discusses what changes might occur in other areas of life in rural Latin America if people's attitude toward religion were to fall into apathy.

Conditions

The panel may use either Spanish or English; discussion should last at least 15 minutes. Membership on the panel is limited to five persons. The presentation will take place at a meeting of the language club.

Criterion

The panel should present the pros and cons of "fatalists" and "realists" as alternate descriptors of the people of San Pedro, and examine nonreligious manifestations of these philosophies. The panel should do this well enough so that 80 percent of the listeners can answer three out of four questions put to them by the teacher. Each member of the panel should speak a minimum of three minutes.

Terminal behavior

Take a quiz that tests how suffering, resignation, and religious processions are related to everyday life in San Pedro.

Conditions

20 minutes will be provided for the exam to be administered during class time.

**Goal 6a. Evaluating Statements about a Culture. The
student can evaluate the relative strength of a
generalization about the target culture.**

Performance Objective 6a: German generalities

To show that you do not indiscriminately accept as factual
everything you hear about German culture, carry out the
following activity.

Terminal behavior

Evaluate ten generalizations about German culture as (a)
probably true, (b) probably false, (c) I don't know whether it
is true or false. For the "probably true" statements, state briefly
the evidence supporting your judgment. For the "probably
false" statements, state briefly the evidence that would tend to
contradict them. For those generalizations in the "don't know"
category, state briefly what additional information you would
need to reach a decision. (You will be awarded the same
number of points for each true and false statement you
correctly identify as for those statements for which you indicate
plausible additional information that is needed.)

Conditions

The ten generalizations will be presented in English and in
writing at examination time. 25 minutes will be given to
respond.

Criterion

Plausible responses must be provided for at least eight of the
generalizations. To borrow a phrase from national contests, "the
decision of the judges (i.e., the instructor) will be final."

Goal 6b. Researching Another Culture. The student has developed the skills needed to locate and organize information about the target culture from the library, the mass media, people, and personal observation.

Performance Objective 6b: The research report

To indicate that you have developed an organizational procedure and a familiarity with relevant sources of information concerning the target culture, carry out the following activities.

Terminal behavior

Identify a question that intrigues you about the target culture and write it down. Then

1. Locate the titles of at least five articles in periodicals and five books that may reasonably be thought to contain information on the topic you identified. At least one of the articles should be from a professional journal. Prepare a separate index card for each title, using a standard bibliographical model.

2. Skim the publications contained in your bibliography for pages relevant to your topic. Indicate the pages on the index cards.

3. Read the pages and transfer the most salient facts to the index cards.

4. Outline the subtopics and sequence of development you would use to develop the topic.

5. List the variables that are most relevant to your topic.

6. Compose twenty questions that might be asked of a native speaker to provide additional information on your topic. Be sure to include several questions to establish the biases of your informant.

7. Prepare a list of ten additional sources of any kind that pertain to your topic. Prepare them on index cards the same way you did before.

8. Present a brief report, either orally or in a paragraph not longer than 250 words, on the feasibility of pursuing the topic you originally identified.

Conditions

Each of the above eight activities should be completed in a week or less. (Some of these activities are a matter of a few minutes' work.) Each completed activity should be shown to the teacher for evaluation and feedback.

Criterion

A possible 10 points will be awarded to each of the first seven activities, and 30 points to the last. The student must score 70 or above.

Refining the Objectives

Some of the performance objectives stated above must be further refined. Students have a legitimate concern over details such as what kind of test will be administered, how long it will last, how much time they will have to prepare for it, how well they have to do to pass it.

In the foregoing examples of end-of-course performance objectives, the same general format was observed in each. This was done to emphasize the component parts of a performance objective (goal statement, terminal behavior, conditions, and criterion), and to make it easier for the reader to follow.

There is, of course, no one way to write performance objectives. For example, what were listed as activities in the foregoing presentation could just as well have been called separate objectives, since each contained the major components of a performance objective.

The process of refining objectives involves gradually removing the ambiguities until a student knows what to expect and until any teacher—not only the student's teacher—can grade the performance. Words like "understanding" and "appreciation" give us something to hide behind; more scrutable aims must be developed. Ultimately, the teacher would want to offer a wide variety of ways in which the student could indicate competency. Students can take a test, write a report, participate in a skit or simulation, or prepare a graphic or literary dramatization. The circumstances surrounding a student's performance of an objective are determined by the familiar exigencies of time and the facilities available for observing and testing the performance, by the maturity of the students, by whether performance can be measured directly, and so on. The writer of performance objectives must anticipate the circumstances that will affect the performance and clarify them in writing. Hindsight is a great aid in doing this.

Different students can be counted on to perform at different levels of proficiency. The teacher must decide what level of performance can realistically be accepted as adequate. If the teacher expects mastery, the student should be expected to perform the objective with 90 to 100 percent accuracy. Failing mastery, the student would be expected either to repeat the performance at another time or to carry out an equivalent activity. Student performance would not, under these conditions, be graded on a curve (norm referenced). The purpose of many activities can be achieved, thankfully, with less than near-perfect performance on the part of the student. Each teacher must make individual decisions about criteria.

There are excellent aids in helping teachers draft performance objectives. The simplest and most helpful is the brief paperback by Mager (1962). You can read it easily in forty-five minutes. A more detailed and technical guide is available in Popham (1970). The most complete exposition aimed specifically at the foreign language teacher is a book written by Valette and Disick (1972). Superb self-instructional materials for language teachers have been prepared by Jenks, Bostick, and Otto (1971). One article has been published that specifically discusses performance objectives for teaching culture (Seelye, 1970). A package of twenty-six booklets of about twenty-two pages each has been published to help teachers develop performance objectives (Popham and Baker, 1973). Steiner (1972, 1975) treats both affective and cognitive objectives. Byrnes and Canale (1987) include cultural issues in their book on defining and developing foreign language proficiency.

Writing performance objectives is not easy. But without them, how is a teacher able to evaluate the extent to which he or she is succeeding in having students learn cultural skills? In the absence of performance objectives, program evaluation must ignore the most important product of the program and the only reason for its existence—what the student learns. Objectives that are not measurable are like desert signposts that advise "Nearing Oasis"—but don't say how near or how big or in what direction the oasis lies.

Suggested Activities

1. What one intercultural communication skill do you want students to develop in your course with the biggest enrollment? Write an end-of-course performance objective for it.

2. Indicate three ways nonverbal communication can be introduced in your classroom in a natural way.

3. Choose one topic (women, clothing, food, social stratification, etc.) and write end-of-year performance objectives for it for each of the six goals.

4. Adapt the end-of-course objectives that appear in this chapter under each goal to the exigencies of a course or workshop you will teach.

References Cited

ACTFL. 1982. *Provisional Proficiency Guidelines*. Hastings-on-Hudson, NY: American Council on the Teaching of Foreign Languages.

Byrnes, Heidi, and Michael Canale, eds. 1987. *Defining and Developing Proficiency: Guidelines, Implementations, and Concepts*. Lincolnwood, IL: National Textbook.

Jenks, Charles L., Nancy G. Bostick, and J. Gregory Otto. 1971. *Deriving Objectives Training Unit 3*. Rev. ed. Berkeley, CA: Far West Laboratory for Education Research and Development.

Ladu, Tora T. 1967. Draft of New Guidelines for Foreign Language Teachers. Presented for discussion at State Conference of Foreign Language Teachers. Raleigh, NC: Department of Public Instruction.

Mager, Robert F. 1962. *Preparing Instructional Objectives*. Palo Alto, CA: Fearon.

Nostrand, Howard L. 1968. "Levels of Sociocultural Understanding for Language Classes," pp. 19-24 in H. Ned Seelye, ed., *A Handbook on Latin America for Teachers: Methodology and Annotated Bibliography*. Springfield, IL: Office of Public Instruction.

Nostrand, Howard L. 1991. "Basic Intercultural Education Needs Breadth and Depth: The Role of a Second Culture," pp. 131-59 in Ellen S. Silber, ed., *Critical Issues in Foreign Language Instruction*. New York: Garland.

Popham, W. James. 1970. *The Teacher Empiricist*. 2nd ed. Los Angeles: Tinnon-Brown.

Popham, W. James, and Eva L. Baker. 1973. *The Prentice-Hall Teacher Competency Development System*. Englewood Cliffs, NJ: Prentice-Hall.

Richardson, Miles. 1970. *San Pedro, Colombia: Small Town in a Developing Society*. New York: Holt, Rinehart and Winston.

Seelye, H. Ned. 1970. "Performance Objectives for Teaching Cultural Concepts." *Foreign Language Annals* 3: 566-78.

Steiner, Florence. 1972. "Behavioral Objectives and Evaluation," pp. 35-78 in Dale L. Lange, ed., *Individualization of Instruction*. ACTFL Foreign Language Education Series, Vol. 2. Lincolnwood, IL: National Textbook.

Steiner, Florence. 1975. *Performing with Objectives*. Rowley, MA: Newbury House.

Valette, Rebecca M., and Renée S. Disick. 1972. *Modern Language Performance Objectives and Individualization: A Handbook*. New York: Harcourt, Brace.

13 Testing Cultural Attitudes and Understandings

Four examples are presented of ways to measure shifts in attitudes toward the target culture by student groups. Most culture tests unfortunately measure superficial knowledge rather than intercultural skill development. This chapter emphasizes the fact that concern for both reliability (i.e., whether the tests are capable of yielding consistent results on repeated trials with the same students) and validity (i.e., whether the tests test what they are supposed to test) is effort well spent in developing norm-referenced tests. Test writers are alerted to threats that commonly undermine the validity of individual test items. After the initial discussion on attitude testing, the rest of the chapter deals with multiple-choice test formats. Six other testing formats also are briefly outlined.

Attitudes toward the Target Culture

Do students alter their opinions of the target culture after studying about its language and society for a semester (or four years)? If attitudes toward the target culture do become more positive as classroom exposure increases, does this positive regard transfer to other cultures as well? Do students of French, in other words, begin to feel more charitable toward Hispanic as well as French culture?

The easiest way to get an objective overview of attitude shift in students is to give them a pretest at the beginning of the course, and a posttest at the end. Note, however, that there are a number of obstacles to getting results that you can really bank on. Simple pre-post measures without randomly assigned subjects to treatment-comparison groups lack experimental controls, and quasi-experimental evaluation models require the investigator to deflate well-known threats to internal and external validity. These threats pose rival explanations of the results. For example, that the scores are higher at posttest just because the students have matured more—because they are older than they were at pretest. See Cook and Campbell (1979) for the technical details. Still, taken cautiously, crude pre-posttest comparisons of your students' attitudes may provide ideas on how to improve course performance.

Before I suggest four specific ways to measure student achievement, I want to emphasize that none of the ways is good enough for drawing conclusions about how any individual student has changed his or her attitudes. The tests may be helpful, on the other hand, in giving the teacher a general idea of the direction of any change in the attitudes of the class as a whole. Attitude tests of the type intercultural communication teachers might administer should be completed anonymously by the students.

There are many reasons why the usefulness of tests may be limited to measuring general group characteristics rather than what an individual knows or feels about a chosen topic. Most of these reasons relate to one or two concerns: validity and reliability. For a test to be valid, it has to test what you want it to, and not, inadvertently, something else. A test also must be reliable. Perfect reliability would be achieved by a test if each time it were given the same students would make the same scores—assuming that nothing happened in the intervals between testing to alter their knowledge or feelings on the topic tested.

But everyone has their good days and their dog days, so student performance at different times is never quite the same. There are a lot of sources of variability in test scores. Besides interference from distractions, headaches, and heart throbs, the wording of some test items is interpreted differently by people of different roles, ages, social classes, and so forth. There is one item in a widely used I.Q. test for children that pictures a man relaxing (he is smoking a pipe) in a rocking chair on the lawn in front of his home during a heavy rainfall. The children are asked what is wrong in the picture. In Mormon Utah, many children answer that what is wrong is that the man is smoking. Within their religious framework, getting wet is certainly a lesser evil than smoking. (Many other than Mormons will agree.)

It is easy, unfortunately, to build ambiguous item choices during test construction. Once I was in charge of coordinating the testing of a dozen sections of a college Spanish course. When it came time to draft the final semester examination, I asked each teacher to choose a different chapter and write ten multiple-choice items for that chapter, each item with four choices—only one of which was to be correct. I then gave the draft version of the test to a half-dozen educated native speakers of Spanish from several different countries and asked them to check all the right answers. For about 90 percent of the items more than one answer was chosen as correct, and for 20 percent of the items all four responses were checked as correct! Although these teachers were fluent in Spanish and well trained (all had graduate degrees), they all introduced "secret" contexts into the test. If all you had learned of Spanish was what chapter 10 had told you, then you would do reasonably well on that part of the test, but if you had learned Spanish from sources outside of the class text then you would be in deep trouble. (The teachers, by the way, were very unhappy to have this state of affairs brought to their attention. They insisted that their right answer was the only right answer.)

Because of all of this unwanted static that creeps into our tests, it is imperative to remember that the measurement of *any* phenomenon *always* contains a certain amount of chance error. That, of course, is why we should be nervous about inferring the competency of any individual student from performance on any one test (or on a string of unreliable tests).

One day I went into the university's testing bureau to pick up the scored tests from several of my classes. In addition to simply scoring tests, the bureau always ran, for the teachers' information, a statistical analysis to measure the tests' reliability. (There are several methods for computing this. Interested readers can consult any text on tests and measurement.) Perfect test reliability would result in a reliability score of 1.00, and no reliability at all would yield a score of zero. Commercial tests are expected to yield reliability scores in the .90's; and teacher-made knowledge tests for classroom use yield reliability scores at least in the .80's if they are reliable enough to use. I said to the bureau's director that I guessed that the science professors routinely got high reliability scores on their tests, since they were testing "exact" things and since they were so proficient with numbers. There happened to be at that moment a stack of printouts on the counter waiting to be picked up by the chemistry department. The director smiled and read me the reliability scores of a dozen exams. To my amazement, the reliability scores ranged from 0 to .14. In other words, the test results were totally unreliable. Still, achievement on these totally unreliable tests determined most of the course grades for those hapless students.

Now that you are forewarned about some of the limitations of tests, let's look at four techniques to measure attitudes. Two of these approaches to measuring cross-cultural attitudes have been used especially extensively by social scientists for many years: social distance and semantic differential scales.

"Social distance" scales attempt to measure the degree to which one separates oneself socially from members of another culture. Developed by Bogardus (1925) to obtain a measurable indication of peoples' reactions to different nationalities or ethnicities, these scales list the target identities (Bogardus called them "racial and language groups") and then asks the respondent to indicate the level at which he or she would accept "an average" member of each group. The respondents were provided with seven different ways of expressing their reactions, namely, in terms of willingness to (1) marry someone of the target group; (2) have them "as chums in one's social club"; (3) have them as neighbors; (4) have them as members of the same occupation; (5) have them as fellow citizens; (6) allow them to enter the country as tourists; (7) exclude them from entry altogether.

A modified social distance scale aimed at students might look something like this:

Check all the statements that you agree wit'
national or ethnic group. Remember to giv
reactions to each group as a whole. Do n(
reactions to the best or the worst members பா.
known. Please work rapidly.

1. I wouldn't mind if my brother or sister married one.

2. I wouldn't mind having one as a close friend.

3. I would not object to having them move in next door as neighbors.

4. I wouldn't mind working on the job with them.

5. They should be allowed to immigrate to our country and become citizens.

6. They should be allowed to visit our country as tourists.

7. They should be kept out of our country.

A second approach measures the "semantic differential," or distance between two descriptors, with which the rater judges the defined culture group in terms of a number of bipolar traits (Osgood and Suci, 1955). A modification of this technique for use as a classroom attitude scale might result in something like this:

Put a check in the position that best indicated the direction and intensity of your feeling with regard to each pair of descriptors.

Tibetans in general tend to be:

good						bad
beautiful						ugly
clean						dirty
valuable						worthless
kind						cruel

pleasant	☐	☐	☐	☐	☐	unpleasant
happy	☐	☐	☐	☐	☐	sad
nice	☐	☐	☐	☐	☐	awful
honest	☐	☐	☐	☐	☐	dishonest
fair	☐	☐	☐	☐	☐	unfair

The ten descriptors used in the above semantic differential proved to be useful in cross-cultural studies of many countries. Teachers may choose to identify the bipolar items by having the class/grade/school indicate in an open-ended exercise what the students feel to be the strengths and weaknesses of specified groups (e.g., Chicanos, African-Americans, French). The teacher then constructs from these descriptors the bipolar items for a semantic differential scale. This way, one uses terms that are in currency among the students and, presumably, mean something to them. (The psychometric properties of these scales, of course, will not be known.)

A third approach to measuring attitudes toward a defined group was developed by Grice (1934) and is still in use. This approach presents the respondents with a number of statements (over forty in the original version). The respondent is asked to put a check in front of those statements with which he or she agrees. The following are illustrative:

Following is a list of statements about the people of Gringolandia. Place a check before each statement with which you agree.

1. Show a high rate of efficiency in anything they attempt.
2. Can be depended upon as being honest.
3. Are noted for their industry.
4. Are envious of others.
5. Are highly emotional.

6. Are tactless.

7. Are a God-fearing group.

8. Are self-indulgent.

9. Are quick to understand.

10. Have an ideal home life.

Finally, a fourth approach illustrates another variation in attitude measurement. This forced-choice questionnaire was developed to measure annual changes in the self-esteem of bilingual program students in the primary grades. The items are presented orally and bilingually. Students are asked whether they "mostly agree" or "mostly disagree" with each statement, some examples of which are given below:

1. I am happy with myself.

2. I am happy at home.

3. I like school.

4. My teacher likes me.

5. I am not nervous when my teacher asks me a question.

6. I can do many things well.

7. My friends like me.

8. I like to speak Arabic (or whatever their home language is).

9. I like to speak English.

10. I like to read.

11. I like to do arithmetic.

12. I like music classes.

13. I like art classes.

In a variation of this, you can develop brief written questionnaires for early elementary school bilingual children by writing your own items, one item per page, in big block letters in both the students' home language and English. The students indicate their attitude toward each item by marking one of two faces, as the following examples taken from a student practice sheet illustrate. (The teacher can read the items to the students.)

A. QUIERO A MI MAMA. I LOVE MY MOTHER.

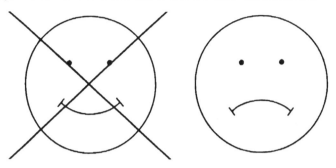

B. ME GUSTA EL DOLOR DE OIDO. I LIKE EARACHES.

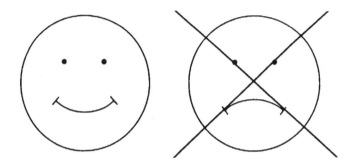

Shaw and Wright (1967) have prepared a compendium of attitudinal scales, along with examples and evaluations of each. There are sections devoted to the nature of attitudes, methods of scale construction, social practices, social issues and problems, international issues, abstract concepts, political and religious attitudes, ethnic and national groups, and social institutions. Two experienced foreign language teachers offer assistance in measuring attitudinal variables, Cooke (1970) for Spanish and Savignon (1972a) for French. Foreign language and bilingual education teachers will find helpful the description of 342 oral and written tests, many of them attitude measures, compiled by the Northwest Regional Educational Laboratory (1978). Cohen's (1979) very useful book on evaluating bilingual programs contains a chapter on affective measurement. An exposition of virtually all the social science postulates concerning ethnocentrism has been prepared by LeVine and Campbell (1972).

Most classroom testing focuses on cognitive learning rather than on student attitude. The rest of this chapter will examine different approaches to measuring cultural skills and knowledge.

Criterion-Referenced Tests

The student performance objectives elaborated in the previous chapter are, in the jargon of the profession, a form of criterion-referenced testing in which the teacher clearly delineates the student competencies to be achieved. Whether the students do or do not achieve enough to pass the unit (or course) depends on whether they meet the criteria spelled out before they are evaluated.

This type of testing is the most useful in giving teachers and students relevant feedback on achievement as it relates to specific intercultural communication goals. Since this was covered at length in the previous chapter, I will go on to a discussion of the most commonly used form of classroom testing: norm-referenced testing.

Standardized Tests

My oldest son, David, picked me up at the airport. He was accompanied by my youngest son, Michael, who had just taken the practice version of college entrance examinations administered to high school juniors. "How did you do on the PSATs?" I asked. Silence. I turned to David and asked how Mike had done. "It depends on who you compare him to," he replied. "Compared to the country, he scored well above average." Then, after a pause, "Compared to his brothers he didn't do as well." And that is the essence of norm-referenced testing.

Norm-referenced test scores are evaluated within the context of how an individual student scores in relation to how a group (the classroom or some national group) scores on the same test. These tests are often curved so that "average" achievement is awarded a C, and so on. (Criterion-referenced tests, on the other hand, are evaluated in terms of what percentage of the test items the student answers correctly.) Two familiar examples of norm-referenced testing are the standardized college entrance exams and the teacher-made, end-of-course multiple-choice tests.

Several states have, from time to time, administered standardized culture tests to their secondary students. New York State, through the Regents Examinations, has the longest tradition of this. Some years ago I was invited by the New York Department of Education to critique these examinations. Based on a review of 83 test items appearing in six different Spanish exams, I found 82 of the items tested knowledge of the following five areas:

1. recognition of historical events and persons (22 items)
2. recognition of trivial facts (19 items)
3. recognition of toponyms (17 items)
4. ability to define vocabulary (13 items)
5. familiarity with plastic arts, especially architecture (11 items)

While the narrow scope reflected in the above breakdown may no longer be true of the Regents Examinations, it does highlight many endemic weaknesses in the few culture tests in recent use.

Another common weakness, the confusion of literary knowledge with behavior patterns, is exemplified in many culture tests. Dates, historical facts, and literary bits can easily be misused. The most common items appearing on most culture tests, unfortunately, can be correctly answered by a superficial familiarity with geographical and historical facts.

Most norm-referenced testing is not of the "standard test" type described above. It is done by a classroom teacher in the form of end-of-semester exams. This type of testing is ideally suited for a department where two or more instructors teach the same levels and where a uniform evaluation criterion is desired.

The designer of a cross-cultural test, if a purist who follows the classical prescription, begins by defining his or her specific objectives. The designer then elaborates on the areas of culture that bear upon the stated objectives. This elaboration consists of mapping out the thematic character of the "universe" of relevant test items. Will the test objectives support items concerned with art and literature, for example? Will the items have to be tied directly to linguistic units?

One testing project (Seelye, 1968b), designed to measure the biculturation of the American colony in a Latin American country, divided test items into two major categories: (1) items that are associated with the ability to function in a society, and (2) items that measure knowledge not overtly associated with functioning in the society. Falling into the latter category are items based on abstract or implicit patterns of which the native is not aware (although these patterns may well indirectly affect behavior), erudite academic knowledge, and patterns for which there is not wide concordance in the target culture (patterns peripheral to the core culture). Ideal patterns of belief that do not occur frequently (false patterns) and patterns that present a cultural anomaly in that they deviate from a major value of the culture (dysfunctional patterns) probably should be avoided unless they are clearly identified in the test as anomalous patterns. In this research, the ability to use the target cultural patterns to satisfy societal conventions was measured through items that had been shown to differentiate empirically the cultural stranger and the target native.

The six cultural goals described in chapter 3 provide an excellent frame for devising purposeful test items for the classroom.

Validating Test Items

It would seem to belabor the obvious to observe that the correct response to a test item should itself be correct. Yet we are whimsically casual about requiring documentation to back up a "right" answer. This is especially easy to observe in tests of discrete units of culture where the student selects the correct response from among several choices offered. In spite of extensive experience over four decades in a large number of countries of Latin America, Europe, Africa, and Asia, and over thirty years as an educator, I still find myself making a few simple errors in designing cross-cultural test situations.

The most common error lies in generalizing beyond the legitimate extension of a cultural practice. Test questions that contain wording such as "In X situation, a Latin American would act in Y manner," have repeatedly been shown to be dangerous. The test designer who is drawing a situation from either personal experience or a written source should attempt to be specific in the wording of the item. More likely of success are items worded "A Mexican can be expected to do X in Y situation," or better still, "A middle-class Peruvian male living in Lima can be expected to do X in Y situation." Little work has been done to provide a "cultural atlas" of varieties in cultural patterning within any given geographic area, so the test designer had best tread with caution.

Certain patterns that have come to be regarded as "typical" offer a particular dilemma in test construction, for we want the test to avoid reinforcing clichés and half-truths. Groups are often stereotyped along the lines of several patterns of behavior that are infrequent in the group but may be even less frequent in other groups. Perhaps these infrequent patterns can be tested best within the context of in-group approval or disapproval, rather than in terms of the frequency of the pattern. For example, rather than ask whether German men often have mistresses, the item could be phrased, "Would a German politician running for office be discredited were it to become known that he supported a mistress in addition to his wife?"

Validation techniques might be as rigorous as polling a representative sample of target subjects in order to establish the distribution of a cultural pattern or as lenient as the simple acceptance of a generalization based on an anecdote of the classroom teacher or returning a tourist. While the ultimate strength of the test will depend in large part on the rigor of the validation techniques employed, there are many occasions when the exigencies of the classroom relegate sophisticated methods to the realm of the impractical. Three quite different methods of documenting the validity of a cultural pattern— classroom authority, pretesting with the target people, and expert opinion—differ widely in their relevance for the classroom teacher.

Classroom Authority

In those cases where the classroom teacher is well-grounded in the target culture, the authority of his of her word usually suffices. This is probably satisfactory if one does not take oneself too seriously; most of us have discovered that what is accepted with adulation in the classroom often gets quite another reception at a staff meeting. The usefulness of an item validated solely by the classroom teacher is necessarily local. While this is obviously the most expedient technique for teachers and trainers at the battlements, it is important to recognize that great modesty becomes the instructor rash enough to insist on the validity of a pattern so documented.

Pretesting

The acid test of whether an item forms part of the explicit or conscious culture of a people is to administer it to them, controlling for relevant variables such as age, sex, residence, and social class differences. Although 95 percent agreement can be expected on the correct response to a language test administered to educated natives of a target culture, the best that can realistically be expected on a widely administered culture test is 65 percent agreement. In one study (Seelye, 1968a), cultural items achieving 51 percent or more agreement with a Latin American test group (of varied age, sex, social class, and educational background composition) were retained when they significantly contrasted with the performance of North Americans on the same items.

The obvious disadvantage of quantitative methods of validation is that they are difficult to implement. How many of us can commission scientific opinion polls? The method most accessible to teachers who want to document a cultural pattern by an independent source is to use the expressed opinion of specialists in the target culture as documentation.

Although objective tests are somewhat difficult to compose, their ease in correction is especially appreciated when large numbers of students are tested. Once the test is designed, correction is completely objective and can be accomplished by practically anyone—and without prejudice (something that cannot be said for essay questions).

Expert Opinion

As we all know, experts differ in opinion. Naroll (1962), an anthropologist, discusses an elaborate and highly sophisticated means of checking the credibility of a reporter by a method he calls data quality control (see especially his chapters 1 and 7). He suggests, for example, a six-level classification reflecting the authority of the investigator or source depending on the nearness to the actual data ("source proximity") (1) datum report, "where an artifact or a statement is itself the trait being studied"; (2) participant report, "where an event or culture pattern is described by a participating culture bearer"; (3) observer's report, "where an event or culture pattern is described by an eyewitness who is not himself a participant in the culture or subculture pattern involved"; (4) derivative report, "an account by a non observer based on a report of another which is no longer available for study"; (5) scholar's report, "an account by a non observer, based on existing primary sources which the comparativist does not find it convenient to consult directly"; (6) reader's report, "an account by a non observer based on other writings, in which specific passages in primary sources covering the data in question are not cited." The level of source proximity can be further evaluated for reporting bias by introducing such control factors as length of stay of the reporter in the target culture, explicitness and generality of the report, and familiarity with the target language.

A less rigorous method of validation along the lines of the technique just mentioned would be to document the accuracy of a cultural pattern with three independent sources, but without an elaborate assessment of source proximity and reporter bias.

Some Illustrative Mistakes

Some years ago in Guatemala a colleague, Tom Daiglé, and I began designing a culture test (we wanted to measure the acculturation of Americans there) by thinking of specific items of Guatemalan cultural behavior that differed in form, distribution, and meaning from an analogous United States pattern, then casting them into test form. As it became increasingly difficult to recollect from memory new contrastive items, we began working from topics such as religion or death. As a third means of identifying contrastive patterns, we took statements made in anthropological reports and attempted to devise questions from them. Of the three methods, we found the first to yield the most successful test items, the second to be the next most productive technique, and the third to be the approach most fraught with problems of validation (Seelye, 1966).

Each test item consisted of a stem and four multiple-choice responses constructed on an analogy to the concept of the phoneme. That is, the correct response presented a situation totally unfamiliar to Americans or one that contrasted in form, distribution, or meaning to the pattern Americans recognize as their own. (See Lado, 1957, 1961.)

Two bilingual Guatemalan groups of twenty each were used to pretest the English version of the questionnaire. The contrastive test item would be introduced to one group; then any changes that seemed to be warranted were made. It was then tested on the second group, changed again, retested on the first group, and so on. The main function of this pretest group was to give an indication of what items would be successful and to discover problems that limited their acceptability. The pretest groups also served to point out faux pas. For example, some of our "fictional" names conveyed too much meaning. Because these two groups became quite familiar with the questionnaire, their school was not used in the final testing.

Some of our *unsuccessful* items might illustrate the problems of writing cross-cultural tests. The following is an example of a pattern reported by anthropologists that we then cast into question form.

The most appropriate place for two businessmen to conclude a business transaction is

A. a prestigious bar

B. an intimate soft-drink stand in the central market

C. the home of one of the businessmen

D. the stadium during a soccer game

We expected Guatemalans to answer A, and Americans C. As it developed, however, three times as many Guatemalans answered C as A. We feel that in spite of this the reported pattern is accurate, that Latins do not transact business in the home, and we attribute the failure of the question to two factors. First, the wording is probably faulty. Perhaps a stem such as "What kind of atmosphere would [Latin American] businessmen look for in which to close a big business deal?" might have elicited a better response. Second, there is difficulty in finding a group of sufficient size sophisticated enough in the ways of businessmen to give the pattern a fair test.

Some questions brought out the differing social orientations of the subjects due to sex differences. Two examples will illustrate this.

The president of Guatemala offers Mr. Sánchez the
position of Minister of Education, but he declines the offer
because

A. the salary of public servants is very low

B. he fears assassination

C. traveling would absent him from home too often

D. he fears permanent identification with the government in
   power

It was expected that Guatemalans would answer D, and Americans would be spread over the other three choices, with a concentration on B. Guatemalan males did, in fact, generally answer as expected, but the females had a strong tendency to answer B. The reason for women's answering as they did would seem to be lack of political sophistication; although some of the ministry posts are dangerous—minister of defense, for example—ministers of education had met with controversy but not death as an occupational hazard. (Some years after this testing, minister of education became a more dangerous post.)

Another question on which males unexpectedly performed better than females is the following question that tests nursing customs.

A mother is nursing her infant in public. This would be

A. infrequent and in poor taste

B. common, but only in one or two social classes

C. more or less common on all social levels

D. almost totally unheard of but not reprehensible

Male Guatemalans generally answered the anticipated B, while females tended to select D. Possibly males are more conscious of women nursing in public. (The test results as a whole did not indicate a general tendency for one sex to be more alert to social forms than the other.)

The understandable impulse to see things as they should be ideally rather than as they are was exemplified by several questions. For example:

A young man has political ambitions. He would like, in fact, to become president of the country some day. In choosing a career to help realize his ambition, he would probably choose to go to

A. the seminary and become a priest

B. the university and study medicine

C. the military academy and become an officer

D. the university and study political science

The political history of Guatemala consists of a long procession of military governments. At the time this question was posed, in the previous 140 years only two constitutionally elected presidents had completed the period for which they had been elected. On the other hand, one military dictator this century was in power thirteen years. There have been but a handful of civilian heads of state. Nevertheless, in answer to our question, Guatemalans overwhelmingly answered D—and the university curriculum did not even offer a degree in political science. In fact, there wasn't even a political science department!

Occasionally a question contained two or more responses, instead of just one, that appealed to Guatemalans. The following interesting situation affords an example.

A pretty young woman is waiting for a bus on a busy street corner. A man comes up behind her and pinches her. She would

A. tolerate it, but only during carnival time

B. call a policeman any time of the year

C. laugh and feel proud

D. pretend nothing had happened so people would not notice

Although the largest concentration of Guatemalans chose D as expected, almost a third answered B. As yet, we have not heard of a Guatemalan woman who has called a policeman in this situation. Perhaps they think they should!

Another perplexing pattern of response was provoked by the following question.

A volcano in Antigua erupts. The people of Guatemala City would

A. ask the government for protection

B. rush to see the spectacle

C. deny the possibility of an eruption because the volcano has been inactive for many years

D. prepare to evacuate the city

Most Guatemalans surprisingly answered D; about 30 percent answered B as expected. Possibly the D response is too ambiguously worded: It might not be clear which of the two cities, Antigua or Guatemala, is indicated. Also, we overstated the B response by using the word *rush* instead of a more temperate *go*.

Social classes occasionally replied differently to a question. The upper class, for example, tended to see public school teachers as members of the upper-lower class, whereas the lower class saw them as middle class.

One last example (patterned after an example from Lado, 1961) will illustrate the difficulty of writing successful questions.

It is Sunday afternoon and the soccer game is very exciting. One of the players makes a vital play. The public whistles loudly. This indicates that they are

A. cheering the player

B. asking for a repetition; more of the same

C. showing their displeasure

D. cheering the goal which has just been made

The contestants were equally divided between C and D. This question appears to have four weaknesses in our wording: (1) The stem leads one to believe that a vital play was completed, rather than just attempted; (2) it is not specified whether the whistling public represents the home rooters or the visitors; (3) response C allows that the whistling is done to show displeasure, rather than to ridicule the player; and (4) it is possible the phenomenon of whistling might have more complex meaning and distribution than we realized.

To illustrate some objective test items that did work, I'll take four items from the final version of the test that measured knowledge of Guatemalan culture. All four items relate to food. The correct answers are starred.

---

1. When a Guatemalan gets up from the table after eating, he

   * A. says thank you, or some other pleasantry

   B. just smiles

   C. says nothing, but does not smile

   D. says nothing, but taps his chest lightly

2. Sometimes a store displays a red flag (about 1 foot square) outside its door. This indicates

   A. the employees are striking

   B. the store is closed for repairs or inventory

   * C. they are selling fresh meat

   D. none of the above

3. At which of the following times would a Guatemalan traditionally eat tamales?

   A. Sunday noon

   * B. Saturday evening

   C. For breakfast

   D. There is no preferable custom

4. A lamp with a candle inside is covered with red paper or red cellophane and displayed outside a doorway. This indicates

   A. a party is in progress

   B. it is a theater exit

   * C. tamales are being sold

   D. none of the above

Besides the Guatemalan examples just given, an example taken from the ACSP unit on "Culture as Adaptation to Complex Social Systems: Peasants" (ACSP, 1968) illustrates another approach to objective testing. The student is asked to study a sheet of dialogue typical of a peasant (examples from India and Italy are given). The class is divided into thirds, and each is assigned a different situation. One student from each group is selected to play the role of peasant and another the role of outsider. "First they read given lines, then ad lib as long as they can, trying to say kinds of things (and in a manner) typical of the part played." The student-oriented objective of this is: "Recognize two or more ways in which peasants usually adapt to outsiders and persons who control their lives and explain how they are adaptive: close-knit family, deference, shrewdness, caution, suspicion, humble appearance." The following ACSP test item is appropriate for measuring achievement of the student objective:

Suppose a stranger entered a peasant village and told the first man he met that he was a new government official whose duty was to help the villagers find better ways to farm their land. Which of the following reactions would you expect from the peasant? (Choose three.)

_____ Asking the stranger for his credentials

_____ Claiming that he already had the best farming methods in the village

__X__ Showing a lot of respect for the stranger's authority

_____ Inviting the stranger home for dinner

__X__ Caution in answering the official's questions

_____ Volunteering information about how lucky the village had been in its crops recently

__X__ Appearing interested in the official's advice on farming

---

Recycling Trivial Items

Once the validity of the test items has been subjected to healthy skepticism, the test designer usually has a pile of factual but superficial items such as "What is the capital of France?" These trivial items can be converted into academically defensible items that test specific course objectives.

That testers think of so many trivial things to test is of no great concern. Creativity is not served by an inhibiting and premature preoccupation with quality. Ideas need to be welcomed in whatever form they initially appear; they can be refined later. That teachers actually test so many trivial things *is* of concern.

Trivial items can be reclaimed by reversing the "ideal" process of devising test items directly from specific goals. The tester can reclaim these weak items that seek to test superficial facts by resolving four questions:

1. How does the trivial fact relate to the lives of the target people?
2. What other behavior patterns come to mind when you think of the way the trivial item relates to the lives of people?
3. What, if any, additional facts can be given in the item to provide the raw material for testing skill in problem-solving?
4. Which of the six goals listed in chapter 3 most readily relates to the item as it evolves through the above three questions?

The test item should then be reworked to fit the goal's intention more closely. This process of converting trivial, purposeless items into respectable items is illustrated by the table at the end of chapter 3 and by the "great belly button question" in chapter 4.

There are at least five limitations imposed upon any testing program by chance and circumstance: the aim of the examiner limits the test content; the validation technique employed further limits content; the time available for testing limits both content and the format of the test; the format of the test limits both content and the circumstances of the testing; and, finally, the imagination of the test designer limits everything.

Alternate Testing Techniques

Just as there is a need for culture tests to be more goal-oriented than is presently the case, there is a corresponding need for more experimentation with the format of culture tests. Classroom checklists, simulation, objective questions, and audiovisual, oral, and tactile approaches are some of the formats that may be used in constructing culture tests.

Classroom Checklists

Teachers who manage classrooms that involve students in individualized instruction often develop checklists of student activity. When a student completes a specified activity, either the student or the teacher checks the appropriate box on the checklist. The checklist, in effect, becomes a "test" of successful activities. (This technique also is used in "mastery learning.") The value of the checklist depends on how purposeful and goal-related the activities are.

Exemplary curriculum materials incorporate purposeful student activities. An especially good secondary school series was developed under the direction of the anthropologist Malcolm Collier (ACSP, 1968). These multimedia materials focus on the teaching of a social studies unit on prehistory.

One of the prehistory units, by way of illustration, seeks to develop student ability to interpret evidence in the area of early human societies. To this end, Bushman culture is studied via filmstrips, site maps, readings, and so on. A number of specific student activities are identified: Use imagination and evidence to make inferences about the Bushman way of life; Identify factual evidence to support an inference; Challenge others' inference if evidence or reasoning suggests an alternative inference. For the last of the three mentioned activities, Collier suggests several measurement techniques that lend themselves to checklists, for instance, keeping a record during regular class of which students do challenge others' inferences. Another way to test the objective is by presenting the student with a question such as: "The Kalahari Bushmen eat only meat and other animal products. Can you tell by what evidence this is known?" When the student makes the desired response, this is noted on the checklist. For this example, the proper response would be to challenge the statement and to give contrary evidence (e.g., nutshells).

Collier's approach to introducing anthropology's insights into existing school curricula—rather than as an added course—has implications for other fields as well. Working with teachers from other disciplines can enhance the accomplishment of many culture goals.

Simulation

The ideal way to test the student's ability to operate in a second culture would be to place the student in the target culture and then observe him or her in a series of "foreign" situations. This method lacks economy and, in addition, would be fatiguing for the middle-aged examiner sentenced to observe the young at work and play.

Simulating certain controlled situations would seem to offer a viable alternative to placing the student in the target culture for test purposes. A role is assigned the subject, such as Latin American student leader, president of France, peasant, businessman, or Peace Corps volunteer. A series of problem-solving situations are then presented for resolution in a form consistent with the target reality. This method becomes more feasible the longer the time available for testing, since only a few subjects can be tested concurrently during a 30-minute period. In the longer form the test itself, if intensely oriented to problem-solving situations, can afford an experience that would assist the subject in handling the inevitable "cultural fatigue" of residence abroad. Preparation of experiences of this type require a lot of work.

For help in developing simulations, see Livingston and Stoll, 1973; Zuckerman and Horn, 1973; Stadsklev, 1974, 1975; Fowler, 1986; and Crookall and Oxford, 1990.

Visual Tests

Suppose a short story has been read in class and a lottery vendor figures in the plot. In testing recognition of a lottery vendor several slides of Latin Americans can be projected: one of a corner candy vendor, another of a businessman, a third of a boy selling chewing gum, and fourth slide picturing a lottery vendor. The student would indicate the latter response on his answer sheet. Or, more economically, the student would be asked to identify an entire series of images for which he or she had been given some context from which to deduce the answers. Any pictorial image, such as slides, drawings, or magazine clippings, will do.

Audio Tests

Here the principle is the same as for visual tests, except the student responds to audio stimuli. A taped section might contain a portion of the lottery vendor's spiel, a brief section of a radio announcer's reading of the articles that announce a state of siege, or a humanely brief portion of a radio commercial. Needless to say, the content of the test would depend on what the teacher wanted to measure; here the concern is with test technique, not content. Nostrand develops the audiovisual possibilities for the teaching of cultural content in language courses in a brief article replete with ideas (Nostrand, 1966).

Oral Exams

The interview, or oral exam, has long been a device for eliciting information on almost any topic from a student. Structured interviews have the advantage of being easier to code and evaluate than open-ended interviews and are, consequently, more objective. However, what the structured interview usually amounts to is a multiple-choice test administered orally. Open-ended interviews often produce unexpected information, but sooner or later the mass of information collected has to be coded for appraisal. Then, too, the interviewers of open-ended exams have to be articulately aware of the object of their search, for unless the interview is recorded they will consciously or unconsciously be eliminating many data (most of which might well be extraneous to the purpose of the interview anyway). The critical concept in developing interviews is K.I.S.S. (Keep It Simple, Sweetheart).

Tactile Tests

Object-using tests confront the subject directly with some aspect of the target culture, thus avoiding the abstract artifices that relegate the target culture, as many students perceive it, to the limbo of the lifeless. The student could be given a lottery ticket to check against a newspaper containing the winning numbers. In another situation the student might be given chopsticks and instructions to eat a Japanese meal that is thoughtfully provided him or her. Primary and secondary teachers have used tactile devices (often curios of the airport variety, with but limited potential) more than have college dons, but few teachers have explored the possibilities of tactile tests.

Technical Help

Finally, there are some excellent sources prepared by teachers to assist in the technical aspects of test construction. A wonderfully succinct (37 pages) introduction to teacher-made tests is available free from the Educational Testing Service in Princeton (Diederich, 1964). Lado's superb book (1961) on language testing contains two excellent chapters that are still entirely relevant to readers of this chapter. An excellent, succinct discussion of the preparation of instructional objectives—the key to good testing—is provided by Mager (1962) in his programed book. The testing manual by Valette (1977) also discusses cultural testing.

The nature of each specific test item determines the kind of inquiry it might be subjected to, but some general questions can be asked of most discrete test items to assess their strength:

1. To what extent is the cultural pattern evident to a member of the target culture? (Does it represent an implicit or an explicit pattern?)

2. To what social, sex, residential, and age groups would the pattern apply?

3. What documentation has the teacher required to back up the "right" answer? Do native speakers of the language— except for those involved in teaching the course—score the expected responses?

4. Is the answer to the question either too difficult or too easy for the intended testees? (Item analyses will give this information.)

5. Can the item be recast to test a skill rather than a fact?

6. What is the pedagogical justification for testing the item? Exactly which cultural goal is to be tested?

7. If test items from a number of different objectives are to be included in the same test, in what proportion is each to be represented?

8. Does each item measure just one cultural element?

9. Does test achievement indicate knowledge of the target culture, or does achievement depend mostly on some extraneous skill such as language or reading ability, general intelligence, or imitating the opinions of the teacher?

10. Can the test be objectively scored?

11. Are attitudes that are conducive to cross-cultural understanding measured in a way that will avoid confusing opinion with fact?

12. What is the reliability of the test as determined through item analysis?

Answering these questions will make the results of your classroom tests more interpretable. And why expend energy on tests whose results will not be interpretable?

Suggested Activities

1. Using the topic and activities developed in your performance objectives for the six goals, compose a test with sample items using multiple choice, objective, audio, oral, and tactile techniques.

2. Try to validate your test using the twelve criteria outlined above.

3. Examine a commercial culture test and determine how many items relate to one of the six cultural goals.

4. Develop a ten-item attitude scale, administer it to at least six people, and score the results.

References Cited

Anthropological Curriculum Study Project (ACSP), 1968. *Modern and Traditional Societies* (kit and student readings); *Origins of Humanness* (kit and student readings). New York: Macmillan. (out of print.)

Bogardus, E. S. 1925. "Social Distance Scale," *Sociological Social Research* 17: 265-71.

Cohen, Bernard H. 1979. *Evaluating Bilingual Education Programs*. Hingham, MA: Teaching Resources Corporation.

Cook, Thomas D., and Donald T. Campbell. 1979. *Quasi-Experimentation: Design and Analysis Issues for Field Settings*. Skokie, IL: Rand McNally.

Cooke, Madeline A. 1970. "Suggestions for Developing More Positive Attitudes toward Native Speakers of Spanish," pp. 118-39 in H. Ned Seelye, ed., *Perspectives for Teachers of Latin American Culture*. Springfield, IL: State Superintendent of Public Instruction.

Crookall, David, and Rebecca Oxford, eds. 1990. *Simulation/Gaming and Language Learning*. New York: Harper and Row.

Diederich, Paul B. 1964. *Short-Cut Statistics for Teacher-made Tests*. 2nd ed. Princeton, NJ: Educational Testing Service.

Fowler, Sandra Mumford. 1986. "Intercultural Simulation Games: Removing Cultural Blinders," pp. 71-81 in L. H. Lewis, ed., *Experiential and Simulation Techniques for Teaching Adults*. San Francisco: Jossey-Bass.

Grice, H. H. 1934. "The Construction and Validation of a Generalized Scale Designed to Measure Attitudes toward Defined Groups." *Bulletin Purdue University* 25: 37-46.

Lado, Robert. 1957. *Linguistics across Cultures: Applied Linguistics for Language Teachers*. Ann Arbor: Univ. of Michigan Press.

Lado, Robert. 1961. "How to Test Cross-Cultural Understanding," pp. 275-89 in Robert Lado, *Language Testing; The Construction and Use of Foreign Language Tests*. London: Longmans, Green. (Also, New York: McGraw-Hill, 1964.)

LeVine, Robert A., and Donald T. Campbell. 1972. *Ethnocentrism: Theories of Conflict, Ethnic Attitudes and Group Behavior*. New York: Wiley.

Livingston, Samuel A., and Clarice Stasz Stoll. 1973. *Simulation Games: An Introduction for the Social Studies Teacher*. New York: Free Press.

Mager, Robert F. 1962. *Preparing Instructional Objectives*. Palo Alto, CA: Fearon.

Naroll, Raoul. 1962. *Data Quality Control: A New Research Technique*. New York: Free Press.

Northwest Regional Educational Laboratory. 1978. *Assessment Instruments in Bilingual Education: A Descriptive Catalog of 342 Oral and Written Tests*. Los Angeles: National Dissemination and Assessment Center.

Nostrand, Howard L. 1966. "Audiovisual Materials for Teaching the Social and Cultural Context of a Modern Foreign Language: Their Bearing upon Pre-Service Education." *The Department of Foreign Languages (DFL) Bulletin*, National Education Association 5, 3 (May): 4–6.

Osgood, Charles E., and G. J. Suci. 1955. "Factor Analysis of Meaning." *Journal of Experimental Psychology* 50: 325-38.

Savignon, Sandra J. 1972. *Communicative Competence: An Experiment in Foreign-Language Testing*. Skokie, IL: Rand McNally.

Seelye, H. Ned. 1966. "Field Notes on Cross-Cultural Testing," pp. 77–85 in *Language Learning* 16, 1–2.

Seelye, H. Ned. 1968a. "Item Validation and Measurement Techniques in Culture Tests," pp. 29-33 in H. Ned Seelye, ed., *A Handbook on Latin America for Teachers*. Springfield: Illinois Office of Education. [EDRS: ED 027 797]

Seelye, H. Ned. 1968b. "Measuring the Ability to Function Cross-Culturally," pp. 34-43 in H. Ned Seelye, ed., *A Handbook on Latin America for Teachers*. Springfield: Illinois Office of Education. [EDRS: ED 027 797]

Shaw, Marvin E., and Jack M. Wright. 1967. *Scales for the Measurement of Attitudes*. New York: McGraw-Hill.

Stadsklev, Ron, ed. 1974. *Handbook of Simulation Gaming in Social Education: Part 1—Textbook*. University, AL: University of Alabama, Institute of Higher Education Research and Services.

Stadsklev, Ron. 1975. *Handbook of Simulation Gaming in Social Education: Part 2—Directory*. University, AL: University of Alabama, Institute of Higher Education Research and Services.

Valette, Rebecca M. 1977. *Modern Language Testing: A Handbook*. 2nd ed. New York: Harcourt, Brace.

Zuckerman, David W., and Robert E. Horn. 1973. *The Guide to Simulations/Games for Education and Training*. Cambridge, MA: Information Resources.

14 If I'm Bicultural, Will the Real Me Please Stand Up?

Students who hear one language at home and another in school or on the street are already well on the way to becoming bicultural. Biculturalism conveys important intellectual advantages, but it also can entail stress, especially concerning self-identity. How to deal with issues such as pressures to conform and cultural relativism? The chapter tackles the question of how bicultural people can "become themselves," and it presents models of how other people have become bicultural. The school environment itself often presents problems and challenges.

The Challenge

No one is born bicultural any more than anyone is born fluent in a language. "None is born wise," said Ptahhotep, in 24th century B.C. Egypt. With each skill that one acquires to facilitate communication with people from another culture, one becomes more bicultural.

Students with an enviable head start in acquiring intercultural communication skills frequently enter our classrooms from homes where another language is spoken. ESL and bilingual education classrooms are populated almost solely by students who each day increase their skill in functioning appropriately in diverse cultural settings. Individuals who grow up with each foot in a different culture have a unique opportunity to view objectively what in most people is a conditioned reflex beyond easy scrutiny—the role convention plays in the formation of thought and behavior.

The proportion of Americans claiming minority roots is growing swiftly. While the 1980 census reported one of every five Americans belonged to a minority group, by 1990 the proportion had jumped to one of every four asserting Native American, Hispanic, Asian, or African roots. Add to this the number of first-generation residents who speak a European language other than English in their homes and the numbers of multicultural people in the U.S. is startling.

As is the dreary case with most opportunities for growth, biculturalism is not without its stresses. Cross-cultural contact inevitably provokes some degree of cross-cultural conflict, especially for people who are expected to internalize disparate—and sometimes conflicting—values. When Ruben Snake, a leader of the Winnebago Indian Tribe, was asked why so many Native Americans experience so much stress in their daily lives, he replied, "If you had a cowboy boot on one foot and a moccasin on the other, you'd go around in circles, too." Or, as a Navajo puts it, we are "caught on the horizon, part of neither Earth nor sky" (*Time* magazine, 1990).

This chapter focuses on stresses that students from "minority" backgrounds often experience as they develop their own sense of self. Some of this stress may become counterproductive and lead to undesirable behaviors such as low self-esteem or drug abuse. Much of this excess pressure can be alleviated by teachers sensitive to the personal dilemmas commonly faced by bicultural individuals. Most of the stress, fortunately, provides an opportunity—even an incentive—for the individual to make exciting discoveries about the interaction between self and the world beyond.

Teachers of bicultural students can deal with student identity problems in three ways: ignore the problems inherent in the integration of two separate world views and ways of doing things—and leave the student to his or her own resources; adopt regional and partisan positions and attempt to "sell" the particular version of reality that one country or the other accepts as orthodoxy; or help students deal creatively with the effects of multicultural conditioning. The last choice will appeal to anyone who has read this far in this book.

Resisting Pressures to Conform to Provincial Standards

"The primary reason youngsters need to study multiple cultures is to learn how to develop multiple perspectives," Edmund Gordon, a Yale professor of psychology, is quoted as saying (*Time* magazine, July 8, 1990, p. 19). "This capacity," he goes on, "is essential to developing intelligence." Gordon sees the central issue to be one of enabling students to use "broad, often conflicting bodies of information to arrive at sound judgments."

Bicultural people are essential to the well-being of any society. Besides enriching the collective wisdom with other perspectives of reality, often their language skills and their personal contacts with people who live in other societies contribute meaningfully to the national social and economic life. Geopolitical conditions, in the flash of gunpowder, catapult "obscure" cultures to life-and-death relevancy. People who speak the languages of the former Soviet republics, or of the former Yugoslav states (e.g., Slovenia, Croatia), of Nigeria's Yoruba or Ibo or Hausa, are needed in our national bank of human resources. (Remember when we referred to the U.S.S.R. as "Russia," ignoring the ethnically heterogeneous nature of the union?)

Nevertheless, to be bicultural (or multicultural) in some societies (e.g., middle-class United States) may be to risk appearing a little "different." This is partly because a bicultural person's communicative patterns differ from those of mainstream members of either culture since bicultural people can and do talk to people with whom their peers cannot communicate.

Another reason bicultural people are sometimes viewed with distrust in very provincial societies is that they cannot be counted on to have the values of the dominant culture. The hysterical internment of Americans of Japanese ancestry in the United States during World War II is an example of what can happen in this regard.

Underlying much of the controversy regarding how far publicly financed schools should go in recognizing cultural and linguistic pluralism within their systems is a concern for how much diversity a nation can contain and still maintain its national unity and viability. Two readers of *Time* magazine succinctly articulate (in the letters to the editor section) their unease with cultural pluralism (July 29, 1991):

"Behind the banner of multiculturalism lies the specter of tribalism." Bill Gregory

"Multiculturalism is the intellectual junk bond of the '90s. Are the short-term returns worth the risk of devaluing our proven cultural assets?" Bruce Kidd

Unrest among ethnically identifiable sectors of the population can certainly disrupt national life. Nash (1989) identifies a number of concepts that have been rallying cries for ethnic struggles in the 20th century—political self-rule, economic opportunity, cultural identity, and religious freedom. What are the conditions that make ethnic identity relevant to the riots and rebellion that undermine national unity? The basic condition is the feeling that individuals are being denied society's scarce resources—money, prestige, power— *because* of their ethnic or racial membership. Equal-opportunity societies would have little to fear from ethnic diversity. Seelye and Wasilewski (1979a) argue that biculturalism does not pose any intrinsic threat to national viability.

In many societies everyone is expected to be able to function linguistically and culturally in at least two cultures. Europeans, perhaps pushed by their geopolitical circumstances, are examples of this expectation of multiculturalism. An educated person in India, to use another example, customarily is fluent in five or six languages. I am writing this chapter ten thousand feet up in Ecuador's Andes mountains, where many Spanish-speaking teachers confront classrooms populated almost solely by Quichua-speaking children. (In other parts of South America, Quichua is called Quechua.) The survivors—both children and teachers—are those who can function biculturally. (Since one cannot function within a society without being able to communicate with its inhabitants, bilingualism, or bidialectalism, is a prerequisite of biculturalism.)

One can escape appearing culturally different by forfeiting one of the two cultures—and there is always considerable pressure on economically and politically subservient groups to make this sacrifice—but trading one brand of monoculturalism for another seems an unnecessarily pallid business. Besides, for one person to go from monocultural Chinese-speaking to monocultural Indonesian-speaking (or whatever) requires passing through a state of biculturalism—

and that is where there is the most potential for social learning. To the extent that a culture group also is distinguishable physically from "mainstream" people, then "escape" from being regarded as different is often impossible. (On the other hand, escape from being just another pretty face is a lot easier.)

It is the expectation of many people in the United States (and in many other countries as well) that one's efforts will be amply rewarded when one loses the annoying vestiges of a "foreign" culture and becomes an A*l*l*-*A*m*e*r*i*c*a*n. The realization of this expectation would be as tragic for the intellectual development of the United States as for the person losing one of his or her cultural heritages. In becoming acculturated the child is expected, like Judas, to deny past associations and allegiances, rather than to build on them. Consider the Chicano first-grader, for example, suffering through reading in a language he does not yet know so that in high school he can suffer through classes in Spanish, a language he was made to forget. Extinction of minority cultures is an ill-thought-out wish of many "mainstream" peoples worldwide. In areas where pressures to acculturate and to conform have won out, society has inherited the bitter irony of rootless uniculture, with its attendant alienation and commerce in headache remedies.

Arnberg (1987) offers advice on how to raise little children bilingually.

It is not just mainstream society that resists cultural pluralism— parents, too, can pose a "generational" hurdle. To the extent that parents want Juanito to be a little replica of themselves, talking, acting, and thinking as they do, they are consigned to disappointment. The culture of the parents was a reasoned response to the conditions in which they lived. Often, they lived an agrarian, preindustrial life that bears little resemblance to present urban life in Mexico City or San Juan. It was often a life lived before there were many opportunities for the occupation of the son to differ substantially from that of the father; it was a pre-women's liberation life that allowed the daughter few opinions that differed from those of the mother, and later, perhaps, from those of the mother-in-law; it was life where social classes "knew their place." It was a life enriched by folk art, strong beliefs, and wise adages. And the culture worked; witness the very existence of children from that cultural parentage in our classrooms. But it was a culture that in some regards is largely dysfunctional when transplanted to postagrarian societies. An illustration of this is seen in the daily drama in which thousands of rural people in Latin America flock to cities in hope of a better life. At any rate, it was the culture of another generation, and the prerogative—and necessity—of each generation is to modify the rules of the game.

Nor are children home free who emigrate from an urban culture outside the United States. While the urban cultures of London, Buenos Aires, Mexico City, and Los Angeles probably have more in common with each other than with the rural peasant classes in their own countries, there are still important differences in the life of each of these cities. The culture of each population is a response to present needs as seen through the many-colored but distorted prism of its own unique past experiences.

No, the culture of bilingual children cannot be precisely that of the parents. To be so would be to sacrifice the experience and independence of the children for the expediency of the status quo.

Cultural Relativism

Cultural relativism can be discussed in a classroom from several perspectives: if you wanted people to think you were brave, and you were a male living in the first half of this century as a Shuar in Ecuador, what might you do? What ideas do you have that you would be willing to hurt someone else to keep? If someone from an unfamiliar culture came to your house for dinner and ate spaghetti with his fingers, what would you do? (For what it's worth, I eat pizza with my fingers in the United States and with a knife and fork in Italy.) What if it were against your beliefs to eat any kind of meat and you had not eaten anything for several days and you were invited to a friend's home for dinner and all they served was steak and potatoes?

Teachers can help their students develop insight into the part cultural conditioning plays in the formation of their own identity by having them talk about how large a family they want to have, and how much they want to march to the tune of a different drum beat. Whose drum beat? What type of person are they describing?

Are they comfortable with the description? A puzzle in the inter-relatedness of self-identity and societal feedback that may intrigue older students focuses on a literary dilemma: Is Don Quixote immortal because of Miguel de Cervantes Saavedra, or does Cervantes owe his immortality to Don Quixote?

The French intellectual André Malraux argues that the world is between cultures. Just as the fall of Rome ended one era, the end of European colonization (circa 1950) ended another. We are now living in the interim between a colonial era and a "decolonial" era, he says. David S. Hoopes, a founder of the Society for Intercultural Education, Training, and Research (SIETAR International), refers to the potential that bilingual people have to "mediate" between cultures. Perhaps in the meantime, bicultural man can put his or her mediating imprint on the next, more compassionate, era.

The cultural reality of the U.S. classroom forces its students to deal with the cultural heritage of their home vis-à-vis mainstream U.S. culture. Bilingual teachers can help students who are between cultures interpret both cultures honestly and sympathetically.

Most problems in interaction between an educator of one culture and a pupil or parent of another stem from the implicit, culturally conditioned assumptions each makes about the other. Preparing educators to deal with these "foot in mouth" problems is not an easy task. The most effective approach to date is the sophisticated training method developed by Alfred J. Kraemer. It teaches educators how to recognize and identify the subtle cognitive manifestations of their own cultural conditioning by observing how hidden cultural values affect the behavior of (videotaped) fellow Americans inter-acting with people from different cultures. This training increases one's ability to diagnose, and often prevent, the most pervasive problems in intercultural communication. At a more general level, the training greatly facilitates learning to understand another culture from a nonethnocentric perspective. (School systems that may want to have their teachers trained to use this method and its unique materials can directly contact Dr. A. J. Kraemer, 8418 Masters Court, Alexandria, VA 22308.)

The following brief scenario illustrates how Kraemer uses one mainstream U.S. value (in this case, the tendency to define and describe people primarily in terms of their work and achievements instead of personal attributes) to bring American educators to an understanding of how their values affect intercultural communication.

MRS. RAMÍREZ: Yes, I'm sorry I couldn't come to the party. Did you enjoy it?

MRS. JONES: Oh, yes, I met so many interesting people there. There was one woman, Marlena, who used to be an English teacher, but now she is high up in the office of education. And, oh, there was another man who works for IBM as a computer engineer, and has just been assigned to the Paris office.

MRS. RAMÍREZ: Hmmm?

MRS. JONES: And, let's see, I talked for a long time with another gentleman who would never tell me what he was doing. I called him the mystery man.

MRS. RAMÍREZ: Why did you call him that?

Episodes such as this form part of the workshop exercises. Taken together, these exercises enable the participants to identify the often unspoken values behind Mrs. Jones's behavior and to see in themselves reflections of the same mainstream values. (The presence of a "contrast culture" person [Mrs. Ramírez] merely serves in these exercises to make it easier for American educators to see how their values are culturally conditioned.)

Becoming Yourself

Knowledge of one's values and sense of self can be helpful in itself to individuals who are dealing with identity issues.

There is a big difference in the way human and nonhuman life forms tend to make the adjustments needed to survive. In nonhuman life forms, many behavioral characteristics (e.g., where eagles build nests) are largely determined by genetic selection brought about through the interaction of the species with forces that selectively favor the propagation of certain genes—those favoring great eyesight in eagles, for instance, or tricky prehensile tails in monkeys, or in camels the ability to go a long time without drinking chocolate milkshakes.

In homo sapiens, it is human culture—not so much our genes—that evolves to meet the exigencies of changing life conditions. Culture is the principal adaptive mechanism humans use to cope with life's circumstances. When the pace of the "hunt" is leisurely, one can dawdle over long meals. When these circumstances change, the adaptive mechanism must also change (e.g., fast-food restaurants on every corner). These cultural changes help the individuals within that changing culture to continue as viable organisms. To the extent survival of a society is threatened by behavior that has become dysfunctional (e.g., thermonuclear arms buildup), traditional ways of doing things (e.g., national defense measured by the destructive power of its armaments) become a liability to the group. In homo sapiens there are no subspecies to evolve different genetic directions as there are in birds and bees and cinnamon trees. In humanity there are subcultures, not biological subspecies, that provide the wherewithal to help us adapt to our environment.

Were culture seen simply as an adaptive tool, to use or discard as needed, then cultural change would not evoke the emotional trauma associated with its occurrence. But because human culture, besides being pragmatically adaptive, also provides the vehicle for esthetic and moral satisfaction, even minor changes sometimes evoke major crises by inducing anxiety in the gratification of the most subjective of basic needs, the psychological. An example of this is the consternation among the citizenry of San Francisco, California, when they learned that some of their Southeast Asian neighbors were surviving by eating unwanted dogs. Alas, cultures define friendship and reverence for life as ethnocentrically as any other topic.

Hall (1976) argues that human beings must learn to separate their perception of self from the cultural extensions of their selves that they fabricate in response to adaptive pressures. These cultural responses can easily lose their functionality as circumstances change. People become bicultural in response to adaptive needs. Bicultural individuals are faced with the need to identify those belief forms that have cross-cultural validity in satisfying esthetic and moralistic needs, and to differentiate the form from the need.

Any correlation between "race" and culture is coincidental, not causal. A child begins life with a genetic, chemical, neurological base that will be affected by age, disease, and nutrition. Physical anthropologists have not discovered any gene present in one race or ethnic group that is not found in other races or ethnic groups as well. Although the frequency of specific genes differs in different populations, humans share the same basic gene pool.

Nutrition, unlike race, is an important determinant of behavior and varies more widely from population to population than does the relative frequency of particular genes. To the extent that we are eating better food than our parents, our inborn genetic program acts out its development without as many debilitating hindrances. We are what we eat, some say. The one child in 800 with an extra chromosome on pair number twenty-one (trisomy 21—Down's syndrome), will never have the intellectual capacity to be a nuclear physicist regardless of what he or she eats, but a person with genes that permit him or her to become a genius will never realize this potential if his or her first few years are spent in belly-swollen malnutrition. It is also unrealistic to expect a child from a ghetto environment, where the parents have been unable to resolve the essential problems of food and roof, to come to class disposed to reach for academic excellence for its own sake.

No matter how smart your mother was, or how much vitamin D-enriched milk you drink, you are not going to be a nuclear physicist if you are born—and stay—in a Kapauku Papuan village in New Guinea. Nor are you going to design a suspension bridge (a Pygmy invention) if you live in the Sahara Desert. One realizes potentials within a cultural setting. It is no genetic accident that different cultures experience a flurry of distinguished production in the arts—a Golden Age—at infrequent but discernible periods in their history. It is a cultural accident. Human talents fall in and out of fashion. Facilities for intellectual development in most industrialized nations, as reflected by proffered government scholarships, go to bright children who want to become engineers, not poets. The intellectual capacity for both is there in the gene pool, but cultural elements foster one at the expense of the other. (Some would say that poets thrive in adversity.)

We see ourselves in relation to our environment. The way we perceive this relationship depends on the looking glass we use. Our inborn intelligence, our group-intelligence (the wisdom of the tribe), our language system, and the particular situations in which we find ourselves (including the kind of feedback we get from others) are the major determinants of what we see.

The brilliant Neanderthal who invented the flint knife did not see stone the same way that his or her neighbors did, although they adopted the insight readily enough. Individual intelligence is the source of the folk wisdom of a people. Alan W. Watts (1969) observed that "the stereotyped attitudes of a culture are always a parody of the insights of its more gifted members." Bicultural individuals will develop different world views because—but not only because—of differences in intelligence.

The collective wisdom of one's culture influences one's concept of self in such basic matters as whether we see ourselves as subject and the rest of the world as object (Western thought), or whether we see ourselves at one with the world, a pattern of energy interacting with all things and getting our form from this interaction (Eastern thought). Do we have an identity independent of our interaction with others and with nature? Social psychologists would say no. As products of Western, Protestant thought we rebel against the notion that we are not captains of our ship. But the realization that our self is inseparable from its environment does not take away any of our uniqueness. Who has had the same genetic combination? Who has had the same experiences in life? The possibilities for human uniqueness are infinite both in spite of and because of our dependence on "circumstances beyond our control."

Ironically, one of the least potent ingredients of self-identity in monolinguals is a sense of being part of a national political system. There are only a few occasions yearly when nationality is given ritualistic observance. Other than during an election year, or at times of celebrations such as Independence Day or birthdays for deceased statesmen, one hardly thinks of one's "national" identity. Subnational identities such as family, city, region, or roles such as woman, teenager, athlete, Mormon, steelworker, or high school teacher, powerfully affect everyday behavior.

One's nationality becomes significant by contrast with another in much the same way that ethnocentrism comes into relief when its basic premises are challenged by a different value system. Governments often play upon this reality by making much ado about some political problem involving "outsiders," while at the same time muting criticism of internal affairs. Territorial disputes, for example, are bombastic occasions in which to sound the drums of national identity.

Focusing on a national level of identity can obscure important ethnic differences within any one nationality. Likewise, a narrower focus on ethnic background can overlook important attitudes and behavior that are shared with the national, mainstream culture. One blond, blue-eyed prospective bilingual teacher was berated by an ethnically conscious community worker in Chicago who claimed, with much feeling and some sarcasm, that Puerto Rican students would not be able to identify with her because she was an "Anglo." There are, of course, Puerto Ricans from all kinds of backgrounds and what the community worker did not realize was that this Puerto Rican teacher hailed from one of them. She was the real McCoy but did not match the stereotype.

For an individual residing within the country of his or her birth, ethnic background is more important than nationality. Where I lived for several years in Italy, people were first *Vicentini* (from the town of Vicenza), second from Veneto (the northeast region), third from Northern Italy, and only fourth, Italian. When we go abroad, however, national identity assumes greater importance—the *Vicentino* is Italian, the Alabaman in Mexico is a *yanqui*, and the Welshman in France is an *anglais*. One of the characteristics of living in a second country is that one finds oneself dealing frequently with what was hitherto a minor aspect of self-identity—nationality. One is generally, by consequence, ill equipped to deal with the national aspect of one's identity unless one is confronting the behavior of a different nationality.

The teacher may be more effective in buttressing the self-esteem of a child when ethnic identities are not lost in the national conglomerate. When the first student language census was taken in Illinois schools in the 1970s, teachers often reported that their students spoke "Indian" instead of Urdu or Hindi or Tamil, or any of the 500 other languages of India, Pakistan, and Sri Lanka that their students actually spoke. Today, many teachers remain unsophisticated about the languages spoken by their students. Likewise, few teachers are aware of which tribe—there are over 500—their Native American students identify with.

A big step in liberating ourselves from the caprices of cultural conditioning is taken when we soberly perceive the immense importance it plays in the determination of our sense of identity. In discovering this sense of self, the multicultural person does not deny the influence of one or another culture on his or her character—the multicultural person accepts being a product of all his or her experiences. The Spanish philosopher José Ortega y Gasset expressed the interaction of self and culture in this way: *Yo soy yo y mis circunstancias* (I am myself and my circumstances). Once one knows how the game of life is played, and that it is a game—complete with arbitrary rules and plaster of Paris incentives—one is free to take, if one wishes, a more sporting attitude toward the human scene.

A powerful predictor of behavior is knowledge of a person's cultural background, especially when subcultural variables such as age, sex, social class, religion, occupation, and place of residence are taken into consideration. A useful outline for focusing on the cultural origins of ideas and behavior was prepared by Kraemer (1973), adopted from the anthropologists Kluckholm and Murray:

Every person thinks and acts in some respects

    (a) like all other persons
    (b) like some other persons
    (c) like no other person

    (b1) like other persons of the same sex
    (b2) like other persons of the same occupation
    (b3) like other persons of the same age
    (b4) like other persons in the same role
    (b5) like other persons in the same situation

One way in which teachers can use this outline is to have students offer personal examples for each item on the outline.

If one is the product of cultural conditioning, then bicultural people are the product of two contrasting forms of cultural conditioning. This makes it harder to predict the behavior of bicultural people. It is fun to watch bicultural strangers interact at parties, when each knows the first-culture patterns of the other. In this situation, the conventions governing appropriate behavior forms are up for grabs. For instance, an American guest might bow to a Japanese guest at the same time that the latter extends his hand to shake the American's hand. Anthropologists have dubbed the resulting mix of behavior "bobbing." Each party-goer responds unexpectedly to the first-culture patterns of the other.

Classroom activities can provide explicit help in integrating conflicting values. There are activities to highlight these cross-cultural conflicts (Weeks et al., 1977), but there is no pat way to dispatch the confusion that accompanies the ensuing conflict. Tender loving care seems to be the response that inspires the most confidence. Uvaldo Palomares's (1974) technique of the magic circle may bring some of these affective confusions to light for subsequent discussion. (In this activity, a dozen or fewer children sit in a circle and share their personal feelings on a given topic. Topics cover areas such as: I can show you something I feel good about [kindergarten]; I didn't know I'd get in trouble [second grade]; I had a hard time choosing between two things [third grade].) For older students, value clarification exercises may make the problem easier to deal with. Some value clarification exercises are described in Pfeiffer et al. (1969-1975), Simon et al. (1973), Weeks et al. (1977), and Seelye (1979).

How Other Bicultural People Cope

Looking at the behavior of people who have attempted to "make peace" with disparate cultural systems, molding conflicting experience into an integrated sense of self, it is clear that there are many different ways to accomplish this. The models that other people provide can help students see where they are in the process of biculturation. These models can also help students judge the usefulness that different forms of adaptation may have for their own lives.

Eight divergent ways in which individuals respond to situations of marginality or uprootedness were identified (in an unfunded proposal) in 1950 by Donald T. Campbell, the eminent social psychologist, from descriptions found then in the social science literature: (1) to become an agent of change through a personal and creative deployment of innovation; (2) to have one's ego damaged, as characterized by neurotic indecisiveness, aimlessness, schizoid withdrawal, self-depreciation, cynicism, and destructiveness; (3) to convert a relativism of values into a stable standard of reference and a way of life; (4) to adapt to situations by focusing on the interplay between role and reference group, letting one's behavior be guided by several discrete "generalized others"; (5) to retain one's first cultural goals (e.g., money) while abandoning the culturally prescribed means of achieving them; (6) to reestablish an orthodoxy, often more rigid than the "natural born" variety, characterized, perhaps, by a reactionary return to an ancestral culture; (7) to overconform rigidly to the second culture, resulting sometimes in anti-egalitarian, anti-lower-class attitudes on the part of the socially mobile; (8) to adopt, in concert with other uprooted persons, a novel orthodoxy, differing from and probably hostile to all the traditional cultures whose contact may have produced the marginality.

Real-life models cover the wide range of strategies suggested by Campbell: Amish farmers following the customs of rural farmers of two centuries ago—even though the descendants of their ancestors who remained in Germany no longer share that culture; Eskimo fishermen who return home after years of medical treatment in sanatoriums in urban Canada, never to mention anything that happened during those "foreign" years; nativistic South Sea Islanders who create a glorious, ancient culture the way they imagine it to have been; the person who changed his name from Hipólito Pérez Ramos to Hal Rome, and says he's of Italian descent if anyone asks; the angry militant who rejects all cultural values; the Buddhist bodhisattva, who sees life as a game in which one avoids confusing social role with self-identity; the person who neatly compartmentalizes values into separate boxes, one for each culture; and so on. The expatriate writer Salman Rushdie wrote (in *Grimus*, 1974) that "It is the natural condition of the exile, putting down roots in memory."

For adolescents from non-Western backgrounds, dress is an area that commonly provokes particular stress (Brah, 1978; Louden, 1978; Saunders, 1982). Nor are adolescents the only ones affected by concern for dress. Many Muslim women who are comfortably veiled in their home countries are made to feel uncomfortable in most areas of the United States when they wear veils. When a Quichua Indian student I had taught in Ecuador arrived in the United States on a scholarship, she had severe difficulties in changing dress patterns that were part of her ethnic identity. When I picked her up at the airport it was twenty degrees below zero and there was a foot of snow on the ground. She arrived in sandals and held out for several days before donning the boots she was given upon arrival.

A study that viewed second-culture coping strategies as healthy, nonpathological attempts to deal with daily exigencies suggests that all intercultural coping, which includes the thousands of behavioral choices that are made, falls into one of five categories (Seelye and Wasilewski, 1979b; also recounted in Brislin, 1981, pp. 277-79):

1. *Adherence* to first-culture patterns and an avoidance, a nonacceptance, of second-culture patterns. (Example: A woman from India moves to the United States and continues to wear a *sari*.)

2. *Substitution* of second-culture patterns for first-culture patterns. (Example: The Indian woman wears Western dress exclusively.)

3. *Selective addition* of second-culture patterns to first-culture patterns. (Example: She wears *saris* or Western dress, depending on the circumstances.)

4. *Hybridization*, synthesis or recombination of behavior from first and second cultures, where both cultural influences are simultaneously apparent. (Example: She wears a *sari*, but combines it with leather boots and a long-sleeved blouse or sweater.)

5. *Innovation*, where an original integration of the influences of two cultures is effected, resulting in a novel "third-culture" pattern. (Example: She designs *haute couture* based on abstractions from the dress designs of both cultures.)

After interviewing 200 bicultural adults, Seelye and Wasilewski found that 75 percent reported using three or more different coping strategies to meet different demands at different times in their lives. These researchers stress that one does not begin by using "adherence" as a response to all situations and then evolve toward "innovation" as the preferred strategy. Rather, one draws on many or all of the coping strategies; choice of a strategy depends on the nature and context of the cultural demand and on how one is disposed at the moment.

If a student can find "kindred spirits" among the school staff, perhaps someone of the same ethnic background, the student may see his or her attempts to succeed within the system as a more achievable goal. But teachers should not make the mistake of thinking that they are all things to all students. Sensitive teachers can bring to the student's attention a wide range of models found in literature or in examples of people living in the student's community.

Students can be given the assignment of interviewing people in their family or community who are bicultural to see how they describe their attempts at integrating cultural differences. Though there is no one right way to become bicultural, some ways are healthier than others. The healthier ways use all experience as a springboard to greater awareness of the interrelatedness of self and the universe; they do not deny experience.

To generate further insight into the dynamics through which minority persons effectively cope and adapt in multicultural environments, Jacqueline Howell Wasilewski (1982) described the strategies used by people who successfully adapted to life in the United States without turning their backs on their home cultures. She determined which strategies were prominent in the experiences of four major minority groups. Wasilewski based her ethnographic study on several hundred life histories that were published in English. Her study focused on three major domains: the environments in which interpersonal interaction takes place (both physical and psychological); the competencies of the actor (abilities to appraise social situations and to transform reality); and the behaviors exhibited in the environments by the actor (abilities to deploy behavior appropriately, to accept one's own diversity, to accept assistance from the dominant group). Wasilewski developed a checklist that can be used to indicate—from the perspective of the minority person doing the coping and adapting—the presence of important patterns.

Recurring patterns emerged from Wasilewski's study that are particularly helpful in enabling minority people to cope and adapt to multicultural conditions. Successful copers have

1. *A superordinate goal* (e.g., concern for someone else's welfare, perhaps by participating in an organization or movement or by internalizing an organization's goals)

2. *Role models and mentors*

3. *The ability to choose (internally) to be one's complex self* in the face of cultural and interpersonal pressures to simplify (e.g., "I'll never be Japanese enough for my grandmother or American enough for my friends, so I'll just have to be myself")

4. *The ability to behave (externally) in accordance with one's complex self.* (This leads, oftimes, to improvement in the environment's ability to accept the diversity inherent in culturally plural individuals.)

5. *The ability to transform negative energy* (e.g., bitterness) into positive energy (e.g., deciding one is not going to spend energy in self-destructive ways, then going on to use one's energies to develop a skill or build something)

6. *A large repertoire of coping strategies* from which to choose behaviors appropriate to a particular situation (e.g., when to behave actively, when to behave passively)

In other research (Seelye and Wasilewski, 1981) into how bicultural children develop the skills they need to function simultaneously in different cultural settings (a Spanish-speaking home, with black peers, and in an urban, all-English school), it was discovered that one of the most important correlates of success in school was whether they made a friend the first day of school. Further, success in the other domains was related to whether they had a close confidant with whom they could talk about anything.

In a school in Dearborn, Michigan, a teacher asked one sixth-grade ESL class to write what they felt about school. An Arabic-speaking student emphasized in her brief heartfelt essay the importance of friends.

I always want to be nice to people but I don't know how. I give people my stuff just so they can be my friends. I sometimes act like them so they can be my friends. I hate teasing people but if you want to have some friends, well

that's what I did, but it didn't work. In Lebanon I used to
be quiet and nice and did all my work and got good
grades. These days I'm getting good grades. But in class
people talk to me so I talk back to them so they don't get
mad at me. I know I complain. I know I take some things
serious but I'm trying not to. I cry because I try to be that
person's friend, but then they start calling me names. Girls
start coming to me and saying that some of the girls and
boys are saying that I'm the ugliest girl and they all hate
me. There is another way I try to be their friend, and that
is acting like them but I think they don't like the way they
act. The real me is nice, kind, generous, sweet, and quiet.
But that is not the way I act in class. I'm just telling you
on paper how I really feel and how I used to be and the
truth.

Examples such as these of how others worked through typical
bicultural problems let students know they are not alone and that
there are many ways to accomplish cultural integration. By projecting
his or her own concerns into someone else's problem, the student
can retain privacy while gaining insight into some of his or her own
frustrations.

"Messages" from School

A factor to be considered consciously by a bicultural student is the
extent to which he or she receives satisfaction from group endeavor
in comparison to individual accomplishment. Each society has people
of every ilk, but some societies are oriented around one type more
than another. In the United States, for example, the Protestant ethic,
the frontier spirit, laissez-faire government, a high degree of social
and geographic mobility, and the large size of the country have
produced a lot of Captain Marvels who change the rest of the world
to suit themselves by shouting, "SHAZAM!" In Mexico, on the
other hand, the extended family often affords the setting within
which one achieves psychological satisfaction. In some socialist
countries a major attempt is being made to have individuals sublimate
their own cravings into societal priorities so that the good of the

group has more psychological force than drives toward individualization.

A person who is highly ego-centered can expect frustration in a society whose institutions are based too efficiently on subordinating individual interests to group goals. Likewise, a person who feels comfortable in working for the good of the many will experience distress in a society where one is expected to contribute as an individual, without aid of family, friends, or work cohorts.

Schools, too, sometimes pit the institution against the individual, and they have six hours a day, nine months a year, for twelve years (or more) to get their message across. The dialects of academia sometimes serve as armaments in the employ of the institution in its struggle for student minds. Classification systems, especially those constructed by monocultural social scientists, often are biased against bicultural people. For example, the following continuum popular among Western psychologists is one semantic trap to avoid in a discussion of ego:

strong ego.........................weak ego

This dichotomy implies a positive value on "strong ego" and a negative value on "weak ego." Whenever a classification system places a person in categories with negative overtones, it is time to counterattack with another classification more sympathetic to our complexity. One antidotal continuum that might turn the tables here associates "weak ego" with a desirable quality—a strong sense of context:

weak sense of universe..........strong sense of universe

strong ego.........................weak ego

Here, strong ego is synonymous with weak sense of universe. One also can conceptualize classifications where none of the categories are appealing: Unamuno, in El Sentido trágico de la vida, said that the intellectual world is divided into two classes—dilettantes on the one hand and pedants on the other.

Some people view bilingualism, the most overt sign of biculturalism, as a desirable condition only of the upper class or of people from the non-English world. Middle- and working-class U.S.

children and adults are expected to remain ignorant of other languages. This view, of course, negates the worth per se of bilingualism and would limit its utility to jet-set peregrinations to the health spas of Europe or as a communicative tool for "foreign" or "minority" peoples to discourse with American monolinguals. The self-esteem of the bicultural student is enhanced by the presence of teachers, administrators, and peers of the mainstream culture who are fluent in the language and customs of the minority ethnic group. It is also positively affected by the presence of adult bilingual-bicultural models from the minority culture as well. It is a lot easier for a student to see the value of bilingualism and biculturalism when it is sought after by people from all cultural backgrounds.

What's in a Name?

The most important sounds in the universe are those that say your name. It's your ticket on the train of life. I know that teachers love to anoint their foreign-born students with American names.

On an Arab student's first day in his Michigan classroom, the teacher asked him what his name was. "Abdul Naser," he replied. "Hmmm," the teacher cogitated. "We'll call you Al." To this, the student replied, "Abdul yesterday, Abdul today, Abdul tomorrow." Later, in high school, Abdul became a very popular student and star on the football team; nobody calls him Al.

I have a colleague from Texas who works in migrant education, Alfredo del Barrio. He told me that he understood the difficulty many of his teachers had in pronouncing his name. They would say Alfreedou del Bariou and that didn't bother him. I asked him if they called him Freddie. "Some did," he said, "but I always called myself Alfredo."

My son Michael came home from his high school Spanish class with a new name, Jesús. Why, I asked, didn't the teacher call you Miguel, the name your mother has always called you? "Because Miguel was already taken," he said, mirroring the twisted logic of formal education.

"Last" names are a problem. Americans assume that the last name is your father's surname. But this isn't the case in many cultures. The naming system in the Hispanic world, for example, is a little complex (it would take five or ten minutes to explain), but generally speaking, one's father's surname is the next to the last name. The last name is your mother's surname. Imagine how disconcerting it is for a father to be addressed with his wife's surname instead of his own. (Gorden, 1968, has made an excellent study of Hispanic surnames.)

Swapping Languages or Adding Languages?

Besides keeping your names, it is nice to keep your fluency in the language of your grandparents.

Some weeks after my first child entered kindergarten in Illinois, the teacher called my wife and me in for a conference. David, it seemed, was not speaking. He didn't say anything at all to anybody. One of the kindergarten teachers knows some Spanish but when she spoke to David in Spanish he smiled but didn't break his silence. The teacher suggested a solution. "I think the problem is David is not hearing enough English. If you and your wife would speak to him in English at home, I believe his English would improve."

The trouble with this suggestion was that his English would improve at the expense of his Spanish. He would be isolated from half his relatives, not to mention from his mother. The human brain can handle many languages and we saw no compelling reason to give up on one of David's two incipient languages. Forget Spanish in kindergarten so he could struggle relearning it in high school foreign language classes?

David went almost the whole year without uttering a single word in kindergarten class. (At home he wasn't very verbal in Spanish or English, either.) In May the conscientious teacher was elated. David had spoken to another kid in class. The kid had asked David whether he wanted a graham cracker (it had jelly on it) and David said "Yes." "You know," the teacher enthused, "I believe that with all of the English David is going to hear this summer, playing with his friends and listening to TV, he'll be ready for first grade in the fall." She was happy that she could in good faith recommend David for first grade. I told her that the day after kindergarten, I was shipping the family to Central America for the summer and that he wouldn't hear a word of English. And that's what happened.

But another thing happened too. David spent the summer running free with his dozens of cousins and their friends, playing soccer, riding horses, and learning which life forms you could pet and which were poisonous. His Spanish became more impressive. Larger vocabulary, more complex sentence structure, more verbality. He returned to Illinois the evening before school began. The next day he immediately transferred his newfound Spanish language ability into English and has done well since.

A couple of years later, David's younger brother Alan entered first grade. One noon, a month or so into first grade, Alan came home for lunch. My wife and I were talking in the kitchen. Alan stood by us and gave us a disgusted look. "Why don't you speak English—*bright* people speak English." We looked down at this little-worm-of-an-idea with an expression of our own. Alan didn't raise the issue again.

Earlier this week Alan, now an industrial engineer, was mediating a labor dispute between a Russian factory worker and his Colombian foreman. Alan apparently managed to look bright while translating between Russian and Spanish.

The Hidden Curriculum

Schools make many culturally based assumptions about kinship. "Parents and guardians" is a common phrase in the school lexicon. Yet many cultures define the significant relationships differently. Among the Hopi, for instance, the mother's brother is a more significant "parent" than the child's biological father. In many cultures, extended families view child-rearing responsibilities quite differently from the way many Americans view them. Maybe we ought to look into this.

The management style of U.S. classroom teachers constitutes another way in which the dominant culture sends "messages" to unsuspecting bicultural students. These messages constitute a "hidden curriculum" with which the students must successfully interact. Through intensive study of a small number of classrooms, Margaret LeCompte (1981) identifies five rules that students were expected to internalize and that were embedded in the teachers' "management-type behavior." These rules were:

1. Do what the teacher says.

2. Live up to teacher expectations for proper behavior.

3. Stick to the schedule.

4. Keep busy.

5. Keep quiet and keep still.

LeCompte suggests that schools teach children how to manage these "hidden" rules of classroom behavior.

All sorts of unintended messages (to give the benefit of the doubt) are conveyed by teacher behavior. In one bilingual education program that I evaluated, the teachers (uncharacteristically for bilingual teachers) used Spanish solely for punitive purposes: "Shut up." "Sit down." "Be quiet." The medium for academic content and praise was English.

Respect

A few years ago a colleague and I studied academic and social competency development in a sample of Hispanic children who attended about five all-English elementary schools. As part of the study (Seelye and Wasilewski, 1981), we invited the students' teachers to identify the strengths and weaknesses of each child. Without exception, each teacher identified as a weakness the child's lack of fluency in English. In not one case, however, did a teacher list as a strength that the kid spoke two languages. In fact, not a single teacher identified a single ethnically related skill such as skill in declaiming verses in Spanish, social graces, cooking and dancing abilities, abilities to function in culturally diverse settings. They were blind to what happened off the English-language stage.

The American concept of classroom fairness gave many of the children difficulty. Teachers who strove to treat all children the same were perceived by many Hispanic students as not caring for them as the special individuals they were. Eldest Hispanic children who were used to the perquisites that came from being surrogate parents to their younger siblings were offended at being treated by their teachers as irresponsible children.

Tiedt (1990) suggests a number of practical ways teachers can help build a positive concept of self. The authors outline ideas for activities such as welcoming the student, the "me" collage, writing projects (e.g., What I Like about Me, Ten Things about Me), It's Okay to Be Afraid (students write fears on slip of paper, put in box anonymously, slips are drawn, and the whole class discusses the fear), the fantasy trip (close your eyes, think back to the time you first . . . how did you feel?; think of a time something unpleasant happened in school . . . what should the teacher have said to make it all right?), names (my name, what my parents call me, what my friends call me), family roots.

These authors list teaching strategies that they recommend be avoided:

1. Activities in which there is only one winner.
2. Publicizing the "A" papers or those that got 100 percent on the spelling test. (This ignores the children who need a boost the most.)
3. Putting a grade on every paper a child completes.
4. Teaching to mastery. (Fluency and employment [of reading] are more important.)
5. Expecting the same answer to everything.

Ethnic minority students are exposed to the trials and trivia, heroes and villains of both their home culture (or the culture of their parents) and U.S. mainstream culture. The challenge is for these students to integrate what they hear. I studied Mexican history in Mexico and U.S. history in the U.S. Only after several hours of history lectures about the United States Southwest did I realize that my U.S. teacher was talking about the same historical period that my Mexican teacher had addressed previously. In the area of overlap, there were two completely different histories! This observation— that each society puts its own interpretation on events—can be enlightening.

It is hard to feel good about yourself if everyone except your mother is telling you what a dud you are. From the age of six to eighteen or twenty-two, anybody who gets mediocre or worse grades in school suffers from loss of self-esteem. Successful school experiences are like jolts of energy that recharge the batteries of self-esteem. Efforts to strengthen pupils' self-esteem must include skill development. The concluding observation made by Lieberman, Yalom, and Miles (1973) in their impressive study of encounter groups is pertinent for all educators:

> The participant must be able to carry something out of the group experience that is more than a simple affective state. He must carry with him some framework, though by no means necessarily well-formulated, which will enable him to transfer learning from the group to his outside life and to continue experimenting with new types of adaptive behavior.
> . . . Most small groups will spontaneously evolve into a social unit which provides the affective aspects of the intensive group experience; the leader's function is to prevent any potential obstruction of the evolution of the intensive experience, and in addition to be a spokesman for tomorrow as he encourages group members to reflect on their experiences and to package them cognitively so that they can be transported into the future. [p. 439]

Success in the "noncultural" cognitive areas of the curriculum bolsters a healthy sense of self-esteem in bicultural students. So, in a real sense, the math or gym teachers are aiding the cause of self-identity when they ply their trades to get children to do things they could not do before.

Two mistakes commonly accompany cognitive skill development in programs aimed at students for whom English is a second language. The more common of the two is to assume falsely that the learning style of the "average" Anglo child, as embodied in course syllabi, will snugly fit the Hispanic (or other) child if only it is translated into Spanish (or another "foreign" language). The other mistake is to assume falsely that most Spanish-speaking children share the same learning style, even if it is seen as differing from the Anglo. The trick—and it does not matter which ethnic group you happen to be teaching—is to be prepared to help a student learn concepts and skills in the best way for him or her. One can expect nearly as much variance within ethnic groups as between them.

In recent years, schools have attempted to select instructional materials that portray people and problems with which students of diverse backgrounds can identify. A student booklet developed by the Peace Corps in Ecuador entitled *Ñucanchi Mundoca Cashnami* (This Is How Our World Is) contains graphics of a Quichua woman nursing her child, of growing corn, of a carpenter at work, etc. It was made expressly for Quichua-speaking *otavaleño* children to learn about the world around them through images that really belong to their world. The book has been a success—among *otavaleños*. When the book was used with Quichua-speaking children in other locations in Ecuador, the pictures provoked laughter—the corn was all right, but the headdress of the woman looked weird and the long braid of the *otavaleño* carpenter struck them as even weirder. The teachers were faced with a dilemma: to publish different editions for each subcultural division of the Quichua world, or to broaden the child's world by including graphics of many different Quichua-speaking people at the expense of total relevance to any one regional group. The latter decision was made by the Peace Corps and the results are encouraging.

In the case of the excellent instructional materials developed by Ralph Robinette for reference only et al. (1973) in Florida, the decision was made to develop three versions of their materials: a Mexican version for the Southwest, a Cuban-Puerto Rican version for the East, and a version for use in areas such as Illinois where there is a mixture of Mexicans, Puerto Ricans, Cubans, and other Hispanic nationalities. The economics of the situation heavily weights the decision. No one in the United States, for example, is getting out versions of their materials that would allow a Guatemalan or Argentine child to relate immediately to them. However, to shrink the world that a child is exposed to unduly would duplicate the error of previous U.S. textbook writers and illustrators who thought the world was populated solely by WASPs. In deciding how culturally specific to make instructional materials, some compromise can be healthy. In fact, the only version of Robinette's materials that was published commercially was the multiethnic edition.

Knowledge of one's ethnic and/or national background serves to provide a sense of one's own continuity with the past and provides the feeling (some would say illusion) that the traditional ways are being retained, if only in memory. The Shuar Indians of Ecuador are doing just this in their bilingual programs through transcriptions of stories told by old shamans. This is especially important where an awareness of continuity is threatened by loss of language or by a sudden, drastic change in what one does or how one dresses. These threats can be alleviated. Knowledge of historic accomplishments can instill pride in one's background and give one a sense of cultural roots. Examples taken from contemporary life have an immediate appeal to youth; they are a call to action. For some students of mathematical aptitude, modern mathematicians like Einstein may be more effective models than ancient giants like Aristotle.

Rapid cultural change breeds alienation if the change is imposed by outside forces. It is common for cultures to experience a confrontation-depression-revival cycle as a result of contact with a culture perceived to be dominant. The whole cycle takes about one hundred years. Teachers can help combat the alienation people in the cycle experience by involving parents and students in as many educational decisions as is practical. Alienation is reduced when one thinks of oneself as choosing the "best" of the second culture; the potential for alienation increases when one adopts wholesale a different way of life in place of one's own.

Educators have just begun to scratch the surface in helping bicultural students to realize their creative potential. This potential will remain elusive as long as teachers, current curricula, and curricula developers remain monocultural in experience and outlook. Everyday role changes that we all experience manifest a subcultural flexibility inherent in our species. This daily shifting from one set of ground rules to another as we go from home to work to play can provide us important insights into the process of biculturation.

The critical integration in the process of becoming bicultural is a personal, psychological one that can be helped by teachers who themselves understand the process explicitly. At present, this understanding is intuitive and fragmentary.

Those Group Categories

My third son, Michael, was born in the United States, unlike his two brothers. When it came time to register his birth in Cook County some twenty years ago, I wanted to know what the options were: the father was white, the mother Hispanic of African ancestry. I talked on the phone to a lady, obviously black, who worked in the birth registration department. I explained the situation. "Well," she said, "there are a lot of choices." She read me a list of about twenty races and ethnicities. "Filipino has been quite popular," she told me. It made me feel good to know that the world's major cultural groupings were my son's oyster.

When my oldest son, David, was filling out the student college scholarship form, he came and asked me what race he was. We studied the responses noted on the form and quickly narrowed it down to four: white, black, Hispanic, and "other." This was not disconcerting to him, just amusing how some people categorize others.

When my second son, Alan, began looking for a summer job to help him continue his college studies, I offered my sympathies. I guessed summer jobs were hard to find since so many high school and college students were out there looking too. "Not for minority students," he said. And which minority are you? I asked. "Being Hispanic never got me anywhere," he said. "I'm putting down black."

Ah, to have the flexibility to glide back and forth among identities.

Many people—Americans married to people from other cultures—have told me that they were concerned that their spouses, after a few years in the United States, found themselves between countries. They weren't Zimbabweans anymore (you can't go back home) but they weren't fully accepted as Americans, either. They were without a country, without an identity, sympathized the American spouses. My sympathies, however, go to the *monocultural* spouse—it's so much more fun to be bicultural! Millions of bicultural people the world over are faced with the same situation. You can function in several cultures and yet develop a third culture that you can share with millions of other bicultural folk. Feeling sorry for multicultural people is like pitying people with high IQs because they don't share all the values of less gifted people.

I appreciate people who allow me to celebrate their ethnicity with them. On St. Patrick's Day, everyone is Irish. Half of the U.S. Native American population lives in urban areas where it often is not feasible to restrict ritual events to people of one tribal affiliation, so there are great inter-tribal events that have comfortably loose prerequisites for participation. A few years ago, an hour or so into dancing in a Pow Wow, I experienced viscerally something I had never felt in such a physical fashion before: profound, syncopated unity with an ancient tradition. And for this I am grateful to some Native Americans who opened a part of their culture to a "pinkskin." Many societies are as generous.

This chapter has focused on biculturalism, but in a world with ever permeable boundaries, multiculturalism often is a more accurate descriptor of a person's cultural conditioning. Multiculturalism is a complex collage of knowledge, affect, and skills. It conveys important advantages to oneself and to society. I am tempted to say that if you've got it, flaunt it.

Suggested Activities

1. Using Kraemer's outline for focusing on the cultural origins of ideas and behavior, give three examples from your own life of each of the seven items in Kraemer's outline.

2. Together with three or four of your colleagues, locate yourselves on a 10-point continuum: from strong sense of ego to strong sense of universe. How does this affect the way you make decisions in areas such as career and marriage?

3. Tape-record or write an ethnic history of yourself, starting as far back in your family tree as you can.

References Cited

Arnberg, Lenore. 1987. *Raising Children Bilingually: The Pre-School Years.* Avon, Eng.: Multilingual Matters. (Available from Taylor & Francis)

Brah, Artar. 1978. "South Asian Teenagers in Southall," *New Community* 6, 3: 197-206.

Brislin, Richard W. 1981. *Cross-Cultural Encounters: Face-to-Face Interaction.* New York: Pergamon.

Gorden, Raymond L. 1968. *Spanish Personal Names as Barriers to Communication between Latin Americans and North Americans.* Yellow Springs, OH: Antioch College.

Hall, Edward T. 1976. *Beyond Culture.* New York: Anchor Press/Doubleday.

Kraemer, Alfred J. 1973. *Development of a Cultural Self-Awareness Approach to Instruction in Intercultural Communication*. Alexandria, VA: Human Resources Research Organization.

LeCompte, Margaret D. and Anthony G. Dworkin. 1991. *Giving Up on School: Student Dropouts and Teacher Burnouts*. Newbury Park, CA: Corwin Press.

Lieberman, Morton A., Irvin D. Yalom, and Matthew B. Miles. 1973. *Encounter Groups: First Facts*. New York: Basic Books.

Louden, D. 1978. "Self-Esteem and Locus of Control." *New Community* 6, 3: 218-34.

Nash, Manning. 1989. *The Cauldron of Ethnicity in the Modern World*. Chicago: Univ. of Chicago Press.

Palomares, Uvaldo H., and Geraldine Ball. 1974. *Magic Circle: An Overview of the Human Development Program*. La Mesa, CA: Human Development Training Institute.

Pfeiffer, J. Williams, W. Jones, and John E. Jones, eds. 1969-1975. *A Handbook of Structured Experiences for Human Relations Training*. vols. I-V. Iowa City, IA: University Associates Press.

Robinette, Ralph F., et al. 1973. *SCDC Spanish Curricula Units*. Trenton, NJ: Crane.

Rushdie, Salman. 1991. *Grimus*. New York: Viking.

Saunders, Malcolm. 1982. *Multicultural Teaching*. New York: McGraw-Hill.

Seelye, H. Ned. 1979. "Individualizing and Sequencing Training for Inter-Cultural Communication," pp. 146-57 in J. D. Arendt, D. L. Lange, and P. J. Myers, eds., *Foreign Language Learning, Today and Tomorrow: Essays in Honor of Emma M. Birkmaier*. New York: Pergamon.

Seelye, H. Ned, and Jacqueline Howell Wasilewski. 1979a. "Historical Development of Multicultural Education," pp. 39-61, in M. D. Pusch, ed., *Multicultural Education: A Cross-Cultural Training Approach*. Yarmouth, ME: Intercultural Press.

Seelye, H. Ned, and Jacqueline Howell Wasilewski. 1979b. "Toward a Taxonomy of Coping Strategies Used in Multicultural Settings." Paper presented at the meetings of the Society for Intercultural Education, Training, and Research, Mexico City, March.

Seelye, H. Ned, and Jacqueline Howell Wasilewski. 1981. *Social Competency Development in Multicultural Children, Aged 6-13: Final Report of Exploratory Research on Hispanic-Background Children*. [EDRS: ED 209 363]

Simon, Sidney B., Leland W. How, and Howard Kirschenbau. 1973. *Composition for Personal Growth: Values Clarification through Writing*. New York: Hart.

Tiedt, Pamela L. 1991. *Multicultural Teaching: A Handbook of Activities, Information and Resources*. 3rd ed. Boston: Allyn and Bacon.

Wasilewski, Jacqueline Howell. 1982. Effective Coping and Adaptation in Multiple Cultural Environments in the United States by Native, Hispanic, Black, and Asian Americans. Ph.D. dissertation, University of Southern California, Los Angeles.

Watts, Alan W. 1969. *Psychotherapy East and West*. New York: Ballantine.

Weeks, William H., Paul B. Pedersen, and Richard W. Brislin, eds. 1977. *A Manual of Structured Experiences for Cross-Cultural Learning*. Yarmouth, ME: Intercultural Press.

15 A Global Village in Every Classroom*

This chapter has been coauthored by Jacqueline Howell Wasilewski

Intercultural educators can be on the cutting edge of a schoolwide curriculum that thrives on cultural differences. Diverse, culturally conditioned learning styles can be recognized and learning enhanced by curricular innovations. Students of every ethnic background can develop the whole range of skills and understandings that are possible in a multicultural curriculum, but the teaching and testing of ethnically distinct children requires special sensitivity to cross-cultural differences in learning styles. This chapter offers many suggestions for implementing the kind of education that will help students of all ethnic backgrounds acquire intercultural communication skills.

We live in a multicultural world. An education that helps students acquire intercultural communication skills is a necessity for everyone, not just for the culturally "deprived" or distinct, but for all children. We are all cultural beings. A contemporary author expresses this in engagingly simple language:

---

* An earlier version of this chapter appeared in Margaret D. Pusch, ed., *Multicultural Education: A Cross-Cultural Training Approach.* Yarmouth, ME: Intercultural Press, 1979.

I've often thought there ought to be a manual to hand
to little kids, telling them what kind of planet they're on,
why they don't fall off, how much time they've probably
got here, how to avoid poison ivy, and so on. . . . And one
thing I would really like to tell them about is cultural
relativity. I didn't learn until I was in college about all the
other cultures, and I should have learned that in the first
grade. A first grader should understand that his or her
culture isn't a rational invention; that there are thousands of
other cultures and they all work pretty well; that all cultures
function on faith rather than truth; that there are lots of
alternatives to our own society. Cultural relativity is
defensible and attractive. It's also a source of hope. It means
we don't have to continue this way if we don't like it.
(Vonnegut, 1974, p. 139)

To adopt the perspective of cultural relativity is to recognize
that different cultures provide different behavioral options for satisfying the universal physical and psychological needs of Homo sapiens.
This point was the main thrust of chapter 9. An understanding that
cultural conventions are created by people to serve ourselves lays
the foundation for a kind of cultural literacy, the acceptance of
humans as cultural beings. Aristotle said the human being is a political
animal, which is much the same thing.

Not only do we live in a multicultural world, we are inextricably
tied to lesser developed countries. John Maxwell Hamilton, in two
books, *Main Street America and the Third World* (1988) and *Entangling
Alliances: How the Third World Shapes Our Lives* (1990), persuasively
and entertainingly exposes some of the connections. In a chapter
entitled "The Long-Distance Call" (in the latter book), Hamilton
describes the booming business of offshore data processing for the
banks and businesses of industrial nations. (See also Meadows [1991]
for a general discussion of "the global citizen.")

One eye-opening book describes the epic effects that American
Indians, north and south, had on the world (Weatherford, 1988).
It highlights how the Indians of the Americas initiated or transformed
vast areas such as money capitalism, the birth of corporations,
industrialization, agricultural technology, food, and medicine.

It is a much smaller world than casual acquaintance would suggest. It has been said that any individual in the world is only five people away from someone we know. A commendable approach to closing the gap between monocultural teachers (of a variety of subjects) and their multicultural students is available in Grant and Sleeter (1989).

One eminent anthropologist (Hall, 1976) says that culture is dictatorial unless it is understood and examined. Just as a fish never discovers water as long as it remains immersed, so it is that only when we are called upon to function in another culture are our basic assumptions revealed. Until an alternate is known, the medium of life is an unexamined given.

Teachers can make a difference in the way we see ourselves. We can structure the curriculum so that students can examine the many ways cultural conditioning affects the quality of human thought and actions. This chapter provides teachers and teacher trainers with ideas culled from many sources to increase curricular relevancy in a multicultural word.

The Checkered History
of Multicultural Education

O. Henry, that master of surprise endings, is reported to have said that the Statue of Liberty "offered a cast-ironical welcome to immigrants." These immigrants—and all American groups save one are of immigrant background—have affected the evolution of American education. (And even the one exception—Native Americans—originated elsewhere.) Two books trace this effect. Weiss (1982) reconstructs the period between 1840 and 1940, and Gollnick (1980) focuses on the history of education from 1943 to the present. There have been many permutations ranging from education in ethnically specific private schools, through ethnic studies in public schools, to an emergent but beleaguered multicultural or global education.

Appel and Appel (in Weiss, 1982) observe, in an article entitled "The Huddled Masses and the Little Red School House," that in the early years of this century the United States changed from a largely rural, small-town, homogeneous, white Protestant society to an industrial, urban, heterogeneous, ethnically diverse, secular society. These authors argue that the "little red school house" had always been a compelling symbol for education in that former era. But as yet there are no compelling symbolic substitutes for the little red school house in our present heterogeneous society. Appel and Appel reason that educational symbols are needed to "provide rallying points for what is strong, appealing, and excellent with respect to the education of minorities." These symbols "would help groups with divergent views to articulate shared ideas and values better than the ubiquitous symbol of recent history, the school bus!" The authors added that it is as difficult to live up to unsymbolized aspirations as it is to live down harmful stereotypes.

Berrol (in Weiss, 1982) states that in no case was school the central or most important acculturative experience for the ethnic groups. Rather, it was the expanding economy of the turn of the century that offered a job to even the greenest newcomer that provided a locus where the newcomer could learn how the American system worked. Fellow workers, bosses, and union leaders taught them. They learned politics from district leaders and ward bosses. Ethnic newspapers made them aware of all kinds of social developments, including how to play baseball. Mothers and children learned from the streets, the former while doing marketing, the latter while playing with peers. Settlement houses also made a profound contribution to immigrant adaptation.

A pithy history of multicultural education between 1924 and 1941 (Montalto, in Weiss, 1982) examines the "tolerance" professed during that period toward people of diverse ethnicity. Montalto notes that along with this "tolerance" came an accompanying fear that to foster greater awareness of cultural distinctiveness would also foster "minority chauvinism." This fear, along with World War II, effectively killed the movement toward multicultural education. Montalto states that the "persistence of our divisions, whether they be ethnic, regional or class in nature, is still a disturbing reality, a reality with which we have only begun to deal." (See also Ogbu, 1978; Wasilewski and Seelye, 1979; Walsh, 1979; Davis, 1980; García, 1982; Gollnick and Chinn, 1986.)

Two acute pressures inhibit the growth of global education— a wartime mentality and economic hard times. Since teachers cannot directly affect either, what can we do to help prepare students for the real world—a multicultural planet? The answer is obvious: we can implement a curriculum that enthusiastically acknowledges the polycultural setting of our species.

Curriculum Adjustments

The adaptation of course content already in the curriculum is the most easily implementable way to achieve multicultural objectives. As one educator observes,

> every school subject, if taught truthfully and realistically, requires a plural culture perspective. Science, literature, the behavioral sciences, all must be freed from the monocultural ethnocentric focus that characterizes most standard course work. . . . We can no longer tolerate nor afford to permit a subject area to be called generally "music," "history," "psychology," "political science," when it is really a culture specific music, history, psychology, or political science. (Hilliard, 1975)

Course content can be made more global in two ways. First, teachers, with the help of specialists, can exploit opportunities to illustrate existing course objectives with examples that serve additionally to increase knowledge of other cultures. An example of this approach might be a math unit that rightly credits the Mayas of what is now Mexico and Guatemala with the world's first use of the zero, followed several centuries later by the Arabs.

A second approach involves developing new instructional objectives that allow multiculturally oriented units to fit into existing courses. Let's say, for example, that one such objective is to illustrate the interdependence of cultures. The math curriculum could cull many examples of cultural diffusion, such as why the invention of the zero by the Arabs (influenced by the East Indians) spread widely throughout the world, whereas the same invention by the Mayas did not diffuse widely.

Whichever of these two general approaches is employed to integrate cultural objectives into existing courses, curriculum development teams and teacher-training institutions can greatly facilitate the process by aiding the identification and production of relevant objectives for all courses at all levels. One should not forget the potential inherent in sports and the arts. The former provides grist for understanding the relation between competition and cooperation, whereas the latter affords opportunities to experience and express cultural symbolism.

Any attempt to get school curricula to better articulate the multicultural world in which we live obviously must involve classroom teachers directly. Teachers, as well as students, learn by doing, and teachers learn side by side with their students. (Since teachers usually learn more than students, try activities that put the students in the role of teacher.) When classroom learning openly acknowledges its two-way nature, new instructional styles often place less emphasis on verbal exposition (the resplendent teacher-talk that occupies so much classroom time) and on narrowly focused teacher-student interactions ("Johnny, why do the Masai drink camel blood?" "Gee, I don't know, Miss Stern, I left my book at my cousin's last night and couldn't . . ."). More emphasis is placed on getting students to learn from one another, on developing group activities, and on cultivating a zest for learning by showing that the teacher shares in the excitement of learning. McLaughlin's (1976) study of how to implement change stresses that "mutual adaptation is the best way to ensure that change efforts are not superficial, trivial, or transitory."

The type of preservice and inservice teacher training that can best help teachers prepare for working in a global curriculum, therefore, is characterized by an emphasis on exploration and experimentation, in which much learning is accomplished through demonstrations, modeling, simulations, and deduction (Gay, 1977). John Dewey stated it simply: We learn by doing.

Excellent guides for introducing global education into the classroom are available. Elder and Carr (1987) focus on the primary school. Ferguson (1987) focuses on the whole school system, as does Gollnick and Chinn (1986). Wurzel (1988) edits nineteen insightful articles on multicultural education.

There is some controversy revolving around the proper focus of global education. (How could there possibly be global education without animated differences of opinion?) One informed position taken by the National Council for the Social Studies (Banks et al.,

1976) argues that ethnic pluralism and not cultural pluralism should be the focus of curriculum reform. "Cultural pluralism suggests a type of education which deals with the cultural contributions of all groups within a society. Consequently, that concept is far too broad and inclusive to set forth effectively the boundaries of an area encompassing both the contributions of ethnic groups and the problems resulting from ethnic discrimination in American society." Still, it is not yet clear that this distinction is a necessary one once we begin dealing with specific intercultural skills on operational levels. This chapter will focus on the broader concept of cultural pluralism. (Chapter 14 included a discussion of ethnic identity versus national identity.)

An easy to read, nuts-and-bolts aid to classroom activities relevant to intercultural education is presented by Tiedt (1990). The author covers topics such as building positive self-concepts, determining the role of language (including various dialects of English), fostering intergroup relations, developing activities around a multicultural calendar, creating teacher materials, and identifying available resources. For other activities appropriate to a multicultural curriculum, see Baldwin and Wells (1980), Hicks (1981), Edith King (1980), Lurie (1982), Baker (1983), and Woyach and Remy (1989).

A brief look at the "hard core" curricula areas will generate additional ideas and illustrations of how adjustments can be effected to exploit the multicultural content implicit in all curricular areas.

Math, Science, and Technology

Mathematics is perhaps the only world language of the present day. The Western hegemony during the last several centuries has been largely due to the preeminence of science and technology: Spanish guns in Mexico and Peru in the sixteenth century and English steam engines 200 years later. (This latter development of industrial technology was perhaps ultimately dependent on the fact that sixteenth-century Britain ran out of firewood and turned to coal to heat the foggy isle, and this adoption of a new fuel set in motion the chain of events that culminated in the Industrial Revolution [Nef, 1977].)

Yet the development of a technological culture is fraught with ironies. The Arabic concept of zero, which resolved a mathematical problem that neither the Greeks nor the Romans had been able to solve and which facilitated the mathematical description of the world, sprang from the Hindu culture, which perceived the world quite differently from the Greek. The Greeks demarcated space, described and measured the dimensions of shapes and volumes, had their eye caught by the concrete, the discrete, the something. The spaces between "somethings" were seen as vacuums, as the opposite of "somethings." Hindu culture, on the other hand, saw the world as pattern on pattern, as cyclic and blending, and as kaleidoscopically transforming. Space was a manifesting field, the universe played hide-and-seek with itself, nothing was something, potentially anything (Dass, 1974).

The West puzzles over why the Chinese used gunpowder only for fireworks, while it took the West 1000 years to adopt the wheelbarrow from China. And speaking of wheels, the Mayas used wheels but only on toys (Casson et al., 1977).

Or a completely different tack might be taken by teachers to introduce "culture" into technical subjects. For instance, the principles of probability might be demonstrated through use of card games popular with different ethnic groups represented in the classroom (Gay, 1977).

There are excellent resources that put mathematics into international perspective: Ascher (1991), Joseph (1991), Schwartz (1990).

Social Sciences

Social studies is, of course, the "natural" arena for introducing multicultural content since virtually every social studies objective can be illustrated rather arbitrarily by examples from hundreds of cultures.

A good source of material for social problems that typically are faced by ethnic groups is the ethnic press. Sharon Murphy (1974) lists black, Chicano, and Native American newspapers (186 publications for Native Americans alone). In an award-winning article, Seelye and Day (1971) illustrate how to go about developing student activities from newspaper sources; the examples are based on Spanish-language newspapers.

An excellent text on minority relations in the United States is available in Vander Zanden (1983). Wallace (1990) discloses the interrelatedness of the world's economic systems.

Language and Literature

Language can serve as the core curriculum of a multicultural school. Language is, of course, a major vehicle for the transmission of culture. Learning the cultural roots of a language is essential for meaningful fluency. The preceding chapters of this book have provided innumerable exercises and activities for revealing the patterns of culture while learning a second (or third) language.

A plural society is an intercultural society, a society that effectively communicates across cultural boundaries. A crucial skill in such a society is the ability to be expressive and articulate, whether on behalf of oneself or one's group (Freire, 1974). The clearest form of communication usually is accomplished through language.

In mainstream U.S. society, the value placed on the ability to manipulate language in many of its forms, oral and written, has a great deal to do with student achievement, which, in turn, affects subsequent success in the workplace (Massad, 1972; Goodenough, 1976). Further, researchers generally believe that positive self-concept can best be nurtured in an environment that respectfully accepts a child's first culture (e.g., Seelye and Wasilewski, 1981). Of course, inherent in this situation there may be a conflict: What if a child's first culture does not value expressive, articulate children?

In U.S. society, even a child from a cultural background that does not value articulation and expressiveness will have to be articulate and expressive enough to communicate that very characteristic of his or her group. In fact, a curriculum focus on cross-cultural communication patterns may contribute to the child's ability to cope on his or her own terms, so that he or she can "understand himself and his behavior in a social context and learn to make wise choices with which he can live" (Ammons, 1969).

The techniques teachers develop to help individual students learn a pattern of responses appropriate to various cultural contexts are likely to be quite idiosyncratic. Self-concept cannot be evaluated independently of the standard used: the standard of the mainstream culture, of the child's first culture, or of the children themselves (Saville-Troike, 1973). Llabre, Ware, and Newell (1977) indicate that even the structures underlying the self-concept of children are not the same across gender and ethnic groups.

It is in using language to communicate that children learn a language well, whether it is their first, second, or third language (Paulston, 1974), especially if what they are communicating is "purposeful and significant" to them. One student in a bilingual program that encouraged writing about things of deep significance to the students themselves said, "This is the first time that anybody in a course like this ever asked me to tell them what I know" (Rivers, 1975).

Students are, above all else, interested in themselves and their friends. Every student, no matter what his or her level of ability, is an expert in at least one thing, their own feelings. An intriguing challenge for older students in creative writing courses lies in developing ethnic identity in a world where even the most disparate of cultures are coming into daily contact. Such courses can help students develop the ability to articulate the difficulties and opportunities they may experience in living on cultural boundaries.

The ability to enter a literary world may be akin to the ability to enter another culture. In both, one suspends "usual" conventions to accept a different set of premises. The ways in which a novelist builds his literary world, the techniques of literary analysis, the use of literature by anthropologists as a social science tool: these are topics that can stimulate fruitful classroom discussion. A number of books can help the teacher to enrich his or her students by illustrating literary responses to life's dramas (e.g., Goonetilleke, 1977; Lewis and Jungman, 1986).

In a seminal anthology written by a broad range of specialists, Albrecht, Barnett, and Griff (1970) discuss art and literature from many perspectives. The authors examine many issues: forms and styles, socialization and careers, social position and roles, distribution and reward systems, tastemakers and publics, and the methodology, history, and theory of analyzing art and literature.

In operation, a classroom activity to assist student entry into a literary world may look like this: The students prepare two products:

(1) an essay, drama, song, or painting on the major themes of a recently read novel (e.g., the individual as a stranger, solitude, lack of known parentage or ancestry); and (2) a personal statement, through prose, poetry, visual, impression, or analysis of one's own background. Both products can be shared with the class at large and discussed. The final class product would be a "bound" edition of the students' work, along with photographs and "reviews" of the nonprint products. The volume can also include notes of some points made by classmates. One group of students named their book "The I I Know."

After World War II, a girl of Chinese immigrant parents entered public elementary school in Stockton, California. Today she teaches college English. One of her books, *The Woman Warrior: Memoirs of a Girlhood among Ghosts* (Kingston, 1976) won the National Book Critics Award for the best book of nonfiction published that year. This book is a chronicle of Maxine Hong Kingston's own particular experiences growing up on the Chinese-American cultural boundary and of her continued attempts to find an American song that can be accompanied by Chinese instruments. The "ghosts" of the title are not ancestral memories of China; rather, they refer to anyone who is not Chinese. You see, only the Han people are real. "You must not tell anyone," my mother said, "what I am about to tell you . . . "

Classroom activities such as a personal statement of one's background may help future "warriors" to understand in themselves a process that too often ends dialogue rather than begins it.

New Courses

The approaches to achieving the multicultural objectives mentioned above are not the only ways to add global perspectives to the curriculum. Sometimes secondary schools are tempted to add a new course (universities practically always see this as the solution) to achieve objectives not already being addressed.

An example of a new course developed by classroom teachers is Dimitriou's (1977) "Suburban Ethnicity: A Case Study of the American-Greek Experience in Southern California," a teaching and resource manual for an intercultural studies curriculum developed ιυι junior and senior high school students at Palos Verdes High School, Palos Verdes Estates, California. It was developed to reveal the Greek immigrant experience in southern California and includes slide and tape materials. This general format can serve teachers as a model for developing materials about other ethnic groups in either English or the ethnic language. Activities include

1. Student preparation of three-generation family trees

2. An inquiry into ethnic characteristics and ethnic stereotyping, both positive and negative, which begins with each student listing five positive and five negative stereotypes for his or her ethnic group (or, for the student who is multiethnic, the group he or she selects to study)

3. An introduction to sociological and anthropological field research by having each student conduct interviews of (a) an older acquaintance or relative with a strong ethnic background; (b) a second-generation American; and (c) a third-generation "ethnic"

4. Visits to a church, mosque, Buddhist temple, or synagogue to be reported on orally or in writing by responding to a predeveloped list of study questions

5. An investigation of ethnic dances as a means of exploring different worlds (e.g., what do the dance configurations tell about the values of the culture?)

6. Preparation of an ethnic cookbook (a particularly savory assignment in multiethnic classes) that can be handed out or sold to the rest of the school (the dishes can be prepared by volunteers and eaten by the entire school and accompanied by any folk songs and dances that have been learned)

Such activities create opportunities in which evaluation techniques other than written examinations can be employed: for example, oral interviews, audio recordings of student performances, peer evaluations, diaries, and "demonstration" evaluations.

An example of a "demonstration" activity is a student production of a play based on the ethnic experience (see Dimitriou, 1977; Gay, 1977). A multiethnic sociodrama of *Manchild in the Promised Land, Down These Mean Streets*, "I Am Woman," "I Am Joaquin," *An*

American Dilemma, or "It Bees That Way" are some specific instances of a demonstration activity. These can give evidence of ability to understand ethnic cultures and experiences, to select and organize a variety of materials, to present different ethnic perspectives on the same issues, and to use knowledge gained from many disciplines, multimedia techniques, and multiethnic perspectives to develop an idea, issue, or event into a coherent message.

Field Experiences

The dramatic break in routine afforded by field trips can be used to advantage by teachers who avoid the common pitfalls that tend to trivialize this type of academic experience. Besides visits to things of interests, visits to people are exciting when students are prepared for the event ahead of time. Simply bringing people into contact is not enough. The history of education in U.S. overseas dependent schools is a case in point. Though these schools are often, geographically speaking, right in the middle of a foreign culture, the curricula barely reflect this. Almost no use is made of the fact that Germany, Spain, or Japan is quite literally right outside the school door. Frequently, classes in the host language are not even offered.

For field experiences to be effective, it helps to have formed careful liaison between the schools and the communities by people comfortable working outside their own ethnic and social class enclaves. Charles Taylor (1989) explains how to sponsor a minority cultural retreat.

Thinking Cross-Culturally

Lurking in the shadows of consciousness is the "hidden curriculum," the values, assumptions, and managerial techniques used in schools to implement the formal program. It has many origins.

More and more, the task of teaching is to discover ways to elicit the behaviors we are interested in developing. Cole et al. (1971) and Cole and Scribner (1974) show unequivocally that cognition is not culture-free, that it is not a trait, but a process, "an adaptive instrument suited to the demands of an environment as seen by the subject." Finding out which environmental demands elicit which behaviors can generate "positive statements relating behavior to occasions" (Glick, 1969). Many of the most surprising of these "statements" have originated with the hapless experiences of teachers and researchers as they attempt to test knowledge and skills cross-culturally.

One interesting approach to measuring cognition was developed when a given test did not elicit the desired performance. The test was changed until it fit the social situation in which the skills to be tested were usually exhibited so that the desired performance could be elicited. Seemingly minor variations in contextual variables sometimes affect even the kinds of tasks that "all rational people" would perform reasonably.

> [W]e wanted to use everyday objects as things to sort. Accordingly, we chose something that was highly familiar to our African subjects—beer bottles of various heights and colors. . . . Our African subjects, though familiar with these objects and their differences, refused to sub-classify them—all bottles were heaped in a single category. We had made the mistake of using empty bottles, which were clearly garbage and nothing else. Preliminary observations with filled bottles show that these can be classified. (Glick, 1974)

The performance measures were not so much related to the ability to classify as to the culturally conditioned constraints of reasonableness that would allow the subjects to use the classification to be tested.

There have been many fascinating studies done in cross-cultural settings that have yielded interesting hypotheses.

Two famous theories of cognition have received extensive cross-cultural treatment, Piaget's theory of cognitive development and Witkin's theory of cognitive style. The former theory stresses universal stages of development, whereas the latter stresses differences in style. Both literatures are thoroughly reviewed in Cole and Scribner (1974) and in Scribner and Cole (1981). Extensive reviews of Piagetian research in cross-cultural areas are available in Dasen (1972) and Goodnow (1969), and of cognitive style research as it applies to cross-cultural areas in Dawson (1967) and Berry (1966).

Cole and Scribner (1974) extensively review the research literature on the interrelationships between culture, cognition, language, perception, conceptual processes, learning, memory, and problem-solving. In almost every area of research reviewed, the research subjects have been shown to be sensitive to a whole host of factors connected with the research problem: the specific demands of the task; the materials used in the performance of the task; the way the problem is worded; what responses are requested. Because little attention has been paid to these factors, researchers have, according to Cole and Scribner, "altogether neglected motivational, attitudinal, and other factors" in their studies of how people think.

Witkin et al. (1977), in an article on the educational implications of field-dependent and field-independent cognitive styles, caution "against using the relations now found to exist between cognitive style and . . . performance to perpetuate a self-fulfilling prophecy." (In essence, a field-dependent person is one who is especially sensitive to the characteristics and desires of those with whom he or she must interact; a field-independent person is more self-actualized and ego-centered, and, therefore, more independent of environmental concerns.)

Research in cross-cultural contexts has generated questions about just how to respond to differences in cognitive style. U.S. school systems are thought to favor field-independent cognitive mode with positive reward accruing to self-seeking, aggressive students who are able to work independently. Yet most hunting-gathering peoples—the epitome of field-independence—have been among the worst academic performers in the learning environments we provide. The sophisticated study by Cole and Means (1981) demonstrates how cognitive differences have led to prejudicial interpretations that result in mental differences being perceived as mental defects.

Ramírez and Castañeda (1974) point out that just because a child has a Hispanic name does not mean that his or her preferred cognitive style is field-dependent. There is great diversity in the Hispanic community; the child's early environment may be traditional, dualistic, or atraditional.

Cole and Scribner stress the importance of assuming nothing when teaching children from another culture. A test of simple inference in which an apparatus consisted of a key, a locked box with three compartments, and a piece of candy (the goal) presented all sorts of difficulties for the subjects in their study. In different permutations of this experiment, it became apparent that

> the difficulty that young children and tribal Liberians experience with our simple inference task is that they do not know how to begin. For some reason, the process involved in obtaining a key from the side panel of the original apparatus interferes with later phases of the response sequence. Cultural differences seem in this case to reside in the kinds of initial situations that promote a good beginning for problem solution, not in the ability to link separately learned elements in order to solve the problem. (Cole and Scribner, 1974)

Preferred cognitive style may be related to which hemisphere of the brain is dominant in mental operations, the left hemisphere for field-independence, the right hemisphere for field-dependence. According to this theory, verbal-analytical processes are carried out in the left hemisphere, and nonverbal, spatial skills are right-brained phenomena. Cross-cultural research on brain-damaged individuals has revealed some interesting wrinkles in this sharply dichotomous picture, however. Frenchmen suffering from aphasia lose their written language if damage occurs to the left hemisphere, their spoken language if the damage is more to the right. Japanese aphasics, on the other hand, lose their spoken language if damage is more to the left, their written language if the damage is more to the right. It is also interesting to note that dyslexic Japanese children are usually dyslexic in the Katakana alphabet (the phonetic alphabet), and almost never in Kanji (the idiographic alphabet) (Samples, 1977). What does this all mean in terms of our conventional dichotomies about the verbal and the nonverbal, about alphabets and art? It means that we still have a lot to learn.

Research indicates that humans have extraordinary powers of recovery and that even "the mind may have some of the qualities of an elastic surface, easily deformed by shearing forces, but able to rebound when those forces are removed" (Kagan, 1978).

So many aspects of human personality that used to be considered as fairly stable "traits" now appear to be learned behaviors. For instance, altruism, generosity, personal consideration, and sharing are all prosocial behaviors that are learned (Mussen and Eisenberg-Berg, 1977). Different cultures and different child-rearing practices help or hinder to varying degrees the development of these behaviors. However, because prosocial behavior is learned, it can also be modified. And more and more we are seeing how different environments elicit different behaviors. Even a value as universal as ethnocentrism is context-bound (Brewer, 1977).

The fruitfulness of perceiving cognition as an adaptive process responsive to context, and the desirability of concentrating on what people can do rather than on what they cannot do, are powerfully demonstrated by Fraiberg's (1977) book, *Insights from the Blind: Comparative Studies of Sighted and Blind Infants.* Fraiberg noted that despite the absence of communicative expression in the faces of blind children, they do convey expression—in their hands. "The hands give meaning to emotional experience," Fraiberg says of blind children. Sighted children get so locked into reading faces that they miss the expressiveness of the blind. (When Fraiberg showed film clips to Piaget of blind Robbie adaptively pursuing a sound-making toy to the place where it was "lost," thereby demonstrating that he had reached the level of "object permanence," Piaget threw his beret in the air and cheered.) Two other books relevant to the culture of the blind are Lucas (1989) and Padden and Humphries (1988).

This necessity of discovering ways of enabling children to grow is also exemplified in the work of Maria Montessori, who provides a model for those instances where "a genuine cultural difference can interfere with academic process" (Carlson, 1976). Her system of education, developed for Roman slum children at the turn of the century, assumes no previous knowledge, even of basic concepts. Everything is taught from scratch in its most concrete form, from what is round to how you hang up your coat. This formal learning occurs in a highly structured environment in which the hidden curriculum also reinforces the cognitive patterns (problem solving, independence of action, responsibility) being developed in the formal part of the curriculum. (It is interesting to note in view of our present difficulty in teaching people to read, that Montessori believed in teaching children to write before they learned to read. Expressive functions first!)

The multicultural child begins life less able than the monocultural child to indulge in "thinking as usual" because already he or she is the inheritor of a cultural pattern that provides alternative "recipes" for "typical solutions for typical problems available for typical actors" (Schutz, 1964). Nothing is given. Everything must be negotiated. Commonalities must be established. In a multicultural context a child is always learning new responses to old stimuli, old responses to new stimuli, and totally new stimulus-response patterns. The child is always engaged in trying to figure out when to generalize a response across situations and when to contextualize responses—that is, how to behave appropriately in different contexts. This enriching experience is, in a multicultural curriculum, available to "ethnics" and mainstream students alike.

The optimum environment for doing all this effectively is one that is characterized by a high tolerance for flexibility, ambiguity, and paradox. Most cultural environments are not so constituted, since one of the main functions of culture thus far in human history has been to provide those nice comfortable "recipes" for action within the boundaries prescribed.

Once again, the importance of situation-specific variables cannot be emphasized enough. The familiar nursery school activity of having children mix flour and water to make paste fails completely when Native American children refuse to make the paste because flour is food and one does not play with food (Rivlin, 1977). A teacher unfamiliar with this prohibition would have great difficulty "extracting" this piece of cultural information from these students, especially early in the school year, because of the additional social custom of keeping silent initially with unfamiliar people in unfamiliar situations (Saville-Troike, 1978).

An extended discussion of student rights within a multicultural classroom appears in García (1982). Several points made by García are particularly salient: (1) Students must know what their rights are before they can practice them; (2) majority rule should not quell individual student rights; (3) students have the right to be different; and (4) students have the right to a positive self-concept.

Some students may feel pressure to conform because of an American penchant for decision making. Perhaps one reason for the emphasis on making decisions and choices in American society is the tension arising from a dominant cultural tradition that assumes that, once all the information is in and all the data processed, one is able to choose the one right answer. (Black is black and white's right.) However, India, another culturally diverse society, presents us with a contrasting dominant pattern, one with an opposite assumption: that it is not necessary to make choices. "The Westerner's choice is to make choices; the Hindu's is to lose his choosing self" (Gilliat, 1972). And to do that the Indian has developed a "habit of ignoring the obvious [and] making a detour to preserve his calm" (Theroux, 1975).

So, in the words of Maxine Hong Kingston, we are left with the problem of how we can learn "to make [our] mind large, as the universe is large, so that there is room for paradoxes" (Kingston, 1976). Peter Adler (1976) says that a multicultural style can evolve when an individual is capable of negotiating the conflicts and tensions inherent in cross-cultural contacts. This ability to negotiate is greatly facilitated in pluralistic societies with their many "alternatives and equivalent ways of reaching the top" (King, 1975).

Children who are multicultural can realize that they are heirs to a tradition that offers the possibility of seeing the world whole. They will perhaps have the chance to build a future that allows for more complex kinds of wholeness. At present the people who are engaged in this task are a growing community of poets, writers, dancers, scientists, teachers, lawyers, scholars, philosophers, entrepreneurs, students, and citizens for whom the old boundaries are irrelevant.

Ackermann (1976) believes that perhaps the challenge of our time is "helping man to relate to unknown man." Intercultural skill is thus the ability to function as a stranger and to interact with strangers (Bochner, 1973; Schutz, 1964).

In this encounter with strangeness, the stranger tries to define the new fact; tries to catch its meaning; and then begins to transform it little by little so that the strange fact is compatible and consistent with all his or her other facts. Experience has been enlarged and adjusted.

We know very little about this relating to strangers. There are tribes today in the Amazon basin who kill strangers on sight because the concept of a stranger who is also a human being is lacking. There has been little research into the conditions needed for creating trust among strangers. The same holds true for the development of cultural perceptions, that is, the way in which people differentiate the important from the unimportant patterns in a strange culture. For instance, in U.S. society use of the left hand is purely idiosyncratic; individuals just happen to be born right- or left-handed. In Muslim culture, however, what one does with which hand is a matter of formal culture with severe consequences if one transgresses the rules. (The left hand is used for personal hygiene; therefore it is considered unfit to use for eating, for example.) How does one learn what is a "rule" and what is not and in which cases to apply the rule? In a given social situation, an American might act as an individual whereas a Japanese might act in terms of his role, or vice-versa. Chapter 14 described how some of these confusions can be dealt with effectively.

Connected with multiculturalism but different from it is the question of intercultural skill. One may grow up multicultural in the sense that if one's parents belonged to two different cultural groups one may have learned to function in both. However, unless one has generalized those processes that enable one to participate effectively in two cultures and applied them to learning how to interact with cultures as yet unknown, one could conceivably tolerate the dissonances that are "all in the family," so to speak, but not be so tolerant of those that appear when interacting with "strange" cultures.

Alternate Pedagogies

There are some really different—some would say bizarre—approaches to learning that can be explored in adventuresome, globally oriented classrooms.

One method of broadening the range of learning modes is to develop instructional materials that are descriptive rather than prescriptive, that encourage students to cull structures from experience rather than imposing structures upon experience (Samples, 1977). A simple example of such strategies is to allow symbolic-visual expression if a student falters with symbolic-abstract expression, to encourage him or her to paint, draw, or sculpt his or her response. Later the student would be encouraged to express the idea through speech or writing. (The opposite journey from symbolic-abstract to symbolic-visual expression would be equally interesting for those with an analytic preference.)

Pedagogies that are truly alternatives to the "symbolic-abstract mode" that Samples among others finds prevalent in most formal school systems are currently being discovered or, in many cases, rediscovered. *The Centering Book: Awareness Activities for Children, Parents and Teachers* (Hendricks and Wills, 1975), for example, suggests activities from outside the Western logical linear cognitive tradition. These activities may introduce yoga, Zen, the dream work of the Senoi people of the Central Malay Peninsula, or the Muslim Sufi tradition. Hendricks and Wills have produced an almost programed text with chapters on basic centering, relaxing the mind, expanding perception, relaxing the body, working with dreams, imagery, stretching the body, movement and dance, and storytelling. It is essentially an elementary text for what has come to be called "transpersonal education." It seeks a synthesis in education of intellect and intuition, mind and body, fact and feeling.

Houston and Master's (1973) book, *Mind Games*, presents specific alternative methods of teaching and learning. For instance, it suggests ways to teach mathematics rhythmically, as patterns of sound and movement rather than as symbolic-abstract patterns: clapping, tah-the-tah-the-tah, instead of saying, "Five and five are ten." This method recognizes that mathematical and musical skills often coincide, but opts to approach this linked universe through the music rather than through the geometry of the spheres. Edward Hall (1983) argues that rhythm is the fundamental ingredient of all human interaction. Rhythm, like love and comedy, is a matter of timing. When people feel uncomfortable in an interaction it may be, according to Hall, because their cultural rhythmic styles are different. Learning to communicate across cultures involves developing the appropriate cultural rhythms.

Perhaps the best description of a truly alternative pedagogy in a modern setting (from a U.S. perspective) appears in Rohlen (1974, 1978) in which the author describes the methods of "spiritual education" (*Seishin Kyoiku*) that form part of the corporate training programs for many medium and large Japanese companies. In the course of this training, young executives run marathons, meditate, and do unpaid labor.

Multicultural Environments

What are the characteristics of those settings that elicit multicultural behavior and thereby facilitate the acquisition of intercultural communication skills? How are these settings created in a school?

Environments that engender intercultural skills provide an atmosphere in which children can expand their repertoire of behaviors. No child is forced into an either/or position, where, for instance, he or she must give up speaking Pidgin in order to speak English. Rather, the student is encouraged to use all behaviors appropriately. It is an environment that values uniqueness and idiosyncrasy and facilitates the individual's interaction with the world at large. The microcosm of the school becomes attuned to the community in which it exists.

What does good teaching in a multicultural context look like? Two highly idiosyncratic New Zealand teachers provide possibilities—Silvia Ashton-Warner, who taught in Maori schools for twenty-four years, and Elwyn Richardson, who took a job as schoolmaster in a mixed Maori/European school in an isolated rural area when he could not find a job as a marine biologist. Neither had special funding, just necessities and time.

Sylvia Ashton-Warner (1963) developed an approach based on the simple notion that children learn to read and write more readily from materials affectively important to themselves, preferably those they have written themselves. In Ashton-Warner's school it all began in kindergarten. When each child arrived in class the child would tell the teacher which word he or she would like to learn. The word was written on two cards, one to keep at school and one to carry around all day, take home, and learn. Next morning the words kept at school were dumped onto the floor. Everyone scrambled for their own word. Then the children paired off and taught each other their words. Eventually, the words became sentences and the sentences stories, and the children learned to read by reading their own and each other's stories.

Meanwhile, in Oruaiti School, a square wooden room built in 1889, roofed with red-painted corrugated iron, gable-ended, weatherboarded, and with three windows, Elwyn Richardson was creating a community of artists and scientists out of rural Maori and European schoolchildren, children whose only "academic" resource at home was the Bible. They set about learning by collecting specimens—words, seashells, different spellings, new thoughts—gradually sorting out observations, discarding stock responses, testing generalizations, and evaluating their inventions over long periods.

> The primary demand on the child was that he should think through exactly what he observed, felt, or believed. . . . [A] great deal of careful training went into eliminating the merely stock response and the expected answer. But combined with this demand for . . . a personal view, and of course necessary to it, was the willing acceptance of idiosyncrasy and the affectionate acceptance of the strengths and limitations of each member of the group. (Richardson, 1964)

There are other schools described in the literature that seem to be providing promising environments for diversity. Frances Sussna's multicultural school in San Francisco uses bicultural teachers to assist in the teaching of specialized knowledge and skills in a context where both the accomplishments of one's own group and interaction with other groups are stressed. The program thus fosters individual self-confidence and situations of meaningful intergroup contact. In the mornings the students interact in mixed groups to learn basic skills, and in the afternoons they meet in their ethnic groups for history and language. When each group has a holiday, the others are invited to help celebrate it. Stress is on pride in one's own heritage and respect for the heritage of other groups. The aim is to stimulate interaction among groups who feel themselves to be equal (D. Lewis, 1976).

There is a public school in Urbana, Illinois, the Martin Luther King School, in which half the students speak one of twenty-one different languages (Bouton, 1975). One striking point about this school is that every person on the staff, from the principal to the janitor, is culturally "literate." They all have intercultural skills. On one occasion, for example, the janitor was able to take care of an East Indian boy who in his first week at school had an attack of diarrhea on the playground. The janitor handled the situation with such sensitivity that the boy's considerable embarrassment was greatly alleviated despite a language barrier. In another case, aides were able to help a new Japanese student understand that the boy who had hit her had done so accidentally. She thought she had been attacked.

Longstreet (1978) gives teachers the tools for doing their own observational action research on the effect of ethnicity on their students' scholastic experience. She includes sample profiles and checklists that critically define the impact of ethnicity on verbal and nonverbal communication, on intellectual styles, and on social value patterns. Renwick (1980) provides an extensive and practical elaboration of how to evaluate multicultural education programs.

Duane Campbell (1980) suggests that teachers develop their own curriculum packages and gives examples based on an inquiry approach to learning. One package, for example, deals with the dynamics of values and social action.

Insights into multicultural education continue to be published at a rapid rate: For example, Banks (1988), Bennett (1990), Boulding (1988), Damen (1987), Donaldson (1987), Fradd (1989), Heltshe (1991), Hernández (1989), Hulmes (1989), Lynch (1986, 1989), Matiella (1990), Ramsay (1987, 1989), Robinson (1985), Ryan (1989), Scarcella (1990), and Tiedt (1990).

In a study of classroom integration, Slavins (1979) makes the startling observation that there was only one strategy that led to improved interpersonal relations and increased academic performance, measured by more time-on-task behavior—the assigning of interracial partners on schoolwork teams. This strategy was found to be much more effective than workshops, biracial student advisory committees, minority history courses, or multiethnic texts.

A study of effective teachers of Eskimo and Indian students (Kleinfeld, 1975) identified two teacher factors that were associated with student success: the establishment by the teacher of an atmosphere of emotional warmth that encouraged students to develop personalized relationships; and teacher demand for high quality academic work.

If there is an overriding theme to the examples of successful implementation of multicultural education cited in this chapter, it is that in each case the reality of where the children are at that particular time is being responded to: It is no good wishing they were someplace else. Adventurous teachers are designing a creative curriculum that fits the multicultural world in which we live.

Suggested Activities

1. Take a basal text in a subject area such as math or science (or any curriculum area of special interest to you) and identify ten locations where a relevant multicultural mini-unit could be developed.
2. Develop one of the multicultural mini-units you identified above.
3. Briefly sketch out a plan to incorporate Seishin Kyoiku methods in a course you teach or plan to teach; or, if you are not planning to teach, apply them to some other job-related area.
4. Pick a book from among those referred to in this chapter, read it, and report on it.

References Cited

Ackermann, Jean Marie. 1976. "Skill Training for Foreign Assignment: The Reluctant U.S. Case," pp. 298-306 in Larry A. Samovar and Richard E. Porter, eds., *Intercultural Communication: A Reader*. Belmont, CA: Wadsworth.

Adler, Peter S. 1976. "Beyond Cultural Identity: Reflections on Cultural and Multicultural Man," pp. 362-80 in Larry A. Samovar and Richard E. Porter, eds., *Intercultural Communication: A Reader*. Belmont, CA: Wadsworth.

Albrecht, Milton C., James H. Barnett, and Mason Griff, eds. 1970. *The Sociology of Art and Literature: A Reader*. New York: Praeger.

Ammons, Margaret. 1969. "Communication: A Curriculum Focus," in Alexander Frazier, ed., *A Curriculum for Children*. Washington: National Education Association, Association for Supervision and Curriculum Development.

Appel, John J., and Selma Appel. 1982. "The Huddled Masses and the Little Red Schoolhouse," pp. 17–30 in Bernard J. Weiss, ed., *American Education and the European Immigrant, 1840–1940*. Urbana: Univ. of Illinois Press.

Ascher, Marcia. 1991. *Ethnomathematics: A Multicultural View of Mathematical Ideas*. Pacific Grove, CA: Brooks/Cole.

Ashton-Warner, Sylvia. 1963. *Teacher*. New York: Bantam.

Baker, Gwendolyn C. 1983. *Planning and Organizing for Multicultural Instruction*. Reading, MA: Addison-Wesley.

Baldwin, J., and H. Wells. 1980. *Active Tutorial Work, Books 1 to 4*. London: Basil Blackwell.

Banks, James A., ed. 1973. *Teaching Ethnic Studies*. Washington: National Council of the Social Studies.

Banks, James A. 1988. *Multiethnic Education: Theory and Practice*. 2d ed. Needham, MA: Allyn & Bacon.

Banks, James A., Carlos E. Cortés, Geneva Gay, Ricardo L. García, and Anna S. Ochoa. 1976. *Curriculum Guidelines for the Social Studies*. Arlington, VA: National Council for the Social Studies.

Baptiste, H. Prentice, Jr., Mira L. Baptiste, and Donna M. Gollnick. 1980. *Multicultural Teacher Education*. Washington: Commission on Multicultural Education, American Association of Colleges for Teacher Education.

Bennett, Christine I. 1990. *Comprehensive Multicultural Education*. Boston: Allyn & Bacon.

Berrol, Selma. 1982. "Public Schools and Immigrants: The New York City Experience," pp. 31–43 in Bernard J. Weiss, ed., *American Education and the European Immigrant, 1840–1940*. Urbana: Univ. of Illinois Press.

Berry, J. W. 1966. "Temme and Eskimo Perceptual Skills." *International Journal of Psychology* 1, 3: 207-29.

Bochner, S. 1973. "The Mediating Man and Cultural Diversity." *Topics in Culture Learning* 1: 23-27.

Boulding, Elise. 1988. *Building a Global Civic Culture*. New York: Columbia Univ. Teachers College.

Bouton, Lawrence F. 1975. "Meeting the Needs of Children with Diverse Linguistic and Ethnic Backgrounds." *Foreign Language Annals* 8, 4 (Dec.): 306-16.

Brewer, Marilynn B. 1977. "Perceptual Processes in Cross-Cultural Interaction," pp. 22-31 in D. S. Hoopes, P. B. Pederson, and G. W. Renwick, eds., *Overview of Intercultural Education, Training and Research*. Vol. I, *Theory*. Yarmouth, ME: Intercultural Press.

Brewer, Marilynn B., and Donald T. Campbell. 1976. *Ethnocentrism and Intergroup Attitudes: East African Evidence*. New York: Wiley.

Campbell, Duane E. 1980. *Education for a Democratic Society*. Cambridge, MA: Schenkman.

Carlson, Paul E. 1976. "Toward a Definition of Local Level Multicultural Education." *Anthropology and Education Quarterly* 7, 4 (Nov.): 26-30.

Casson, Lionel, Robert Claiborne, Brian M. Fagan, and Walter Karp. 1977. *Mysteries of the Past*. Marion, OH: American Heritage Books.

Cole, Michael, John Gay, Joseph A. Glick, and Donald W. Sharp. 1971. *The Cultural Context of Learning and Thinking: An Exploration in Experimental Anthropology.* New York: Basic Books.

Cole, Michael, and Barbara Means. 1981. *Comparative Studies of How People Think: An Introduction.* Cambridge, MA: Harvard Univ. Press.

Cole, Michael, and Sylvia Scribner. 1974. *Culture and Thought: A Psychological Introduction.* New York: Wiley.

Coles, Robert. 1967. *Children of Crisis.* Vol. 1, *A Study in Courage and Fear.* Boston: Little, Brown.

Coles, Robert. 1971a. *Children of Crisis.* Vol. 2, *The South Goes North.* Boston: Little, Brown.

Coles, Robert. 1971b. *Children of Crisis.* Vol. 3, *Migrants, Sharecroppers, Mountaineers.* Boston: Little, Brown.

Coles, Robert. 1977. *Children of Crisis.* Vol. 4, *Eskimos, Chicanos and Indians.* Boston: Little, Brown.

Damen, Louise. 1987. *Culture Learning: The Fifth Dimension in the Language Classroom.* Reading, MA: Addison-Wesley.

Dasen, P. R. 1972. "Cross-Cultural Piagetian Research: A Summary." *Journal of Cross-Cultural Psychology* 3: 23-29.

Dass, Ram. 1974. *The Only Dance There Is.* Garden City, NY: Anchor.

Davis, Renee. 1980. *Cultural Pluralism as a Social Imperative in Education.* New York: Vantage.

Dawson, J. L. M. 1967. "Cultural and Physiological Influences upon Spatial-Perceptual Processes in West Africa, Part 1." *International Journal of Psychology* 2: 115-28.

Dimitriou, James F. 1977. "Suburban Ethnicity: A Case Study of the American-Greek Experience in Southern California. A Teacher's Manual and Curriculum Guide for Activities and Resources." Palos Verdes Estates, CA: Palos Verdes High School.

Donaldson, Judy P. 1987. *Transcultural Education Model.* Holmes Beach, FL: Donaldson.

Elder, Pamela, and Mary Ann Carr. 1987. *World Ways: Bringing the World into the Classroom.* Reading, MA: Addison-Wesley.

Ferguson, Henry. 1987. *Manual for Intercultural Education.* Yarmouth, ME: Intercultural Press.

Fradd, Sandra H. 1989. *Meeting the Needs of Culturally and Linguistically Different Students.* Boston: Little, Brown.

Fraiberg, Selma. 1977. *Insights from the Blind: Comparative Studies of Blind and Sighted Infants.* New York: Basic Books.

Freire, Paulo. 1974. *Pedagogy of the Oppressed.* New York: Seabury.

García, Ricardo L. 1982. *Teaching in a Pluralistic Society.* New York: Harper & Row.

Gay, Geneva. 1977. "Curriculum for Multicultural Teacher Education," pp. 31-62 in Frank H. Klassen and Donna M. Gollnick, eds., *Pluralism and the American Teacher: Issues and Case Studies.* Washington: American Association of Colleges for Teacher Education.

Gilliat, Penelope. 1972. "The Current Cinema: Self-Colloquy. About a Sub-Continent." (Review of Malle's *Phantom India.*) *The New Yorker,* July 8.

Glick, Joseph. 1974. "Culture and Cognition: Some Theoretical and Methic Order. New Concerns," pp. 373-81 in George D. Spindler, ed., *Education and Cultural Process: Toward an Anthropology of Education.* New York: Holt, Rinehart and Winston.

Gollnick, Donna M. 1980. *Multiculturalism in Contemporary Education.* Bloomington, IN: School of Education, Indiana University.

Gollnick, Donna M., and Philip C. Chinn. 1986. *Multicultural Education in a Pluralistic Society.* 3d ed. Columbus, OH: Merrill. (Available from Macmillan.)

Goodenough, Ward H. 1976. "Multiculturalism as the Normal Human Experience." *Anthropology and Education Quarterly* 7, 4 (Nov.): 4-6.

Goodnow, J. J. 1969. "Research on Culture and Thought," in D. Elkind and O. H. Flavell, eds., *Studies in Development.* New York: Oxford Univ. Press.

Goonetilleke, D. C. R. A. 1977. *Developing Countries in British Fiction.* New York: Macmillan.

Grant, Carl A., and Christine Sleeter. 1989. *Turning On Learning: Five Approaches for Multicultural Teaching Plans for Race, Class, Gender, and Disability.* Columbus, OH: Merrill. (Available from Macmillan.)

Hall, Edward T. 1976. *Beyond Culture.* New York: Anchor.

Hall, Edward T. 1983. *The Dance of Life: The Other Dimension of Time.* Garden City, NJ: Anchor Press/Doubleday.

Hamilton, John Maxwell. 1988. *Main Street America and the Third World.* Cabin John, MD: Seven Locks.

Hamilton, John Maxwell. 1990. *Entangling Alliances: How the Third World Shapes Our Lives.* Cabin John, MD: Seven Locks.

Heltsche, Mary Ann. 1991. *Multicultural Explorations.* Englewood, CO: Teacher Ideas Press.

Hendricks, Gay, and Russel Wills. 1975. *The Centering Book: Awareness Activities for Children, Parents and Teachers.* Englewood Cliffs, NJ: Prentice-Hall.

Hernández, Helen. 1989. *Multicultural Education.* Columbus, OH: Merrill.

Hicks, D. W. 1981. *Minorities: A Teacher's Resource Book for the Multiethnic Curriculum*. London: Heinemann.

Hilliard, A. 1975. "Cultural Pluralism: The Domestic International Connection." Paper presented at the American Association of Colleges for Teacher Education Conference, Fort Lauderdale, Florida.

Houston, Jean, and Robert E. L. Master. 1973. *Mind Games*. New York: Dell.

Hulmes, Edward. 1989. *Education and Cultural Diversity*. New York: Longman.

Joseph, George Gheverghese. 1991. *The Crest of the Peacock: Non-European Roots of Mathematics*. New York: Tauris. (Distributed by St. Martin's Press.)

Kagan, Jerome. 1978. "The Baby's Elastic Mind." *Human Nature* 1, 1 (Jan.): 66-73.

King, Edith W. 1980. *Teaching Ethnic Awareness*. Glenview, IL: Scott, Foresman.

King, Edmund J. 1975. *Other Schools and Ours: Comparative Studies for Today*. New York: Holt, Rinehart and Winston.

Kingston, Maxine Hong. 1976. *The Woman Warrior: Memoirs of a Girlhood among Ghosts*. New York: Knopf.

Kleinfeld, Judith S. 1975. *Eskimo School on the Andreafsky: A Study of Effective Bicultural Education*. New York: Praeger.

Lewis, Diane K. 1976. "The Multicultural Education Model and Minorities: Some Reservations." *Anthropology and Education Quarterly* 7, 4 (Nov.): 32-37.

Lewis, E. Glyn. 1976. "Bilingualism and Bilingual Education: The Ancient World to the Renaissance," appendix in Joshua A. Fishman, ed. *Bilingual Education: An International Sociological Perspective*. Rowley, MA: Newbury House.

Llabre, Maria M., William B. Ware, and John M. Newell. 1977. "A Factor Analytic Study of Children's Self-Concept in Three Ethnic Groups." Paper presented at the Annual Meeting of the National Council on Measurement in Education, April.

Longstreet, Wilma. 1978. *Aspects of Ethnicity: Understanding Differences in Education*. New York: Teachers College Press.

Lucas, Ceil, ed. 1989. *The Sociolinguistics of the Deaf Community*. San Diego, CA: Academic Press.

Lurie, Walter A. 1982. *Strategies for Survival*. New York: Ktav.

Lynch, James. 1986. *Multicultural Education*. Boston: Routledge and Kegan Paul.

Lynch, James. 1989. *Multicultural Education in a Global Society*. New York: Falmer.

Massad, Carolyn Emrick. 1972. "The Developing Self: World of Communication," pp. 26-53 in K. Yamamoto, ed., *The Child and His Image*. Boston: Houghton Mifflin.

Matiella, Ana Consuelo. 1990. *The Multicultural Caterpillar*. Santa Cruz, CA: Network Publications.

McLaughlin, Milbrey Wallin. 1976. "Implementation as Mutual Adaptation: Change in Classroom Organization." *Teachers College Record* 77, 3 (Feb.): 339-51.

Meadows, Donella H. 1991. *The Global Citizen*. Washington: Island Press.

Montalto, Nicholas V. 1982. "The Intercultural Education Movement, 1924–41: The Growth of Tolerance as a Form of Intolerance," pp. 141–160 in Bernard J. Weiss, ed., *American Education and the European Immigrant, 1840–1940*. Urbana: Univ. of Illinois Press.

Murphy, Sharon. 1974. *Other Voices: Black, Chicano, and American Indian Press*. Dayton, OH: Pflaum/Standard.

Mussen, Paul, and Nancy Eisenberg-Berg. 1977. *The Roots of Caring, Sharing and Helping: The Development of Prosocial Behavior in Children*. San Francisco: W. H. Freeman.

Nef, John U. 1977. "An Early Energy Crisis and Its Consequences." *Scientific American* 237, 5 (Nov.): 140-42, 146-51.

Ogbu, John U. 1978. *Minority Education and Caste*. New York: Academic.

Padden, Carol, and Tom Humphries. 1988. *Deaf in America: Voices from a Culture*. Cambridge, MA: Harvard Univ. Press.

Paulston, Christina Bratt. 1974. *Implications of Language Learning Theory for Language Planning: Concerns in Bilingual Education*. Washington, DC: Center for Applied Linguistics.

Pusch, Margaret D, ed., *Multicultural Education: A Cross-Cultural Training Approach*. Yarmouth, ME: Intercultural Press, 1979.

Ramírez, Manuel III, and Alfredo Castañeda. 1974. *Cultural Democracy, Bicognitive Development and Education*. New York: Academic Press.

Ramsay, Patricia G. 1987. *Teaching and Learning in a Diverse World: Multicultural Education for Young Children*. New York: Columbia Univ. Teachers College Press.

Ramsay, Patricia G. 1989. *Multicultural Education*. New York: Garland.

Renwick, George W. 1991. *A Fair Go for All: Australians and Americans*. Rev. by Reginald Smart and Don L. Henderson. Yarmouth, ME: Intercultural Press.

Richardson, Elwyn S. 1964. *In the Early World*. New York: Pantheon.

Rivers, Wilga M. 1975. "Motivation in Bilingual Programs," pp. 114-22 in Rudolph C. Troike and Nancy Modiano, eds., *Proceedings of the First Inter-American Conference on Bilingual Education.* Washington, DC: Center for Applied Linguistics.

Rivlin, Harry N. 1977. "Research and Development in Multicultural Education," pp. 81-113 in Frank H. Klassen and Donna M. Gollnick, eds., *Pluralism and the American Teacher: Issues and Case Studies.* Washington: American Association of Colleges for Teacher Education.

Robinson, Gail L. 1985. *Cross-Cultural Understanding.* New York: Pergamon.

Rohlen, Thomas P. 1974. "*Seishin Kyoiku* in a Japanese Bank: A Description of Methods and Consideration of Some Underlying Concepts," pp. 219-29 in George D. Spindler, ed., *Education and Cultural Process: Toward an Anthropology of Education.* New York: Holt, Rinehart and Winston.

Rohlen, Thomas P. 1978. "The Education of a Japanese Banker." *Human Nature* 1, 1 (Jan.): 22-30.

Ryan, Margaret W. 1989. *Cultural Journeys.* Holmes Beach, FL: Learning Publications.

Samples, Bob. 1977. "Mind Cycles and Learning." *Phi Delta Kappan* (May): 688-92.

Samples, Bob, Cheryl Charles, and Dick Barnhart. 1977. *The Whole School Book: Teaching and Learning in the Twentieth Century.* Reading, MA: Addison-Wesley.

Saville-Troike, Muriel. 1973. *Bilingual Children: A Resource Document.* Washington, DC: Center for Applied Linguistics.

Saville-Troike, Muriel. 1978. *A Guide to Culture in the Classroom.* Rosslyn, VA: National Clearinghouse for Bilingual Education.

Scarcella, Robin C. 1990. *Teaching Language Minority Students in the Multicultural Classroom.* Englewood Cliffs, NJ: Prentice Hall.

Schutz, Alfred. 1964. *Collected Papers. Vol. II: Studies in Social Theory.* The Hague: Martinus Nijhoff.

Schwartz, Richard H. 1990. *Mathematics and Global Survival.* New York: Ginn.

Scribner, Sylvia, and Michael Cole. 1981. *The Psychology of Literacy.* Cambridge, MA: Harvard Univ. Press.

Seelye, H. Ned, and J. Laurence Day. 1971. "Penetrating the Mass Media: A Unit to Develop Skill in Reading Spanish Newspaper Headlines." *Foreign Language Annals* 5, 1 (Oct.): 69-81.

Seelye, H. Ned, and Jacqueline Howell Wasilewski. 1979. "Historical Development of Multicultural Education," pp. 39–61, in M. D. Pusch, ed., *Multicultural Education: A Cross-Cultural Training Approach.* Yarmouth, ME: Intercultural Press.

Seelye, H. Ned, and Jacqueline Howell Wasilewski. 1981. *Social Competency Development in Multicultural Children, Aged 6-13: Final Report of Exploratory Research on Hispanic-Background Children.* [EDRS: ED 209 363]

Slavins, R. E. 1979. "Effects of Biracial Learning Teams on Cross-Racial Friendships." *Journal of Educational Psychology* 71: 381-87.

Spindler, George D., ed. 1974. *Education and Cultural Process: Toward an Anthropology of Education.* New York: Holt, Rinehart and Winston.

Taylor, Charles A. 1989. *How to Sponsor a Minority Cultural Retreat.* Madison, WI: Praxis.

Theroux, Paul. 1975. *The Great Railway Bazaar: By Train through Asia.* New York: Houghton Mifflin.

Tiedt, Pamela L. 1990. *Multicultural Teaching: A Handbook of Activities, Information and Resources.* 3rd ed. Boston: Allyn & Bacon.

Vander Zanden, James W. 1983. *American Minority Relations.* 4th ed. New York: Knopf.

Vonnegut, Kurt, Jr. 1974. "Afterword," in Francine Klagsbrun, ed., *Free to Be . . . You and Me.* New York: McGraw-Hill.

Wallace, Iain. 1989. *The Global Economic System.* Boston: Unwin Hyman.

Walsh, John E. 1979. *Humanistic Culture Learning.* Honolulu: East-West Center, University Press of Hawaii.

Wasilewski, Jacqueline Howell, and H. Ned Seelye. 1979. "Curriculum in Multicultural Education," pp. 62-84 in M. D. Pusch, ed., *Multicultural Education: A Cross-Cultural Training Approach.* Yarmouth, ME: Intercultural Press.

Weatherford, Jack. 1988. *Indian Givers: How the Indians of the Americas Transformed the World.* New York: Fawcett Columbine.

Weiss, Bernard J., ed. 1982. *American Education and the European Immigrant, 1840-1940.* Urbana, IL: Univ. of Illinois Press.

Witkin, H. A., C. A. Moore, D. R. Goodenough, and P. W. Cox. 1977. "Field-Dependent and Field-Independent Cognitive Styles and Their Educational Implications." *Review of Educational Research* 47, 1 (Winter): 1-64.

Woyach, Robert B., and Richard C. Remy. 1989. *Approaches to World Studies: A Handbook for Curriculum Planners.* Denver: Center for Teaching International Relations, University of Denver.

Wurzel, Jaime. 1988. *Toward Multiculturalism: Readings in Multicultural Education.* Yarmouth, ME: Intercultural Press.

16 Additional Resources

References that were cited in the preceding chapters are not duplicated here. These listings serve as additional sources. They are divided into three sections:

1. General Professional Interest
2. Country- or Area-Specific
3. International Business

1. General Professional Interest

Adler, Nancy J. 1986. *International Dimensions of Organizational Behavior.* The Kent International Business Series. Boston: Kent.

Albert, Ethel M., and Clyde Kluckhohn. 1959. *A Selected Bibliography on Values, Ethics and Esthetics in the Behavioral Sciences and Philosophy.* Glencoe, IL: Free Press.

Allport, Gordon. 1958. *The Nature of Prejudice.* New York: Anchor Books.

Altman, Howard B., and Victor E. Hanzeli, eds. 1974. *Essays on the Teaching of Culture: A Festschrift to Honor Howard Lee Nostrand.* Detroit, MI: Advancement Press of America.

American Association of Colleges for Teacher Education. 1972. *No One Model American: A Statement on Multicultural Education.* Washington: American Association of Colleges for Teacher Education.

Asante, Molefi K., William B. Gudykunst, and Eileen Newmark. 1989. *Handbook of International and Intercultural Communication.* Newbury Park, CA: Sage.

Augustin, Barbara. 1989. *Marriage across Frontiers*. Avon, Eng.: Multilingual Matters. (Available from Taylor & Francis.)

Axtell, Roger E. 1990. *Do's and Taboos of Hosting International Visitors*. New York: Wiley.

Barbour, Alton, and Alvin A. Goldberg. 1974. *Interpersonal Communication: Teaching Strategies and Resources*. Urbana, IL: ERIC Clearinghouse on Reading and Communication Skills.

Baruth, Leroy G., and M. Lee Manning. 1991. *Multicultural Counseling and Psychotherapy*. New York: Macmillan.

Becker, Tamar. 1968. "Patterns of Attitudinal Changes among Foreign Students." *American Journal of Sociology* 73 (Jan.): 431-41.

Benson, Philip G. 1978. "Measuring Cross-Cultural Adjustment: The Problems of Criteria." *International Journal of Intercultural Relations* 2, 1: 21-26.

Berelson, Bernard, and Gary A. Steiner, eds. 1964. *Human Behavior: An Inventory of Scientific Findings*. New York: Harcourt, Brace.

Berry, J. W. 1971. "Ecological and Cultural Factors in Spatial Perceptual Development." *Canadian Journal of Behavioral Science* 3, 4: 324-36.

Birkmaier, Emma, and Dale L. Lange. 1968. "Selective Bibliography on the Teaching of Foreign Languages, 1920-1966." *Foreign Language Annals* 1: 318-53.

Bode, Janet. 1989. *Different Worlds: Interracial and Cross-Cultural Dating*. New York: Franklin Watts.

Boucher, Jerry, Dan Landis, and Karen Arnold Clark, eds. 1987. *Ethnic Conflicts: International Perspectives*. Newbury Park, CA: Sage.

Bouraoui, Hédi A. 1971. *Parole et action*. Philadelphia: Center for Curriculum Development.

Bourque, Jane M. 1974. "Study Abroad and Intercultural Communication," in Gilbert A. Jarvis, ed., *The Challenge of Communication*. ACTFL Review of Foreign Language Education, Vol. 6. Lincolnwood, IL: National Textbook.

Bozell, Brent L. III, and Brent H. Baker, eds. 1990. *And That's the Way It Is(n't): A Reference Guide to Media Bias*. Alexandria, VA: Media Research Center.

Bransford, Louis A., ed. 1974. *Cultural Diversity and the Exceptional Child*. Chicago: Council on Exceptional Children.

Brembeck, Cole S., and Walker H. Hill, eds. 1973. *Cultural Challenges to Education: The Influence of Cultural Factors in School Learning*. Lexington, MA: D.C. Heath, Lexington Books.

Brislin, Richard W., and Michael P. Hamnett, eds. *Topics in Culture Learning.* Vol. 2 (1974), Vol. 3 (1975), Vol. 4 (1976), Vol. 5 (1977). Honolulu, HI: East-West Center.

Brislin, Richard W., and Paul B. Pederson. 1976. *Cross-Cultural Orientation Programs.* New York: Gardner.

Brislin, Richard W. 1978. "Structured Approaches to Dealing with Prejudice and Intercultural Misunderstanding." *International Journal of Group Tensions* 8, 142: 33-47.

Brislin, Richard W., ed. 1990. *Applied Cross-Cultural Psychology.* Newbury Park, CA: Sage.

Burger, Henry G. 1968. *Ethno-pedagogy: A Manual in Cultural Sensitivity, with Techniques for Improving Cross-Cultural Teaching by Fitting Ethnic Patterns.* Albuquerque: Southwestern Educational Laboratory. (Available only from ERIC Documentation Service, Washington: U.S. Office of Education, [SP 001 971].)

Campos Martínez, Luis. 1975. *Lo Cinematográfico como expresión.* Bogotá, Colombia: Ediciones Paulinas.

Carlson, Elliot. 1969. *Learning through Games: A New Approach to Problem Solving.* Washington: Public Affairs Press.

Carmines, Edward G., and Richard A. Zeller. 1979. *Reliability and Validity Assessment.* London: Sage.

Casse, Pierre. 1979. *Training for the Cross-Cultural Mind: A Handbook for Cross-Cultural Trainers and Consultants.* Washington: SIETAR International.

Casse, Pierre, and Surinder Deol. 1985. *Managing Intercultural Negotiations: Guidelines for Trainers and Negotiators.* Washington: SIETAR International. (Available from Intercultural Press.)

Casteel, J. Doyle, and Clemens Hallman. 1974. *Cross-Cultural Inquiry: Value Clarification Exercises.* Gainesville: University of Florida, Center for Latin American Studies.

Casteel, J. Doyle, and Miriam Williford. 1976. *Planning Cross-Cultural Lessons.* Gainesville, FL: National Seminar.

Chomsky, Noam. 1959. "A Review of 'Verbal Behavior' by B. F. Skinner." *Language* 35, 1: 26-58.

Chomsky, Noam. 1989. *Necessary Illusions: Thought Control in Democratic Societies.* Boston: South End Press.

Christian, Chester C., Jr., and John M. Sharp. 1972. "Bilingualism in a Pluralistic Society," pp. 341-75 in Dale L. Lange and Charles J. James, eds., *Foreign Language Education: A Reappraisal.* ACTFL Review of Foreign Language Education, Vol. 4. Lincolnwood, IL: National Textbook.

Clark, John L. D. 1972. *Foreign Language Testing: Theory and Practice.* Skokie, IL: Rand McNally.

Cohen, David, ed. 1975. *Multi-Ethnic Media: Selected Bibliography in Print.* Chicago: American Library Association.

Cohen, Maurice. 1968. "Reflections on the Role of Philosophy in Studying Other Cultures." *Culture* 29 (Sept.): 240-51.

Condon, E. C. 1973a. Acculturation Problems in Adult Education. Mimeographed. Series C, Teacher Training Materials, Reference Pamphlets on Intercultural Communication. Rutgers, NJ: Rutgers Graduate School of Education.

Condon, E. C. 1973b. Conflicts in Values, Assumptions, Opinions. Mimeographed. Series C, Teacher Training Materials, Reference Pamphlets on Intercultural Communication. Rutgers, NJ: Rutgers Graduate School of Education.

Condon, E. C. 1973c. Introduction to Cross-Cultural Communication. Mimeographed. Series C, Teacher Training Materials, Reference Pamphlets on Intercultural Communication. Rutgers, NJ: Rutgers Graduate School of Education.

Condon, E. C. 1973d. Nonverbal Communication. Mimeographed. Series C, Teacher Training Materials, Reference Pamphlets on Intercultural Communication. Rutgers, NJ: Rutgers Graduate School of Education.

Condon, E. C. 1973e. Selected Bibliography on Culture and Cultural Materials. Mimeographed. Series A, Teacher Training Materials, Reference Pamphlets on Intercultural Communication. Rutgers, NJ: Rutgers Graduate School of Education.

Condon, John C., and Fathi S. Yousef. 1975. *An Introduction to Intercultural Communication.* New York: Bobbs-Merrill.

Cronbach, L. J., and P. J. D. Drenth, eds. 1972. *Mental Tests and Cultural Adaptation.* The Hague: Mouton.

Curt, Carmen Judith Nine. 1976. *Teacher Training Pack for a Course on Cultural Awareness.* Fall River, MA: National Assessment and Dissemination Center for Bilingual Education.

D'Souza, Frances, ed. 1991. *Information, Freedom, Censorship: World Report.* Chicago: American Library Association.

Davey, William G., ed. 1981. *Intercultural Theory and Practice: A Case Method Approach.* Washington: SIETAR International. (Available from Intercultural Press.)

Davis, Martha. 1972. *Understanding Body Movement: An Annotated Bibliography.* New York: Arno.

Debyser, Francis. 1967. "Le Rapport langue-civilisation et l'enseignement de la civilisation aux débutants." *Le Français dans le Monde* 48: 21-24 (Part 1); 49: 16-21 (Part 2).

Dee, Rita, ed. 1977. *Planning for Ethnic Education*. Rev. ed. Chicago: Illinois Office of Education, Ethnic Studies Section.

Deusch, Karl W. 1966. *Nationalism and Social Communication—An Inquiry into the Foundations of Nationality*. Cambridge, MA: MIT Press.

Devereaux, G. 1969. *Reality and Dream: Psycho-Therapy of a Plains Indian*. New York: New York Univ. Press.

Dewey, John. 1938. *Experience and Education*. New York: Macmillan.

Dewey, John. 1939. *Freedom and Culture*. New York: Capricorn Books.

Dewey, John. 1961. *Democracy and Education*. New York: Macmillan.

Dezly, Glen Caudill. 1977. *The Public Man: An Interpretation of La América and Other Catholic Countries*. Amherst: Univ. of Massachusetts Press.

Dil, Anwar S., ed. 1972. *Language, Psychology, and Culture: Essays by Wallace E. Lambert*. Stanford, CA: Stanford Univ. Press.

Dimitriou, James F. 1972. *Other Words, Other Worlds: Language-in-Culture*. Reports of the Working Committees, Northeast Conference on the Teaching of Foreign Languages. New York: MLA Materials Center.

Dodd, Carley H., and Frank T. Montalvo, eds. 1987. *Intercultural Skills for Multicultural Societies*. Washington: SIETAR International. (Available from Intercultural Press.)

Dowling, Peter J., and Randall S. Schuler. 1990. *International Dimensions of Human Resource Management*. Boston: PWS-Kent.

Dumont, Robert V., Sr., and Murray L. Wax. 1976. "Cherokee School Society and the Intercultural Classroom," pp. 205-16 in Joan I. Roberts and Sherrie K. Akinsanya, eds., *Schooling in the Cultural Context*. New York: David McKay.

Echols, John M. 1971. "A Bibliography of Morris Opler," in Mario D. Zamora et al., eds., *Themes in Culture: Essays in Honor of Morris E. Opler*. Quezon City, Philippines: Kayumanggi.

Ehrlich, Howard J. 1973. *The Social Psychology of Prejudice*. New York: Wiley.

Elkins, Robert J., Theodore B. Kalivoda, and Genelle Morain. 1972. "Teaching Culture through the Audio-Motor Unit." *Foreign Language Annals* 6: 61-72.

Epps, Edgar C., ed. 1974. *Cultural Pluralism*. New York: McCutchan.

Epstein, Noel. 1977. "The Bilingual Battle: Should Washington Finance Ethnic Identities?" *The Washington Post*, Sunday, June 5, C1 & 4.

Erassov, Boris S. 1972. "Concepts of 'Culture and Personality' in the Ideologies of the Third World." *Diogenes* 78: 123-40.

Esteves, O. P. 1968. "A Problem-Finding Approach to the Teaching of Social Studies," pp. 3-5 in H. Ned Seelye, ed., *A Handbook on Latin America for Teachers: Methodology and Annotated Bibliography*. Springfield, IL: Office of Public Instruction.

Ferguson, Henry. 1987. *Manual for Multicultural Education*. Yarmouth, ME: Intercultural Press.

Fisher, Glen. 1980. *International Negotiation: A Cross-Cultural Perspective*. Yarmouth, ME: Intercultural Press.

Fisher, Glen. 1988. *The Role of Culture and Perception in International Relations*. Yarmouth, ME: Intercultural Press.

Fishman, Joshua A. 1976. *Bilingual Education: An International Sociological Perspective*. Rowley, MA: Newbury House.

Fishman, Joshua A. 1989. *Language and Ethnicity in Minority Sociolinguistic Perspective*. Avon, Eng.: Multilingual Matters. (Available from Taylor & Francis.)

Forges, Jack D. 1967. *The Education of the Culturally Different: A Multi-Cultural Approach*. Berkeley, CA: Far West Laboratory for Educational Research and Development. [EDRS: ED 013 698]

Garfinkel, Alan. 1972. "Teaching Languages via Radio: A Review of Resources." *Modern Language Journal* 56: 158-62.

Garfinkel, Alan, Robert J. Nelson, Sandra Savignon, and Philip D. Smith, Jr., eds. n.d. *LBRIG Newsletter (Language-by-Radio Interest Group)*. Lafayette, IN: Department of Modern Languages, Purdue University.

Gaston, Jan. 1984. *Cultural Awareness Teaching Techniques*. Brattleboro, VT: Pro Lingua.

Gebser, Jean. 1972. "The Foundations of the Aperspective World." *Main Currents in Modern Thought* 29, 2: 80-88.

Gibson, Margaret Alison. 1976. "Approaches to Multicultural Education in the United States: Some Concepts and Assumptions." *Anthropology and Education Quarterly* 7, 4 (Nov.): 7-18.

Giglioli, Pier Paolo, ed. 1972. *Language and Social Context: Selected Readings*. New York: Penguin.

Gilovich, Thomas. 1991. *How We Know What Isn't So: The Fallibility of Human Reason in Everyday Life*. New York: Free Press.

Glazer, Nathan, and Daniel P. Moynihan. 1970. *Beyond the Melting Pot*. 2nd ed. Cambridge, MA: MIT Press.

Gudykunst, William B., ed. 1983. *Intercultural Communication Theory: Current Perspectives*. Newbury Park, CA: Sage.

Gudykunst, William B. 1991. *Bridging Differences: Effective Intergroup Communication*. Newbury Park, CA: Sage.

Gudykunst, William B., Stella Ting-Toomey, and Lea P. Stewart. 1985. *Communication, Culture, and Organizational Processes*. International and Intercultural Communication Annual, vol. 9. Newbury Park, CA: Sage.

Gudykunst, William B., Stella Ting-Toomey, and Elizabeth Chua. 1988. *Culture and Interpersonal Communication*. Newbury Park, CA: Sage.

Guidelines for the Evaluation and Selection of Ethnically Valid Instructional Materials. 1975. Chicago: Illinois Office of Education, Urban and Ethnic Education Section.

Hall, Edward T. 1961. *The Silent Language.* New York: Fawcett.

Hall, Edward T. 1966. *The Hidden Dimension.* New York: Doubleday.

Hall, Edward T. 1974. *Handbook for Proxemic Research.* Washington: Society for the Anthropology of Visual Communication.

Hancock, Charles R. 1972. "Student Aptitude, Attitude, and Motivation," in Dale L. Lange and Charles J. James, eds., *Foreign Language Education: A Reappraisal.* ACTFL Review of Foreign Language Education, vol. 4. Lincolnwood, IL: National Textbook.

Harding, Edith, and Philip Riley. 1986. *The Bilingual Family: A Handbook for Parents.* New York: Cambridge Univ. Press.

Harris, J. 1980. *Identity, A Study of the Concept in Education for a Multicultural Australia.* Canberra: Australian Gov. Pub. Service.

Harris, Marvin. 1974. *Cows, Pigs, Wars and Witches: The Riddles of Culture.* New York: Vintage.

Hendon, Ursula S. 1980. "Introducing Culture in the High School Foreign Language Class." *Foreign Language Annals* 13, 3: 191-98.

Hickey, Leo. 1980. "Ethnography for Language Learners." *Foreign Language Annals* 3, 6: 475-80.

Hill, Deborah J., ed. 1987. *Innovative Approaches to Curriculum Design in the Study Abroad Program.* Frederick, CO: Renaissance.

Hill, Deborah J. 1990. *Travel Tips International: A Guide for the Practical Traveler.* Frederick, CO: Renaissance.

Hill-Burnett, Jacquetta. 1976. "Commentary: Paradoxes and Dilemmas." *Anthropology and Education Quarterly* 7, 4 (Nov.): 37-38.

Hoffman, Eva. 1989. *Lost in Translation: Life in a New Language.* New York: Dutton.

Hoopes, David S., and Kathleen R. Hoopes. 1990. *Guide to International Education in the United States.* Detroit: Gale Research.

Hoopes, David S., and Paul Ventura. 1979. *Intercultural Sourcebook: Cross-Cultural Training Methodologies.* Yarmouth, ME: Intercultural Press.

Hopkins, Robbins S. 1982. Defining and Predicting Overseas Effectiveness for Adolescent Exchange Students. Ph.D. dissertation, University of Massachusetts.

Howlett, Frederick G. 1972. "Le Rôle de la télévision dans l'enseignement des langues modernes." *Canadian Modern Language Review* 28, 2: 42-49.

Hoxeng, James. 1972. Hacienda. Mimeographed. Amherst: University of Massachusetts, Center for International Education, School of Education.

Hsu, Francis L. K. 1954. *Aspects of Culture and Personality: A Symposium*. New York: Abelard-Schuman.

Humphrey, Grace. 1971. *Stories of the World's Holidays*. Highland Park, NJ: Gryphon.

Hymes, Dell, ed. 1964. *Language in Culture: A Reader in Linguistics and Anthropology*. New York: Harper & Row.

Hymes, Dell. 1972. "The Scope of Sociolinguistics." *Social Science Research Council Items* 26: 14-18.

Integrating Black Studies into Existing Social Studies Curriculum: A Model Unit. 1975. Chicago: Illinois Office of Education, Urban and Ethnic Education Section.

Isaacs, Harold R. 1977. *Deseg: Change Comes to a Boston School*. Boston: Citywide Coordinating Council.

Jakobovits, Leon A. 1970. "Motivation in Foreign Language Learning," pp. 62-75 in Joseph A. Tursi, ed., *Foreign Language and the "New" Student*. Reports of the Working Committees, Northeast Conference on the Teaching of Foreign Languages. New York: MLA Materials Center.

Jameson, Brent L. 1972. Student Attitudes in Culture Capsule Usage. Master's thesis, Brigham Young University, Provo, UT.

Janssen, Gretchen. 1989. *Women Overseas: A Christian Perspective on Cross-Cultural Adaptation*. Yarmouth, ME: Intercultural Press.

Jarvis, Donald K. 1977. "Making Crosscultural Connections," in J. K. Phillips, ed. *The Language Connection: From the Classroom to the World*. Lincolnwood, IL: National Textbook.

Jencks, C. S. 1972. *Inequality: A Reassessment of the Effect of Family and Schooling in America*. New York: Basic Books.

Jenks, Frederick L. 1971. A Schema for the Generation of Educational Objectives Related to the Teaching of Culture in the Foreign Language Classroom. Ph.D dissertation, Wayne State University.

Jenks, Frederick L. 1972. "Teaching Culture through the Use of American Newspapers." *American Foreign Language Teacher* 2, 4: 28-29, 40.

Jenks, Frederick L. 1972. "Toward the Creative Teaching of Culture." *American Foreign Language Teacher* 2, 3: 12-14, 42.

Jenks, Frederick L. 1972. *Planning to Teach Culture: An Instructional Manual*. Detroit: Advancement Press of America.

Jenks, Frederick L. 1974. Any Fifteen-Year-Old Student CAN Do Socio-Cultural Research, pp. 65-71 in *Careers, Communication and Culture*. Lincolnwood, IL: National Textbook.

Jones, Earl, and Frances Dean, eds. 1970. *The Americas and Self-Identification*. Intercultural Education Series. [EDRS: ED 052 100]

Katcher, Roberta. 1971. *Culture Shock: What Problems in Acculturation Can Occur in a New Society?* [EDRS: ED 066 987]

Keesing, R. 1974. "Theories of Culture," in Bernard Siegel, ed., *Annual Review of Anthropology*. Palo Alto, CA: Annual Review.

Kelly, L. G. 1969. *25 Centuries of Language Teaching.* Rowley, MA: Newbury House.

Kennedy, Geraldine, ed. 1991. *From the Center of the Earth: Stories Out of the Peace Corps.* Santa Monica, CA: Cover Park.

Keyfitz, Nathan, and Wilhelm Flinger. 1991. *World Population Growth and Aging: Demographic Trends in the Late Twentieth Century.* Chicago: Univ. of Chicago Press.

Kiev, Ari. 1973. *Transcultural Psychiatry.* New York: Free Press.

Kim, Young Yun, ed. 1986. *Interethnic Communication: Current Research.* International and Intercultural Communication Annual, vol. 10. Newbury Park, CA: Sage.

Kim, Young Yun, and William B. Gudykunst, eds. 1988a. *Cross-Cultural Adaptation: Current Approaches.* International and Intercultural Communication Annual, vol. 11. Newbury Park, CA: Sage.

Kim, Young Yun, and William B. Gudykunst, eds. 1988b. *Theories in Intercultural Communication.* International and Intercultural Communication Annual, vol. 12. Newbury Park, CA: Sage.

King, Edith W. 1971. *Worldmindedness: The World Context for Teaching in the Elementary School.* Dubuque, IA: William C. Brown. [EDRS: ED 052 094]

King, Edmund J. 1976. "Education for Uncertainty," Inaugural Lecture in The Faculty of Education, University of London King's College, Feb.

King, Edmund J., C. H. Moor, and J. A. Mundy. 1975. *Post-Compulsory Education II: The Way Ahead.* Newbury Park, CA: Sage.

King, Nancy, and Ken Huff. 1985. *Host Family Survival Kit: A Guide for American Host Families.* Yarmouth, ME: Intercultural Press.

Klopf, Donald W. 1987. *Workbook for Intercultural Encounters: The Fundamentals of Intercultural Communications.* Englewood, CO: Morton.

Kluckhohn, F., and F. Strodbeck. 1961. *Variations in Value Orientations.* Evanston, IL: Row, Peterson.

Knepler, Henry, and Myrna Knepler. 1990. *Crossing Cultures: Readings for Composition.* 3d ed. New York: Macmillan.

Korzenny, Felipe, and Stella Ting-Toomey, eds. 1990. *Communicating for Peace: Diplomacy and Negotiation.* International and Intercultural Communication Annual, vol. 14. Newbury Park, CA: Sage.

Koslow, Diane R., and Elizabeth Pathy Salett, eds. 1989. *Crossing Cultures in Mental Health*. Washington: SIETAR International. (Available from International Counseling Center, Washington, DC.)

Kraemer, Alfred J. 1976. *Teacher Training Workshop in Intercultural Communication: Instructor's Guide*. Alexandria, VA: Human Resources Research Organization.

La France, Marianne, and Claro Mayo. 1978. "Cultural Aspects of Nonverbal Communication." *International Journal of Intercultural Relations* 1, 2: 71-80.

LaBarre, Weston. 1954. *The Human Animal*. Chicago: Univ. of Chicago Press.

Lado, Robert. 1970. "Language, Thought, and Memory in Language Teaching: A Thought View." *Modern Language Journal* 54: 580-85.

Lafayette, Robert C., ed. 1975. *The Culture Revolution in Foreign Language Teaching: A Guide for Building the Modern Curriculum*. Selected Papers from the 1975 Central States Conference. Lincolnwood, IL: National Textbook.

Lafayette, Robert C. 1978. *Language in Education: Theory & Practice*. Washington, DC: Center for Applied Linguistics.

Laird, Charlton. 1953. *The Miracle of Language*. Cleveland: World Publishing.

Lambert, Wallace E. 1969. "Motivational Variables in Second-Language Acquisition." *Canadian Journal of Psychology* 13: 266-72. [EDRS: ED 031 968]

Lambert, Wallace E., and Otto Klineberg. 1967. *Children's Views of Foreign Peoples*. New York: Appleton-Century-Crofts.

Lambert, Wallace E., Alison d'Anglejan, and G. Richard Tucker. 1972. Communicating across Cultures: An Empirical Investigation. Mimeographed. Montreal: Dept. of Psychology, McGill University.

Landis, Dan, and Judith N. Martin, eds. 1986. *Theories and Methods in Cross-Cultural Orientation*. Washington: Sietar International. (Available from Intercultural Press.)

Lange, Dale L., ed. *Annual ACTFL Bibliography (1969 to 1975)*. Published in May issues of *Foreign Language Annals;* also available through ERIC.

Lauffer, Armand. 1985. *Careers, Colleagues and Conflicts: Understanding Gender, Race and Ethnicity in the Workplace*. Newbury Park, CA: Sage.

Lee, Irving J. 1952. *How to Talk with People*. New York: Harper & Row.

Lee, Irving J. 1954. *Customs and Crises in Communications*. New York: Harper & Row.

Levine, Deena R., and Mara B. Adelman. 1982. *Beyond Language: Intercultural Communication for English As a Second Language*. Englewood Cliffs, NJ: Prentice-Hall.

Linton, Ralph. 1945. *Cultural Background of Personality*. New York: Appleton-Century-Crofts.

Loew, Helene. 1973. "FL Magazines Plus Planning Equal Up-to-Date Culture Units." *Accent on ACTFL* 3, 4: 6-8.

Mackey, William F. 1972. "A Typology of Bilingual Education," pp. 413-32 in Joshua A. Fishman, ed., *Advances in the Sociology of Language II*. The Hague: Mouton.

Martin, Judith, N., ed. 1989. *International Journal of Intercultural Relations* 13, 3. Special Issue: Intercultural Communication Competence.

Maynard, Richard A. 1971. *The Celluloid Curriculum: How to Use Movies in the Classroom*. New York: Hayden.

Mead, Margaret. 1970. *Culture and Commitment: A Study of the Generation Gap*. New York: Natural History Press.

Mead, Margaret, and Rhoda Metraux. 1959. *The Study of Culture at a Distance*. Chicago: Univ. of Chicago Press.

Meltzer, Gail, and Elaine Grandjean. 1989. *The Moving Experience: A Practical Guide to Psychological Survival*. Avon, Eng.: Multilingual Matters. (Available from Taylor & Francis.)

Meyer, Philip. 1973. *Precision Journalism: A Reporter's Introduction to Social Science Methods*. Bloomington: Indiana Univ. Press.

Miner, Horace. 1956. "Body Ritual among the Nacirema." *American Anthropologist* 58 (June): 503-7.

Montagu, Ashley. 1974. *Culture and Human Development: Insights into Growing Human*. Englewood Cliffs, NJ: Prentice-Hall.

Morain, Genelle G. 1972. "Teaching Culture through the Audio-Motor Unit." *Foreign Language Annals* 6 (Oct.): 61-67.

Morain, Genelle G. 1973. "Cultural Pluralism," pp. 59-95 in Dale L. Lange, ed., *Pluralism in Foreign Language Education*. ACTFL Review of Foreign Language Education, Vol. 3. Lincolnwood, IL: National Textbook.

Morain, Genelle G. 1976. "Visual Literacy: Reading Signs and Designs in the Foreign Culture." *Foreign Language Annals* 9, 3 (May): 210-16.

Naroll, Raoul. 1970. *A Handbook of Method in Cultural Anthropology*. Garden City, NY: Natural History Press.

National Council of State Supervisors of Foreign Language. 1972. "Guidelines for Evaluating Foreign Language Programs Abroad for High School Students: A Reappraisal." *Foreign Language Annals* 6 (1973): 453-56. Also in *Connecticut FL News Exchange* 18, 5 (June): 2-5.

Nesbitt, William A. 1971. *Simulation Games for the Social Studies Classroom*. 2nd ed. New York: Foreign Policy Association.

Nierenberg, Gerald I., and Henry Calero. 1973. *Metatalk: Guide to Hidden Meanings in Conversation*. New York: Trident.

Nostrand, Frances. 1970. "Review of *A Language-Teaching Bibliography*." *Modern Language Journal* 54: 39.

Nostrand, Howard L. 1963. *The University and Human Understanding*. Seattle: University of Washington, Department of Romance Languages and Literature.

Nostrand, Howard L. 1963. "Literature in the Describing of a Literate Culture." *French Review* 37 (Dec.): 145-57.

Nostrand, Howard L. 1968. "Levels of Sociocultural Understanding for Language Classes," pp. 19-24, in H. Ned Seelye, ed., *A Handbook on Latin America for Teachers: Methodology and Annotated Bibliography*. Springfield, IL: Office of Public Instruction.

Nostrand, Howard L. 1969. "Theme Analysis in the Study of Literature," pp. 182-97, in Joseph Strelka, ed., *Problems of Literary Evaluation. Yearbook of Comparative Criticism*. University Park: Pennsylvania State Univ. Press.

Nostrand, Howard L. 1970. "The Language Laboratory and the Sociological [read: Sociocultural] Context." *NALLD Journal* 4, 3: 23-38.

Nostrand, Howard L., et al. 1965. *Research on Language Teaching: An Annotated International Bibliography, 1945-64*. 2nd rev. ed. Seattle: Univ. of Washington Press.

Opler, Morris E. 1962. "Cultural Anthropology and the Training of Teachers of Foreign Languages," pp. 90-96, in *Seminar in Language and Language Learning: Final Report*. Seattle: University of Washington, Department of Romance Languages and Literature.

Opler, Morris E. 1969. *Apache Odyssey: A Journey between Two Worlds*. New York: Holt, Rinehart and Winston.

Opler, Morris E. 1969. "Themes of Culture," in Wilhelm Bernsdorf and Friedrich Bülow, eds., *Wörterbuch der Soziologie*. Stuttgart: Ferdinand Enke.

Osterloh, Karl-Heinz. 1981. "Intercultural Differences and Communicative Approaches to Foreign Language Teaching in the Third World." *Studies in Second Language Acquisition* 3, 1 (Fall): 64-70.

Palmquist, Bradley, and Kenneth Darrow, eds. 1977. *Transcultural Study Guide*. 2d ed. Palo Alto, CA: Volunteers in Asia.

Park, Robert E., and Herbert A. Miller. 1925. *Old World Traits Transplanted*. Chicago: Univ. of Chicago Press.

Parker, John R., et al. 1968. "Political Simulation: An Introduction," pp. 25-28, in H. Ned Seelye, ed. *A Handbook on Latin America for Teachers: Methodology and Annotated Bibliography*. Springfield, IL: Superintendent of Public Instruction.

Pasternak, Michael G. Miller. 1979. *Helping Kids Learn Multi-Cultural Concepts: A Handbook of Strategies*. Champaign, IL: Research Press.

Pedersen, Paul. 1986. *Handbook of Cross-Cultural Counseling and Therapy.* Westport, CT: Greenwood.

Pedersen, Paul. 1988. *A Handbook for Developing Multicultural Awareness.* Alexandria, VA: American Assn. for Counseling and Development.

Pedersen, Paul B., Juris Draguns, Walter J. Connor, and Joseph E. Trimble. 1989. *Counseling across Cultures.* 2d ed. Honolulu: Univ. of Hawaii Press.

Perrone, Bobette, H. Henrietta Stockel, and Victoria Krueger. 1989. *Medicine Women, Curanderas, and Women Doctors.* Norman: Univ. of Oklahoma Press.

Philips, Susan U. 1976. "Access to Power and Maintenance of Ethnic Identity as Goals of Multicultural Education: Are They Compatible?" *Anthropology and Education Quarterly* 7, 4 (Nov.): 30-32.

Polcyn, Kenneth A. 1972. "The Joint United States-India Educational Broadcast Satellite Experiment." *Educational Technology* 12, 6: 14-17, 20-25.

Poloma, Margaret M., and George Gallup, Jr. 1991. *The Varieties of Prayer.* Philadelphia: Trinity Press International.

Porter, Rosalie Pedalino. 1990. *Forked Tongue: The Politics of Bilingual Education.* New York: Newbury House.

Prejudice and Ethnocentrism: A Curriculum and Resource Manual for Elementary School Teachers. 1975. Chicago: Illinois-Chicago Project for Inter-Ethnic Dimensions in Education, Dept. of Policy Studies, University of Illinois at Chicago.

Primus, Pearl E. 1968. *A Pilot Study Integrating Visual Form and Anthropological Content for Teaching Children Ages 6 to 10 about Cultures ... A Danced Presentation with Lecture Interpreting Some of the Cultural Values in West and Central African Communities.* [EDRS: ED 027 095]

Prosser, Michael H., ed. 1978. *USIA Intercultural Communication Course: 1977 Proceedings.* Washington, DC: International Communication Agency.

Prosser, Michael. 1985. *The Cultural Dialogue: An Introduction to Intercultural Communication.* Washington, DC: SIETAR International. (Available from Intercultural Press.)

Pusch, Margaret D., ed. 1979. *Multicultural Education: A Cross-Cultural Training Approach.* Yarmouth, ME: Intercultural Press.

Pusch, Margaret D., H. N. Seelye, and J. H. Wasilewski. 1979. "Training for Multicultural Education Competencies," pp. 85-103, in Margaret D. Pusch, ed., *Multicultural Education: A Cross-Cultural Training Approach.* Yarmouth, ME: Intercultural Press.

Randolph, Gary, Dan Landis, and Oliver C. S. Tzeng. 1977. "The Effects of Time and Practice upon Culture Assimilator Training." *International Journal of Intercultural Relations* 1, 4: 105-12.

Reid, Joy, ed. 1988. *Building the Professional Dimension of Educational Exchange.* Yarmouth, ME: Intercultural Press.

Renwick, George W. 1980. *Evaluation Handbook for Cross-Cultural Training and Multicultural Education.* Yarmouth, ME: Intercultural Press.

Rich, Andrea L. 1974. *Interracial Communication.* New York: Harper & Row.

Rich, Andrea L., and Dennis M. Ogawa. 1976. "Intercultural and Interracial Communication: An Analytical Approach," pp. 24-32, in Larry A. Samovar and Richard E. Porter, eds., *Intercultural Communication: A Reader.* Belmont, CA: Wadsworth.

Romano, Dugan. 1988. *Intercultural Marriage: Promises and Pitfalls.* Yarmouth, ME: Intercultural Press.

Rosen, Harold. 1974. *Language and Class: A Critical Look at the Theories of Basil Bernstein.* Bristol, Eng.: Falling Wall.

Rosenzweig, Mark R. 1966. "Environmental Complexity, Cerebral Chance, and Behavior." *American Psychologist* 21: 321-32.

Samovar, Larry A., and Richard E. Porter, eds. 1991. *Intercultural Communication: A Reader.* 6th ed. Belmont, CA: Wadsworth.

Samovar, Larry A., Richard E. Porter, and Nemi C. Jain. 1981. *Understanding Intercultural Communication.* Belmont, CA: Wadsworth.

Savignon, Sandra J. 1972b. "A l'écoute de France-Inter: The Use of Radio in a Student-Centered Oral French Class." *French Review* 46: 342-49.

Schein, Edgar H. 1991. *Organizational Culture and Leadership.* San Francisco: Jossey-Bass.

Schofield, Janet Ward. 1989. *Black and White in School: Trust, Tension or Tolerance.* New York: Columbia Univ. Teachers College Press.

Scott, Andrew M., William A., and Trudi M. Lucas. 1966. *Simulation and National Development.* New York: Wiley.

Sebeok, Thomas A., et al., eds. 1972. *Approaches to Semiotics.* Transactions of the Indiana University Conference on Paralinguistics and Kinesics. The Hague: Mouton.

Seelye, H. Ned. 1966. "Field Notes on Cross-Cultural Testing." *Language Learning* 16, 1-2: 77-85.

Seelye, H. Ned. 1966. "Social Behavior of Non-Human Primates in Captivity." *Science Education* 50, 1 (Feb.): 69-75.

Seelye, H. Ned. 1968. "Culture in the Foreign Language Classroom." *Illinois Journal of Education* 59, 3 (March): 22-26.

Seelye, H. Ned. 1971. "A Hard Look at Hard Times: A Reaction to Superintendent Lawson's 'Is Language Teaching Foreign or Dead?'" *Modern Language Journal* 55, 6 (Oct.): 358-61.

Seelye, H. Ned. 1972. "Analysis and Teaching of the Cross-Cultural Context," pp. 37-81, in Emma M. Birkmaier, ed., *Foreign Language Education: An Overview.* ACTFL Review of Foreign Language Education, Vol. 1. Lincolnwood, IL: National Textbook.

Seelye, H. Ned. 1972. "Using Cultural Content to Develop Cultural Skills." *Hawaii Language Teacher* 14, 3 (April): 3-6.

Seelye, H. Ned. 1973. "Teaching the Foreign Culture: A Context for Research," pp. 74-89 in Jerald R. Green, ed., *Foreign-Language Education Research: A Book of Readings.* Skokie, IL: Rand McNally.

Seelye, H. Ned. 1975. " 'Like Us or Like You'—The Challenge of Continuing Bicultural Education." *Curriculum Review* 14, 5: 271-75.

Seelye, H. Ned. 1977. "Sociology and Education," pp. 99-103, in *Bilingual Education: Current Perspectives. Vol. 1: Social Science.* Washington, DC: Center for Applied Linguistics.

Seelye, H. Ned. 1977. "Teaching the Cultural Context of Intercultural Communication," pp. 249-55 in Muriel Saville-Troike, ed., *Report of the Twenty-Eighth Annual Round Table on Languages and Linguistics, 1977.* Washington: Georgetown Univ. Press.

Seelye, H. Ned. 1978. "Intercultural Training for the First Six Months of Residence Abroad," pp. 201-3 in *Bridges of Understanding Symposium.* Provo, UT: Brigham Young University, Language and Intercultural Research Center.

Seelye, H. Ned. 1978. "Self-Identity and the Bicultural Classroom," pp. 290-98 in H. La Fontain, B. Persky, and L. H. Golubchick, eds., *Bilingual Education.* Wayne, NJ: Avery.

Seelye, H. Ned, and K. Balasubramonian. 1974. Accountability in Educational Reform Programs through Instrumentation Analyses and Design Variation: Evaluating Cognitive Growth in Illinois Bilingual Programs, 1972-1973. Mimeographed. [EDRS: ED 112 635]

Seelye, H. Ned, and J. Laurence Day. 1992. *Careers for Foreign Language Aficionados and Other Multilingual Types.* Lincolnwood, IL: National Textbook.

Seelye, H. Ned, and Billie N. Navarro. 1977. *A Guide to the Selection of Bilingual Education Program Designs.* Arlington Heights, IL: Bilingual Education Service Center.

Seelye H. Ned, and Joyce A. Sween. 1982. "Quality Circles in U.S. Industry: Survey Results." *The Quality Circles Journal* 5, 4 (Nov.): 26-29.

Seelye, H. Ned, and Joyce A. Sween. 1983. "Critical Components of Successful U.S. Quality Circles: Survey Results." *The Quality Circles Journal* 6, 1 (Mar.): 14-17.

Seelye, H. Ned, and V. Lynn Tyler, eds. 1977. *Intercultural Communicator Resources*. Provo, UT: Brigham Young University, Language and Intercultural Research Center.

Segall, M. H., D. T. Campbell, and M. J. Herkovits. 1966. *The Influence of Culture on Visual Perception*. Indianapolis, IN: Bobbs-Merrill.

Segall, Marshall H., Pierre R. Dasen, John W. Berry, and Ype H. Poortinga. 1990. *Human Behavior in Global Perspective: An Introduction to Cross-Cultural Psychology*. Elmsford, NY: Pergamon.

Shaftel, Fannie. 1967. *Role Playing for Social Values*. Englewood Cliffs, NJ: Prentice-Hall.

Shames, Germaine W., and Gerald W. Glover. 1989. *World-Class Service*. Yarmouth, ME: Intercultural Press.

Shiman, David A. 1979. *The Prejudice Book: Activities for the Classroom*. New York: Anti-Defamation League of B'nai B'rith.

Sikkema, Mildred, and Agnes M. Niyekawa-Howard. 1977. *Cross-Cultural Learning and Self-Growth: Getting to Know Ourselves and Others*. New York: International Association of Schools of Social Work.

Simons, George F. 1989. *Working Together: How to Become More Effective in a Multicultural Organization*. Los Altos, CA: Crisp.

Simonson, Rick, and Scott Walker, eds. 1988. *Multi-Cultural Literacy*. The Graywolf Annual, vol. 5. St. Paul, MN: Graywolf.

Singer, Marshall R. 1976. "Culture: A Perceptual Approach," pp. 110-19, in Larry A. Samovar and Richard E. Porter, eds., *Intercultural Communications: A Reader*. Belmont, CA: Wadsworth.

Singer, Marshall. 1987. *Intercultural Communication: A Perceptual Approach*. Englewood Cliffs, NJ: Prentice Hall (Simon & Schuster).

Skinner, B. F. 1972. *Beyond Freedom and Dignity*. New York: Knopf.

Steiner, Florence. 1971. "Culture: A Motivating Factor in the French Classroom," pp. 28-35, in Charles Jay and Pat Castle, eds., *French Language Education: The Teaching of Culture in the Classroom*. Springfield: Illinois State Superintendent of Public Instruction.

Stening, Bruce W. 1979. "Problems in Cross-Cultural Contact: A Literature Review." *International Journal of Intercultural Relations* 3, 3: 269-78.

Stewart, Edward C. 1978. "The Survival Stage of Intercultural Communication." *International Communications Yearbook*.

Stone, James C., and Donald P. DeNevi, eds. 1971. *Teaching Multi-Cultural Populations: Five Heritages*. New York: D. Van Nostrand.

Sue, Derald Wing, and David Sue. 1990. *Counseling the Culturally Different: Theory and Practice*. 2d ed. New York: Wiley.

Sutman, Francis K. 1979. *Educating Personnel for Bilingual Settings, Present and Future*. Washington: American Association of Colleges for Teacher Education.

Szalay, Lorand B., and Jack E. Brent. 1967. "The Analysis of Cultural Meanings through Free Verbal Associations." *The Journal of Social Psychology* 72: 161-87.

Szalay, Lorand B., and James Deese. 1978. *Subjective Meaning and Culture: An Assessment through Word Association*. Hillsdale, NJ: Erlbaum, Wiley and Sons.

Szalay, Lorand B., et al. 1978. *The Hispanic American Cultural Frame of Reference: A Communication Guide for Use in Mental Health, Education, and Training*. Washington: Institute of Comparative Social Studies.

Tanenbaum, Joe. 1989. *Male and Female Realities: Understanding the Opposite Sex*. Incline Village, NY: Erdmann.

Taylor, James S. 1970. "Direct Classroom Teaching of Cultural Concepts," pp. 42-50 in H. Ned Seelye, ed., *Perspectives for Teachers of Latin American Culture*. Springfield: Illinois State Superintendent of Public Instruction.

Teitelbaum, Herbert, and Richard J. Hiller. 1977. "Bilingual Education: The Legal Mandate." *Harvard Educational Review* 47, 2 (May): 138-70.

Terpstra, Vern. 1985. *The Cultural Environment of International Business*. 3d ed. Cincinnati: South-Western.

Therrien, Melvin G. 1973. "Learning French via Short Wave Radio and Popular Periodicals." *French Review* 46: 1178-83.

Thompson, Marion E. 1971. "A Study of International Television Programming within the Structure of Global Communications." *Dissertation Abstracts International* 32: 3469A (University of Wisconsin).

Tidhar, Hava. n.d. *Using Television for Teaching a Second Language through Dramatized Everyday Situations*. [EDRS: ED 053 578]

Ting-Toomey, Stella, and Felipe Korzenny, eds. 1989. *Language, Communication and Culture: Current Directions*. International and Intercultural Communication Annual, vol. 13. Newbury Park, CA: Sage.

Ting-Toomey, Stella, and Felipe Korzenny, eds. 1991. *Cross-Cultural Interpersonal Communication*. International and Intercultural Communication Annual, vol. 15. Newbury Park, CA: Sage.

Triandis, Harry C. 1977. *Interpersonal Behavior*. Belmont, CA: Wadsworth.

Troike, Rudolph C. 1978. *Research Evidence for the Effectiveness of Bilingual Education*. Rosslyn, VA: National Clearinghouse for Bilingual Education.

Troyanovich, John. 1972. "American Meets German: Culture Shock in the Classroom." *Die Unterrichtspraxis* 5, 2: 67-79.

Trueba, Henry T., and Carol Barnett-Mizrabi, eds. 1979. *Bilingual Multicultural Education and the Professional*. Roley, MA: Newbury House.

Trueba, Henry T., Grace Pung Guthrie, and Kathryn Hu-Pei Au, eds. 1981. *Culture and the Bilingual Classroom.* Rowley, MA: Newbury House.

Turbowitz, Julius. 1969. *Changing the Racial Attitudes of Children.* New York: Praeger.

Tyler, V. Lynn, and James S. Taylor. 1978. *Reading between the Lines.* Provo, UT: Eyring Research Institute.

Upshur, John A. 1966. "Cross-Cultural Testing: What to Test." *Language Learning* 16, iii, iv: 183-96.

Valdés, Joyce Merrill, ed. 1986. *Culture Bound: Language Teaching from a Cultural Perspective.* New York: Cambridge Univ. Press.

Wallace, Anthony F. C. 1963. *Culture and Personality.* New York: Random House.

Wax, Rosalie H. 1976. "Oglala Sioux Dropouts and Their Problems with Educators," pp. 216-26 in Joan I. Roberts and Sherrie K. Akinsanya, eds., *Schooling in the Cultural Context.* New York: David McKay.

Weaver, Gary, ed. 1987. *Readings in Cross-Cultural Communication.* 2d ed. Needham, MA: Ginn.

West, Donnamarie. 1990. *Between Two Worlds: The Human Side of Development.* Yarmouth, ME: Intercultural Press.

Williamson, Kay. 1976b. "Small Languages in Primary Education: The Rivers Reader Project as a Case History." Paper presented to the International African Institute's Fourteenth International African Conference on African Languages in Education, Kinshasa, Zaire, Dec. 13-15.

Williford, Miriam, ed. 1976. *It's the Image That Counts: Cartoon Masters for Latin American Study.* Albuquerque: University of New Mexico, Latin American Studies Association.

Wolcott, Harry F. 1974. "The Teacher as Enemy," pp. 411-25, in George D. Spindler, ed., *Education and Cultural Process: Toward an Anthropology of Education.* New York: Holt, Rinehart and Winston.

Wolfenstein, Martha, and Nathan Leites. 1950. *Movies, A Psychological Study.* Glencoe, IL: Free Press.

Wood, Richard E. 1972. "Shortwave Radio as a Teaching Aid for German." *Die Unterrichtspraxis* 5, 1: 36-40.

Woodward, C. Vann. 1991. *The Old World's New World.* New York: Oxford Univ. Press.

Zaidi, S. M. Hafeez. 1967. "Students' Attitude toward Living with Different Ethnic Groups." *The Journal of Social Psychology* 72: 99-106.

Zijderveld, Anton C. 1974. *The Abstract Society: A Cultural Analysis of Our Time.* Middlesex, Eng.: Pelican.

2. Country- or Area-Specific (excluding business topics)

Abraham, Sameer Y., and Nabeel Abraham, eds. 1981. *The Arab World and Arab Americans: Understanding a Neglected Minority.* Detroit: Center for Urban Studies.

Adams, Henry E., ed. 1983. *Handbook of Latin American Studies.* No. 35, *Social Sciences.* Gainesville: Univ. of Florida Press.

Afful, Elizabeth. 1976. "A Study of Ghanaian Language Teaching in Three Primary Schools in Accra." Paper submitted to the Language Centre, University of Ghana, in partial fulfillment of the requirements for diploma in Ghanaian language. Legon: University of Ghana.

Aguirre Beltrán, Gonzalo. 1972. *La Población negra de México: estudio etnohistórico.* 2da ed. aumentada. México, D.F.: Fondo de Cultura Económica.

Alameda County School Department. 1971. *Cultural Understanding: French, Level I.* Hayward, CA.

Anderson, Beatrix, and Maurice North. 1969. *Cassell's Beyond the Dictionary in German.* New York: Funk & Wagnalls.

Ansre, Gilbert. 1975. "Madina: Three Polyglots and Some Implications for Ghana," in Sirarpi Ohannessian, Charles A. Ferguson, and Edgar C. Polomes, eds., *Language Surveys in Developing Nations.* Arlington, VA: Center for Applied Linguistics.

Armstrong, Robert G. 1968. "Language Policies and Language Practices in West Africa," pp. 227-36 in Fishman, Ferguson, and Das Gupta, eds., *Language Problems in Developing Nations.* New York: Wiley.

Arnott, Peter. 1967. *An Introduction to the Greek World.* London: Macmillan.

Bamgbose, Ayo. 1976. *Mother Tongue Education: The West African Experience.* London: Hodder and Stoughton.

Barnlund, Dean C. 1989. *Communicative Styles of Japanese and Americans: Images and Realities.* Belmont, CA: Wadsworth.

Barnlund, Dean C. 1989. *Public and Private Self in Japan and the United States.* Yarmouth, ME: Intercultural Press.

Bellah, Robert N., Richard Madsen, William M. Sullivan, Ann Swidler, and Steven Tipton. 1986. *Habits of the Heart: Individualism and Commitment in American Life.* New York: Harper & Row.

Bryson, Bill. 1990. *The Mother Tongue: English and How It Got That Way.* New York: William Morrow.

Canfield, D. Lincoln. 1968. *Spanish with a Flourish.* AATSP Culture Unit 1. (See a current issue of *Hispania* for ordering information.)

Caplan, Nathan, John K. Whitmore, and Marcella H. Choy. 1989. *The Boat People and Achievement in America: A Study of Family Life, Hard Work, and Cultural Values*. Ann Arbor: Univ. of Michigan Press.

Carroll, Raymonde. 1987. *Cultural Misunderstandings: The French-American Experience*. tr. Carol Volk. Chicago: Univ. of Chicago Press.

Castle, Pat, et al. 1970. "An Explanation of Three 'Levels' of Competence for Spanish Classes," pp. 150-60 in H. Ned Seelye, ed. *Perspectives for Teachers of Latin American Culture*. Springfield, IL: State Superintendent of Public Instruction.

Concheff, B. 1982. *Cartas de España*. Lincolnwood, IL: National Textbook.

Condon, John C., and Keisuke Kurata. 1974. *In Search of What's Japanese about Japan*. Tokyo: Shufunomoto.

Cooney, D. 1973. *German Culture through Performance Objectives*. Detroit: Advancement Press of America.

Cooper, Robert, and Nanthapa Cooper. 1991. *Culture Shock Thailand*. Portland, OR: Graphic Arts Center Publishing.

D'Alleva, Josephine. 1982. *Incontri Culturali: Cross-Cultural Mini-Dramas*. Lincolnwood, IL: National Textbook.

Dekovic, Gene. 1978. *Unterredungen aus Deutschland: Contemporary Germany as Seen through Actual Interviews*. Lincolnwood, IL: National Textbook.

Dekovic, Gene. 1979. *A Tu Per Tu: Contemporary Italy as Seen through Actual Interviews*. Lincolnwood, IL: National Textbook.

Dindi, Hasan, Maija Gazur, Wayne M. Gazur, and Aysen Kirkkopru-Dindi. 1989. *Turkish Culture for Americans*. Boulder, CO: International Concepts.

Drain, Cathie, and Barbara Hall. 1990. *Culture Shock Indonesia*. Portland, OR: Graphic Arts Center Publishing.

Fishman, Joshua A. 1966. *Language Loyalty in the United States*. The Hague: Mouton,

Fishman, Joshua A. 1966. "Italian Language Maintenance Efforts in the United States and the Teaching of Italian in American High Schools and Colleges." *Florida FL Reporter* 4 (Spring).

Fishman, Joshua A. 1969. "The Breadth and Depth of English in the United States," in Alfred Aarons, Barbara Gordon, and William Stewart, eds., *Linguistic-Cultural Differences and American Education*. *Florida FL Reporter* 7, 1: 41-43, 151.

Forker, Jack D. 1960. *Apache, Navaho and Spaniard*. Norman: Univ. of Oklahoma Press.

Frost, Ellen L. 1987. *For Richer, for Poorer: The New U.S.-Japan Relationship*. New York: Council on Foreign Relations.

Fussell, Paul. 1983. *Class: A Guide through the American Class System*. New York: Summit.

Gay, John. 1972. *Red Dust on the Green Leaves*. Yarmouth, ME: Intercultural Press. [Book describes Liberia]

González Casanova, Pablo, et al. 1970. *Sociología del desarrollo latinoamericano: Una guía bibliográfica para su estudio*. México, D.F.: Universidad Nacional Autónoma de México, Instituto de Investigaciones Sociales.

Greelev, A. M. 1971. *Why Can't They Be like Us? America's White Ethnic Groups*. New York: E. P. Dutton.

Habert, Kjell, and Arild Lillebo. 1988. *Made in Norway: Norwegians as Others See Them*. Bekkestua, Norway: Norwegian School of Management Press.

Habla de la Ciudad de México: Materiales para su estudio, El. 1971. México, D.F.: Universidad Nacional Autónoma de México, Centro de Lingüística Hispánica.

Haddad, Yvonne Yazbeck. 1991. *The Muslims of America*. New York: Oxford Univ. Press.

Hall, Edward T., and Mildred Reed Hall. 1989. *Understanding Cultural Differences: Germans, French and Americans*. Yarmouth, ME: Intercultural Press.

Harris, David P. 1969. *Testing English as a Second Language*. New York: McGraw-Hill.

Huizenga, Jann. 1982. *Looking at American Signs*. Lincolnwood, IL: National Textbook.

Huizenga, Jann. 1983. *Looking at American Food: A Pictorial Introduction to American Language and Culture*. Lincolnwood, IL: National Textbook.

Jonas, Sister Ruth. 1972. *African Studies in French for the Elementary Grades: Phase II of a Twinned Classroom Approach to the Teaching of French . . .* [EDRS: ED 066 994]

Juaire, Dennis. 1970. "The Use of Folksongs to Develop Insight into Latin American Culture," in H. Ned Seelye, ed., *Perspectives for Teachers of Latin American Culture*. Springfield, IL: State Superintendent of Public Instruction.

Kany, C. E. 1951. *American-Spanish Syntax*. Chicago: Univ. of Chicago Press.

Kany, C. E. 1960. *American-Spanish Euphemisms*. Los Angeles: Univ. of California Press.

Kany, C. E. 1960. *American-Spanish Semantics*. Los Angeles: Univ. of California Press.

King, Edmund J., C. H. Moor, and J. A. Mundy. 1974. *Post-Compulsory Education I: A New Analysis in Western Europe*. Newbury Park, CA: Sage.

Kitao, Kenji, and S. Kathleen Kitao. n.d. *Intercultural Communication between Japan and the United States*. Tokyo: Eichosha Shinsha.

Kuh, George D., and Elizabeth J. Whitt. 1988. *The Invisible Tapestry: Culture in American Colleges and Universities*. College Station, TX: Association for Higher Education. (Available from ERIC.)

Ladu, Tora T. 1974. *What Makes the Spanish Spanish, and Their New-World Descendants Different*. Detroit, MI: Advancement Press of America.

Lambert, Wallace E., Howard Giles, and Omer Picard. 1973. Language Attitudes in a French-American Community. Mimeographed. Montreal: McGill University.

Lanier, Alison. 1988. *Living in the U.S.A.* 4th ed. Yarmouth, ME: Intercultural Press.

Latin America: A Catalog of Dissertations. 1984. Ann Arbor, MI: Xerox University Microfilms.

Latin America: Intercultural Experiential Learning Aid. 1976. Provo, UT: Brigham Young University, Language Research Center.

Leñero Otero, Luis. 1971. *Investigación de la familia en México*. 2nda. ed. México, D.F.: Impresora Gálvez.

Lieberman, Samuel. 1972. "Ancient Greek and Roman Culture," in James W. Dodge, ed., *Other Words, Other Worlds: Language-in-Culture*. Reports of the Working Committees, Northeast Conference on the Teaching of Foreign Languages. New York: MLA Materials Center.

Loewenthal, Nessa P. 1990. *Update Germany*. Yarmouth, ME: Intercultural Press.

Logan, Nicole Prevost. 1989. *Update France*. Yarmouth, ME: Intercultural Press.

Loy, Jane M. 1973. *Latin America: Sights and Sounds, A Guide to Motion Pictures and Music for College Courses*. Gainesville, FL: Consortium of Latin American Studies Programs.

Madrid-Barela, Arturo. 1976. "Towards an Understanding of Chicano Experience," pp. 98-106 in Larry A. Samovar and Richard E. Porter, eds., *Intercultural Communication: A Reader*. Belmont, CA: Wadsworth.

Mayers, Marvin K. 1982. *A Look at Latin American Lifestyles*. Dallas, TX: International Museum of Cultures.

McGregor, Joy, and Margaret K. Nydell. 1990. *Update Saudi Arabia*. Yarmouth, ME: Intercultural Press.

Mittman, Karin, and Zatar Ishan. 1991. *Culture Shock Pakistan*. Portland, OR: Graphic Arts Center Publishing.

Morris, Marshall. 1981. *Saying and Meaning in Puerto Rico: Some Problems in the Ethnography of Discourse*. New York: Pergamon.

Nostrand, Howard L. 1964. *Film Recital of French Poems: Cultural Commentary*. Seattle: Univ. of Washington Press. [EDRS: ED 044 955]

Olson, James Stewart. 1991. *The Indians of Central and South America: An Ethnohistorical Dictionary*. New York: Greenwood.

Overholt, Kenneth D. 1982. *Voces de Puerto Rico: Contemporary Puerto Rico as Seen through Actual Interviews*. Lincolnwood, IL: National Textbook.

Padilla, Amado M., and René A. Ruiz. 1973. *Latino Mental Health: A Review of Literature*. Washington: Superintendent of Documents, U.S. Government Printing Office. (#1724-00317)

Pemberton, John E. 1966. *How to Find Out about France. A Guide to Sources of Information*. Oxford: Pergamon.

Phillips-Martinsson, Jean. 1981. *Swedes as Others See Them: Facts, Myths or a Communication Complex*. Kent, Eng.: Chartwell-Bratt.

Putti, Joseph M., and Audrey Chia. 1990. *Culture and Management: A Casebook*. Singapore: McGraw-Hill.

Pye, Lucien. 1985. *Asian Power and Politics: The Cultural Dimensions of Authority*. Cambridge, MA: Harvard Univ. Press.

Pye, Lucien. 1988. *The Mandarin and the Cadre: China's Political Cultures*. Ann Arbor: Univ. of Michigan.

Río, Angel del. 1965. *The Clash and Attraction of Two Cultures: The Hispanic and Anglo-Saxon Worlds in America*. Baton Rouge: Louisiana State Univ. Press.

Rogus, Timothy. 1981. *Lettres de France: Impressions of Contemporary France for Beginning Students*. Lincolnwood, IL: National Textbook.

Roland, Alain. 1988. *In Search of Self in India and Japan: Toward a Cross-Cultural Psychology*. Princeton, NJ: Princeton Univ. Press.

Ruddle, Kenneth, and Donald Odermann, eds. 1972. *Statistical Abstract of Latin America 1971*. Los Angeles: University of California, Latin American Center.

Savaiano, Geraldine. 1974. "Some Indications of Changes in Customs and Attitudes among Certain Latin American Young People of the Middle Class." *Hispania* 57 (May): 254-69.

Savaiano, Geraldine, and Luz María Archundia. 1968. *The Folk Arts of Mexico*. American Association of Teachers of Spanish and Portuguese (AATSP) Cultural Unit III. (Consult current issue of *Hispania* for ordering information.)

Savaiano, Geraldine, and Luz María Archundia. 1968. *The Life Cycle in Mexico*. American Association of Teachers of Spanish and Portuguese (AATSP) Cultural Unit II. (Consult current issue of *Hispania* for ordering information.)

Secundy, Marian Gray, and Lois Nixon. 1991. *Trials, Tribulations and Celebrations: African-American Perspectives on Health, Illness, Aging, and Loss*. Yarmouth, ME: Intercultural Press.

Seelye, H. Ned. 1970. "Spanish Culture," pp. 33-48 in *Spain: Comparative Culture and Government*. Lincolnwood, IL: National Textbook.

Seelye, H. Ned, ed. 1970. *Perspectives for Teachers of Latin American Culture*. Springfield: Illinois Office of Education. [EDRS: ED 047 579].

Seelye, H. Ned. 1970. "The *Yanqui* in the Banana Trilogy of Miguel Angel Asturias," pp. 95-103 in H. Ned Seelye, ed., *Perspectives for Teachers of Latin American Culture*. Springfield: Illinois Office of Education. [EDRS: ED 027 797]

Seelye, H. Ned. 1973. *Culture Tests for Spanish*. 4 levels. Honolulu: Hawaii State Department of Education.

Seelye, H. Ned, Martha González Calat, Margarita López Raquec, Julieta Sánchez Castillo, and Joyce A. Sween. 1979. *Informe final del estudio de base sobre la educación bilingüe rural de Guatemala*. Guatemala City: Ministerio de Educación, Socio Educativo Rural.

Seelye H. Ned, and María Guadalupe Mirón. 1970. "Phenotype and Occupational Mobility in Guatemala City: A Preliminary Survey." *Science Education* 54, 1 (January-March): 13-16.

Seelye, H. Ned, Edward C. P. Stewart, and Joyce A. Sween. 1982. *Evaluating Quality Circles in U.S. Industry*. Arlington, VA: Office of Naval Research. [NTIS: AD A118 649]

Seelye, H. Ned, Edward C. P. Stewart, and Joyce A. Sween. 1983. "Japanese Quality Control Circles: Survey Results." *The Quality Circles Journal* 6, 2 (June): 20-22.

Sen, Sondra. 1978. *The Asian Indians in America*. New York: Ethnic Heritage Studies Project.

Seward, Jack. 1969. *Japanese in Action: An Unorthodox Approach to the Spoken Language and the People Who Speak It*. New York: Walker.

Shilling, Marvina A. 1988. *Update Belgium*. Yarmouth, ME: Intercultural Press.

Sinclair, Kevin, ed. 1991. *Culture Shock China*. Portland, OR: Graphic Arts Center Publishing.

Taylor, Sally A., ed. 1990. *Culture Shock France*. Portland, OR: Graphic Arts Center Publishing.

Tobin, Joseph J., David Y. H. Wu, and Dana H. Davidson. 1991. *Preschool in Three Cultures: Japan, China, and the United States*. New Haven, CT: Yale Univ. Press.

United States Bureau of the Census. 1992. *Statistical Abstract of the United States*. Washington: United States Government Printing Office. Published annually.

Wanning, Esther. 1991. *Culture Shock USA*. Portland, OR: Graphic Arts Center Publishing.

Warton, John. 1986. *Jobs in Japan: The Complete Guide to Living and Working in the Land of Rising Opportunity.* Denver: Global Press.

Wedge, Bryant. 1965. *Visitors to the United States and How They See Us.* Princeton, NJ: Van Nostrand.

Wells, Alan. 1972. *Picture-Tube Imperialism?: The Impact of U.S. Television on Latin America.* Maryknoll, NY: Orbis Books.

Wilgus, Karna, S., comp. 1974. *Latin America Books. An Annotated Bibliography for High Schools and Colleges.* New York: Center for Inter-American Relations.

Williamson, Kay. 1976. "The Rivers Reader Project in Nigeria," in Ayo Bamgbose, ed., *Mother Tongue Education: The West African Experience.* London: Hodder and Stoughton.

Witham, Lynn. 1988. *Malaysia: A Foreigner's Guide.* Waterbury Center, VT: Hornbill.

Wolpert, Stanley A. 1991. *India.* Berkeley: University of California.

Zongren, Liu. 1988. *Two Years in the Melting Pot.* San Francisco: China Books and Periodicals.

3. International Business

Adler, Nancy J., and Dafna N. Izraeli, eds. *Women in Management Worldwide.* Armonk, NY: M.E. Sharpe, 1988. 285 pp.

Axtell, Roger E., ed. *Do's and Taboos around the World.* NY: Wiley, 1990. 200 pp. (Business etiquette.)

Bartlett, Christopher A., and Sumantra Ghoshal. *Managing across Borders: The Transnational Solution.* Boston, MA: Harvard Business School Press, 1989. 274 pp.

Casse, Pierre. *Training for the Multicultural Manager: A Practical and Cross-Cultural Approach to the Management of People.* Washington, DC: SIETAR International, 1982. 191 pp.

Casse, Pierre, and Surinder Deol. *Managing Intercultural Negotiations: Guidelines for Trainers and Negotiators.* Washington, DC: SIETAR International. (or Intercultural Press), 1985. 175 pp.

Chesanow, Neil. *The World-Class Executive: How to Do Business Like a Pro Around the World.* NY: Bantam Books, 1986.

De Mente, Boye. *Chinese Etiquette and Ethics in Business.* Lincolnwood, IL: NTC Publishing Group, 1989. 251 pp.

De Mente, Boye. *Japanese Etiquette and Ethics in Business*, 5th ed. Lincolnwood, IL: NTC Publishing Group, 1988. 152 pp.

De Mente. Boye. *Korean Etiquette and Ethics in Business.* Lincolnwood, IL: NTC Publishing Group, 1988. 158 pp.

Dowling, Peter J., and Randall S. Schuler. *International Dimensions of Human Resource Management.* Boston: PWS-Kent, 1990. 256 pp.

Engholm, Christopher. *When Business East Meets Business West: The Pacific Rim Guide to Practice and Protocol.* New York: Wiley, 1991.

Ferraro, Gary P. *The Cultural Dimension of International Business.* Englewood Cliffs, NJ: Prentice Hall (Simon & Schuster), 1990. 176 pp.

Fieg, John Paul, revised by Elizabeth Mortlock. *A Common Core: Thais and Americans.* Yarmouth, ME: Intercultural Press, 1989. 120 pp. (Includes contrast of Thai and American management styles.)

Fisher, Glen. *International Negotiation: A Cross-Cultural Perspective.* Yarmouth, ME: Intercultural Press, 1980. 69 pp.

Forsgren, Mats, and Jan Johanson, eds. *Managing Networks in International Business.* Philadelphia: Gordon and Breach, 1992. 254 pp.

Graham, John L., and Yoshiro Sano. *Smart Bargaining: Doing Business with the Japanese.* New York: Harper & Row, 1989. 212 pp.

Gudykunst, William B., Stella Ting-Toomey, and Lea P. Stewart. *Communication, Culture, and Organizational Process.* International and Intercultural Communication Annual, Vol. IX. Newbury Park, CA: Sage Publications, 1985. 262 pp.

Habert, Kjell, and Arild Lillebo. *Made in Norway: Norwegians as Others See Them.* Bekkestua, Norway: Norwegian School of Management Press, 1988. 179 pp.

Hall, Edward T., and Mildred Reed Hall. *Hidden Differences: Doing Business with the Japanese.* New York: Anchor Press/Doubleday, 1987. 184 pp.

Hall, Edward T., and Mildred Reed Hall. *Understanding Cultural Differences: Germans, French and Americans.* Yarmouth, ME: Intercultural Press, 1989. 208 pp. (Aimed at business.)

Harris, Philip R., and Robert T. Moran. *Managing Cultural Differences.* Third Edition. Houston: Gulf Publishing, 1991. 639 pp.

Hofstede, Geert H. *Culture's Consequences: International Differences in Work-Related Values.* Abridged ed. Newbury Park, CA: Sage Publications, 1984. 328 pp.

Kras, Eva. *Management in Two Cultures: Bridging the Gap between U.S. and Mexican Managers.* Yarmouth, ME: Intercultural Press, 1989. 110 pp.

Leppert, Paul. *Doing Business in Singapore: A Handbook for Executives.* Sebastopol, CA: Patton Pacific, 1990. 135 pp.

Leppert, Paul. *Doing Business with the Chinese: A Taiwan Handbook for Executives.* Sebastopol, CA: Patton Pacific Press, 1990. 145 pp.

Leppert, Paul. *Doing Business with the Koreans: A Handbook for Executives*, 2nd ed. Sebastopol, CA: Patton Pacific, 1991. 134 pp.

Loden, Marilyn, and Judy B. Rosener. *Work Force America! Managing Employee Diversity as a Vital Resource.* Homewood, IL: Business One Irwin, 1990. 250 pp.

MacLeod, Roderick. *China, Inc.: How to Do Business with the Chinese.* NY: Bantam Books, 1988. 224 pp.

Mead, Richard. *Cross-Cultural Management Communication.* NY: John Wiley & Sons, 1990. 273 pp.

Moran, Robert T. *Getting Your Yen's Worth: How to Negotiate with Japan, Inc.* Houston: Gulf Publishing, 1984. 182 pp.

Phillips-Martinsson, Jean. *Swedes as Others See Them: Facts, Myths or a Communication Complex.* Kent, Eng.: Chartwell-Bratt, 1981. 123 pp. [Advice to Swedes working abroad as well as foreigners working in Sweden]

Rearwin, David. *The Asia Business Book.* Yarmouth, ME: Intercultural Press, 1991. 320 pp.

Rossman, Marlene L. *The International Businesswoman of the 1990s.* Westport, CT: Greenwood Press, 1990. 137 pp.

Scott-Stevens, Susan. *Foreign Consultants and Counterparts: Problems in Technology Transfer.* Boulder: Westview Press, 1987. (Case study of Indonesian economic development project.)

Seelye, H. Ned, and Alan Seelye-James. *Culture Clash: Managing Diversity in a Multicultural World.* Lincolnwood, IL: NTC Business Books, 1995.

Shames, Germaine W., and Gerald W. Glover. *World-Class Service.* Yarmouth, ME: Intercultural Press, 1989. 220 pp. (For managers in international hospitality, travel, and tourism.)

Simons, George F. *Working Together: How to Become More Effective in a Multicultural Organization.* Los Altos, CA: Crisp Publications, 1989. 96 pp.

Simons, George F., and G. Deborah Weissman. *Men and Women: Partners at Work, A Ten-Step Program for Success.* Los Altos, CA: Crisp, 1990. 110 pp. (Aimed at U.S. workplace.)

Terpstra, Vern. *International Dimensions of Marketing.* 2nd ed. Boston: PWS-Kent, 1990. 185 pp.

Terpstra, Vern, and Kenneth David. *The Cultural Environment of International Business.* 3rd ed. Cincinnati: South-Western Publishing, 1985. 252 pp.

Theiderman, Sondra. *Bridging Cultural Barriers for Corporate Success: How to Manage the Multicultural Workforce.* Lexington, MA: Lexington Books, 1991. 256 pp.

Zimmerman, Mark. *How to do Business with the Japanese.* NY: Random House, 1985. 331 pp.

Index

Aacladan, David K., 114
AATF. *See* American Association of Teachers of French (AATF)
Abrazo de año nuevo, 59
Abt Associates, 83
Acculturation. *See* Adaptation
Achievement
    cultural valuation of, 131
    and environment, 244
    of students. *See* Assessment
Ackermann, Jean Marie, 285, 291
ACSP. *See* Anthropological Curriculum Study Project (ACSP)
ACTFL. *See* American Council on the Teaching of Foreign Languages (ACTFL)
Adams, J. C., 85
Adaptation
    cultural, 235–64, 270
    phase, in culture shock, 58
Address, forms of, 196–97
Adherence (in cultural adaptation), 250
Adler, Blossom, 154, 175
Adler, Peter S., 285, 291
Advertisements
classroom use and study of, 5, 108
cultural aspects of, 130, 144–49
Affection, displays of, 59, 196–97
Affective
    exercises, 248
    measurement, 207–14. *See also* Assessment, of cultural competence; Attitudes, to target culture; Self-esteem, assessment of
African-American culture, 274, 321. *See also* Race, and culture
African cultures, 280, 282, 317, 319, 323. *See also* specific countries and peoples
Age, cultural aspects of, xiii, 31, 96–98
Agel, Jerome, 37, 54
Agrarian culture, 239–40. *See also* Peasant attitudes
Agua, Guatemalan connotations of, 3

Albert, Rosita, 163, 185
Albrecht, Milton C., 276, 291
Alienation, cultural, 262
Allophonic variations, 91
Althen, Gary L., 66, 85, 127, 138
Ambiguity, cultural valuation of, 128
Amelung, Carolyn, 107
American Association of Teachers of French (AATF), 189
American Council on Education, vi
American Council on the Teaching of Foreign Languages (ACTFL), viii, 83, 188–89, 205
Ammons, Margaret, 275, 291
Analytical skills, 282, 286–87
Anglo culture. *See* United States culture
Anthropological Curriculum Study Project (ACSP), 226, 233
Anthropology, practice and application of, 15, 129
Anxiety
    in culture shock, 61
    language-learning, 41–43
Apache culture, 318. *See also* Native American cultures
Appel, John J., 269–70, 291
Appel, Selma, 269–70, 291
Arabic culture, 9, 62, 99, 117, 129, 252–53, 271, 317, 320. *See also* Islamic cultures *and* specific countries
Argentinean culture, 143, 145–49. *See also* Hispanic culture; Latin American cultures
Aristotle, 268
Arnberg, Lenore, 239, 264
Aronoff, Joel, 118, 138
Ascher, Marcia, 274, 291
Ashton-Warner, Sylvia, 288, 291
Assessment, 280
    of cultural competence, 187–205, 207–32
Assimilation. *See* Adaptation
Assimilators, culture. *See* Culture assimilators
Ataru, 104